THE
LIFE AND LETTERS OF
LEWIS CARROLL

STUART DODGSON

CHAPTER I

The Dodgsons appear to have been for a long time connected with the north of England, and until quite recently a branch of the family resided at Stubb Hall, near Barnard Castle.

In the early part of the last century a certain Rev. Christopher Dodgson held a living in Yorkshire. His son, Charles, also took Holy Orders, and was for some time tutor to a son of the then Duke of Northumberland. In 1762 his patron presented him to the living of Elsdon, in Northumberland, by no means a desirable cure, as Mr. Dodgson discovered. The following extracts from his letters to various members of the Percy family are interesting as giving some idea of the life of a rural clergyman a hundred years ago:

I am obliged to you for promising to write to me, but don't give yourself the trouble of writing to this place, for 'tis almost impossible to receive 'em, without sendinga messenger 16 miles to fetch 'em.

'Tis impossible to describe the oddity of my situation at present, which, however, is not void of some pleasant circumstances.

A clogmaker combs out my wig upon my curate's head, by way of a block, and his wife powders it with a dredging-box.

The vestibule of the castle (used as a temporary parsonage) is a low stable; above it the kitchen, in which are two little beds joining to each other. The curate and his wife lay in one, and Margery the maid in the other. I lay in the parlour between two beds to keep me from being frozen to death, for as we keep open house the winds enter from every quarter, and are apt to sweep into bed to me.

Elsdon was once a market town as some say, and a city according to others; but as the annals of the parish were lost several centuries ago, it is impossible to determine what age it was either the one or the other.

There are not the least traces of the former grandeur to be found, whence some antiquaries are apt to believe that it lost both its trade and charter at the Deluge.

... There is a very good understanding between the parties [he is speaking of the Churchmen and Presbyterians who lived in the parish], for they not only intermarry with one another, but frequently do penance together in a white sheet, with a white wand, barefoot, and in the coldest season of the year. I have not finished the description for fear of bringing on a fit of the ague. Indeed, the ideas of sensation are sufficient to starve a man to death, without having recourse to those of reflection.

If I was not assured by the best authority on earth that the world is to be destroyed by fire, I should conclude that the day of destruction is at hand, but brought on by means of an agent very opposite to that of heat.

I have lost the use of everything but my reason, though my head is entrenched in three night-caps, and my throat, which is very bad, is fortified by a pair of stockings twisted in the form of a cravat.

As washing is very cheap, I wear *two* shirts at a time, and, for want of a wardrobe, I hang my great coat upon my own back, and generally keep on my boots in imitation of my namesake of Sweden. Indeed, since the snow became two feet deep (as I wanted a 'chaappin of Yale' from the public-house), I made an offer of them to Margery the maid, but her legs are too thick to make use of them, and I am told that the greater part of my parishioners are not less substantial, and notwithstanding this they are remarkable for agility.

In course of time this Mr. Dodgson became Bishop of Ossory and Ferns, and he was subsequently translated to the see of Elphin. He was warmly congratulated on this change in his fortunes by George III., who said that he ought indeed to be thankful to have got away from a palace where the stabling was so bad.

The Bishop had four children, the eldest of whom, Elizabeth Anne, married Charles Lutwidge, of Holmrook, in Cumberland. Two of the others died almost before they had attained manhood. Charles, the eldest son, entered the army, and rose to the rank of captain in the 4th Dragoon Guards. He met with a sad fate while serving his king and country in Ireland. One of the Irish rebels who were supposed to have been concerned in the murder of Lord Kilwarden offered to give himself up to justice if Captain Dodgson would come alone and at night to take him. Though he fully realised the risk, the brave captain decided to trust himself to the honour of this outlaw, as he felt that no chance should be missed of effecting so important a capture. Having first written a letter of farewell to his wife, he set out on the night of December 16, 1803, accompanied by a few troopers, for the meeting-place—an old hut that stood a mile or so from Phillipstown, in King's County. In accordance with the terms of the agreement, he left his men a few hundred yards from the hut to await his return, and advanced alone through the night. A cowardly shot from one of the windows of the cottage ended his noble life, and alarmed the troopers, who, coming up in haste, were confronted with the dead body of their leader. The story is told that on the same night his wife heard two shots fired, and made inquiry about it, but could find out nothing. Shortly afterwards the news came that her husband had been killed just at that time.

Captain Dodgson left two sons behind him—Hassard, who, after a brilliant career as a special pleader, became a Master of the Court of Common Pleas, and Charles, the father of the subject of this Memoir.

Charles, who was the elder of the two, was born in the year 1800, at Hamilton, in Lanarkshire. He adopted the clerical profession, in which he rose to high honours. He was a distinguished scholar, and took a double first at Christ Church, Oxford. Although in after life mathematics were his favourite pursuit, yet the fact that he translated Tertullian for the "Library of the Fathers" is sufficient evidence that he made good use of his classical education. In the controversy about Baptismal Regeneration he took a prominent part, siding on the question with the Tractarians, though his views on some other points of Church doctrine were less advanced than those of the leaders of the Oxford movement. He was a man of deep piety and of a somewhat reserved and grave disposition, which, however, was tempered by the most generous charity, so that he was universally loved by the poor. In moments of relaxation his wit and humour were the delight of his clerical friends, for he had the rare power of telling anecdotes effectively. His reverence for sacred things was so great that he was never known to relate a story which included a jest upon words from the Bible.

In 1830 he married his cousin, Frances Jane Lutwidge, by whom he had eleven children, all of whom, except Lewis Carroll, survive. His wife, in the words of one who had the best possible opportunities for observing her character, was "one of the sweetest and gentlest women that ever lived, whom to know was to love. The earnestness of her simple faith and love shone forth in all she did and said; she seemed to live always in the conscious presence of God. It has been said by her children that they never in all their lives remember to have heard an impatient or harsh word from her lips." It is easy to trace in Lewis Carroll's character the influence of that most gentle of mothers; though dead she still speaks to us in some of the most beautiful and touching passages of his works. Not so long ago I had a conversation with an old friend of his; one of the first things she said to me was, "Tell me about his mother." I complied with her request as well as I was able, and, when I had finished my account of Mrs. Dodgson's beautiful character, she said, "Ah, I knew it must have been so; I felt sure he must have had a good mother."

On January 27, 1832, Charles Lutwidge Dodgson was born at Daresbury, of which parish his father was then incumbent. The village of Daresbury is about seven miles from Warrington; its name is supposed to be derived from a word meaning oak, and certainly oaks are very plentiful in the neighbourhood. A canal passes through an outlying part of the parish. The bargemen who frequented this canal were a special object of Mr. Dodgson's pastoral care. Once, when walking with Lord Francis Egerton, who was a large landowner in the district, he spoke of his desire to provide some sort of religious privileges for them. "If I only had £100," he said, "I would turn one of those barges into a chapel," and, at his companion's request, he described exactly how he would have the chapel constructed and furnished. A few weeks later he received a letter from Lord Francis to tell him that his wish was fulfilled, and that the chapel was ready. In this strange church, which is believed to have been the first of its kind, Mr. Dodgson conducted service and preached every Sunday evening!

The parsonage is situated a mile and a half from the village, on the glebe-farm, having been erected by a former incumbent, who, it was said, cared more for the glebe than the parish. Here it was that Charles spent the first eleven years of his life—years of complete seclusion from the world, for even the passing of a cart was a matter of great interest to the children.

In this quiet home the boy invented the strangest diversions for himself; he made pets of the most odd and unlikely animals, and numbered certain snails and toads among his intimate friends. He tried also to encourage civilised warfare among earthworms, by supplying them with small pieces of pipe, with which they might fight if so disposed. His notions of charity at this early age were somewhat rudimentary; he used to peel rushes with the idea that the pith would afterwards "be given to the poor," though what possible use they could put it to he never attempted to explain. Indeed he seems at this time to have actually lived in that charming "Wonderland" which he afterwards described so vividly; but for all that he was a thorough boy, and loved to climb the trees and to scramble about in the old marl-pits.

One of the few breaks in this very uneventful life was a holiday spent with the other members of his family in Beaumaris. The journey took three days each way, for railroads were then almost unknown; and whatever advantages coaching may have had over travelling in trains, speed was certainly not one of them.

Mr. Dodgson from the first used to take an active part in his son's education, and the following anecdote will show that he had at least a pupil who was anxious to learn. One day, when Charles was a very small boy, he came up to his father and showed him a book of logarithms, with the request, "Please explain." Mr. Dodgson told him that he was much too young to understand anything about such a difficult subject. The child listened to what his father said, and appeared to think it irrelevant, for he still insisted, "*But*, please, explain!"

On one occasion Mr. and Mrs. Dodgson went to Hull, to pay a visit to the latter's father, who had been seriously ill. From Hull Mrs. Dodgson wrote to Charles, and he set much store by this letter, which was probably one of the first he had received. He was afraid that some of his little sisters would mess it, or tear it up, so he wrote upon the back, "No one is to touch this note, for it belongs to C. L. D."; but, this warning appearing insufficient, he added, "Covered with slimy pitch, so that they will wet their fingers." The precious letter ran as follows:—

My dearest Charlie, I have used you rather ill in not having written to you sooner, but I know you will forgive me, as your Grandpapa has liked to have me with him so much, and I could not write and talk to him comfortably. All your notes have delighted me, my precious children, and show me that you have not quite forgotten me. I am always thinking of you, and longing to have you all round me again more than words can tell. God grant that we may find you all well and happy on Friday evening. I am happy to say your dearest Papa is quite well—his cough is rather *tickling*, but is of no consequence. It delights me, my darling Charlie, to hear that you are getting on so well with your Latin, and that you make so few mistakes in your Exercises. You will be happy to hear that your dearest Grandpapa is going on nicely—indeed I hope he will soon be quite well again. He talks a great deal and most kindly about you all. I hope my sweetest Will says "Mama" sometimes, and that precious Tish has not forgotten. Give them and all my other treasures, including yourself, 1,000,000,000 kisses from me, with my most affectionate love. I am sending you a shabby note, but I cannot help it. Give my kindest love to Aunt Dar, and believe me, my own dearest Charlie, to be your sincerely affectionate

MAMA.

Among the few visitors who disturbed the repose of Daresbury Parsonage was Mr. Durnford, afterwards Bishop of Chichester, with whom Mr. Dodgson had formed a close friendship. Another was Mr. Bayne, at that time head-master of Warrington Grammar School, who used occasionally to assist in the services at Daresbury. His son, Vere, was Charles's playfellow; he is now a student of Christ Church, and the friendship between him and Lewis Carroll lasted without interruption till the death of the latter.

The memory of his birthplace did not soon fade from Charles's mind; long afterwards he retained pleasant recollections of its rustic beauty. For instance, his poem of "The Three Sunsets," which first appeared in 1860 in

All the Year Round, begins with the following stanzas, which have been slightly altered in later editions:—

I watch the drowsy night expire,
And Fancy paints at my desire
Her magic pictures in the fire.

An island farm, 'mid seas of corn,
Swayed by the wandering breath of morn,
The happy spot where I was born.

Though nearly all Mr. Dodgson's parishioners at Daresbury have passed away, yet there are still some few left who speak with loving reverence of him whose lips, now long silenced, used to speak so kindly to them; whose hands, long folded in sleep, were once so ready to alleviate their wants and sorrows.

In 1843 Sir Robert Peel presented him to the Crown living of Croft, a Yorkshire village about three miles south of Darlington. This preferment made a great change in the life of the family; it opened for them many more social opportunities, and put an end to that life of seclusion which, however beneficial it may be for a short time, is apt, if continued too long, to have a cramping and narrowing influence.

The river Tees is at Croft the dividing line between Yorkshire and Durham, and on the middle of the bridge which there crosses it is a stone which shows where the one county ends and the other begins. "Certain lands are held in this place," says Lewis in his "Topographical Dictionary," "by the owner presenting on the bridge, at the coming of every new Bishop of Durham, an old sword, pronouncing a legendary address, and delivering the sword to the Bishop, who returns it immediately." The Tees is subject to extraordinary floods, and though Croft Church stands many feet above the ordinary level of the river, and is separated from it by the churchyard and a field, yet on one occasion the church itself was flooded, as was attested by water-marks on the old woodwork several feet from the floor, still to be seen when Mr. Dodgson was incumbent.

This church, which is dedicated to St. Peter, is a quaint old building with a Norman porch, the rest of it being of more modern construction. It contains a raised pew, which is approached by a winding flight of stairs, and is covered in, so that it resembles nothing so much as a four-post bedstead. This pew used to belong to the Milbanke family, with which Lord Byron was connected. Mr. Dodgson found the chancel-roof in so bad a state of repair that he was obliged to take it down, and replace it by an entirely new one. The only village school that existed when he came to the place was a sort of barn, which stood in a corner of the churchyard. During his incumbency a fine school-house was erected. Several members of his family used regularly to help in teaching the children, and excellent reports were obtained.

The Rectory is close to the church, and stands in the middle of a beautiful garden. The former incumbent had been an enthusiastic horticulturist, and the walls of the kitchen garden were covered with luxuriant fruit-trees, while the greenhouses were well stocked with rare and beautiful exotics. Among these was a specimen of that fantastic cactus, the night-blowing Cereus, whose flowers, after an existence of but a few hours, fade with the waning sun. On the day when this occurred large numbers of people used to obtain Mr. Dodgson's leave to see the curiosity.

Near the Rectory is a fine hotel, built when Croft was an important posting-station for the coaches between London and Edinburgh, but in Mr. Dodgson's time chiefly used by gentlemen who stayed there during the hunting season. The village is renowned for its baths and medicinal waters. The parish of Croft includes the outlying hamlets of Halnaby, Dalton, and Stapleton, so that the Rector's position is by no means a sinecure. Within the village is Croft Hall, the old seat of the Chaytors; but during Mr. Dodgson's incumbency the then Sir William Chaytor built and lived at Clervaux Castle, calling it by an old family name.

Shortly after accepting the living of Croft, Mr. Dodgson was appointed examining chaplain to the Bishop of Ripon; subsequently he was made Archdeacon of Richmond and one of the Canons of Ripon Cathedral.

Charles was at this time very fond of inventing games for the amusement of his brothers and sisters; he constructed a rude train out of a wheelbarrow, a barrel and a small truck, which used to convey passengers from one "station" in the Rectory garden to another. At each of these stations there was a refreshment-room, and the passengers had to purchase tickets from him before they could enjoy their ride. The boy was also a clever conjuror, and, arrayed in a brown wig and a long white robe, used to cause no little wonder to his audience by his sleight-of-hand. With the assistance of various members of the family and the village carpenter, he made a troupe of marionettes and a small theatre for them to act in. He wrote all the plays himself the most popular being "The Tragedy of King John"—and he was very clever at manipulating the innumerable strings by which the movements of his puppets were regulated. One winter, when the snow lay thick upon the lawn, he traced upon it a maze of such hopeless intricacy as almost to put its famous rival at Hampton Court in the shade.

When he was twelve years old his father sent him to school at Richmond, under Mr. Tate, a worthy son of that well-known Dr. Tate who had made Richmond School so famous.

I am able to give his earliest impressions of school-life in his own words, for one of his first letters home has been fortunately preserved. It is dated August 5th, and is addressed to his two eldest sisters. A boy who has *ten* brothers and sisters can scarcely be expected to write separate letters to each of them.

My dear Fanny and Memy,—I hope you are all getting on well, as also the sweet twins, the boys I think that I like the best, are Harry Austin, and all the Tates of which there are 7 besides a little girl who came down to dinner the first day, but not since, and I also like Edmund Tremlet, and William and Edward Swire, Tremlet is a sharp little fellow about 7 years old, the youngest in the school, I also like Kemp and Mawley. The rest of the boys that I know are Bertram, Harry and Dick Wilson, and two Robinsons, I will tell you all about them when I return. The boys have played two tricks upon me which were these—they first proposed to play at "King of the Cobblers" and asked if I would be king, to which I agreed. Then they made me sit down and sat (on the ground) in a circle round me, and told me to say "Go to work" which I said, and they immediately began kicking me and knocking me on all sides. The next game they proposed was "Peter, the red lion," and they made a mark on a tombstone (for we were playing in the churchyard) and one of the boys walked with his eyes shut, holding out his finger, trying to touch the mark; then a little boy came forward to lead the rest and led a good many very near the mark; at last it was my turn; they told me to shut my eyes well, and the next minute I had my finger in the mouth of one of the boys, who had stood (I believe) before the tombstone with his mouth open. For 2 nights I slept alone, and for the rest of the time with Ned Swire. The boys play me no tricks now. The only fault (tell Mama) that there has been was coming in one day to dinner just after grace. On Sunday we went to church in the morning, and sat in a large pew with Mr. Fielding, the church we went to is close by Mr. Tate's house, we did not go in the afternoon but Mr. Tate read a discourse to the boys on the 5th commandment. We went to church again in the evening. Papa wished me to tell him all the texts I had heard preached upon, please to tell him that I could not hear it in the morning nor hardly one sentence of the sermon, but the one in the evening was I Cor. i. 23. I believe it was a farewell sermon, but I am not sure. Mrs. Tate has looked through my clothes and left in the trunk a great many that will not be wanted. I have had 3 misfortunes in my clothes etc. 1st, I cannot find my tooth-brush, so that I have not brushed my teeth for 3 or 4 days, 2nd, I cannot find my blotting paper, and 3rd, I have no shoe-horn. The chief games are, football, wrestling, leap frog, and fighting. Excuse bad writing.

Yr affec' brother Charles.

To SKEFF [*a younger brother, aged six*].

My dear Skeff,—Roar not lest thou be abolished. Yours, etc.,——.

The discomforts which he, as a "new boy," had to put up with from his school-mates affected him as they do not, unfortunately, affect most boys, for in later school days he was famous as a champion of the weak and small, while every bully had good reason to fear him. Though it is hard for those who have only known him as the gentle and retiring don to believe it, it is nevertheless true that long after he left school his name was remembered as that of a boy who knew well how to use his fists in defence of a righteous cause.

As was the custom at that time, Charles began to compose Latin verses at a very early age, his first copy being dated November 25, 1844. The subject was evening, and this is how he treated it:—

Phoebus aqua splendet descendens, æquora tingens
Splendore aurato. Pervenit umbra solo.
Mortales lectos quærunt, et membra relaxant
Fessa labore dies; cuncta per orbe silet.
Imperium placidum nunc sumit Phoebe corusca.
Antris procedunt sanguine ore feræ.

These lines the boy solemnly copied into his Diary, apparently in the most blissful ignorance of the numerous mistakes they contained.

The next year he wrote a story which appeared in the school magazine. It was called "The Unknown One," so it was probably of the sensational type in which small boys usually revel.

Though Richmond School, as it was in 1844, may not compare favourably in every respect with a modern preparatory school, where supervision has been so far "reduced to the absurd" that the unfortunate masters hardly get a minute to themselves from sunrise till long after sunset, yet no better or wiser men than those of the school of Mr. Tate are now to be found. Nor, I venture to think, are the results of the modern system more successful than those of the old one. Charles loved his "kind old schoolmaster," as he affectionately calls him, and surely to gain the love of the boys is the main battle in school-management.

The impression he made upon his instructors may be gathered from the following extracts from Mr. Tate's first report upon him:

Sufficient opportunities having been allowed me to draw from actual observation an estimate of your son's character and abilities, I do not hesitate to express my opinion that he possesses, along with other and excellent natural endowments, a very uncommon share of genius. Gentle and cheerful in his intercourse with others, playful and ready in conversation, he is capable of acquirements and knowledge far beyond his years, while his reason is so clear and so jealous of error, that he will not rest satisfied without a most exact solution of whatever appears to him obscure. He has passed an excellent examination just now in mathematics, exhibiting at times an illustration of that love of precise argument, which seems to him natural.

I must not omit to set off against these great advantages one or two faults, of which the removal as soon as possible is desirable, tho' I am prepared to find it a work of time. As you are well aware, our young friend, while jealous of error, as I said above, where important faith or principles are concerned, is exceedingly lenient towards lesser frailties—and, whether in reading aloud or metrical composition, frequently sets at nought the notions of Virgil or Ovid as to syllabic quantity. He is moreover marvellously ingenious in replacing the ordinary inflexions of nouns and verbs, as detailed in our grammars, by more exact analogies, or convenient forms of his own devising. This source of fault will in due time exhaust itself, though flowing freely at present.... You may fairly anticipate for him a bright career. Allow me, before I close, one suggestion which assumes for itself the wisdom of experience and the sincerity of the best intention. You must not entrust your son with a full knowledge of his superiority over other boys. Let him discover this as he proceeds. The love of excellence is far beyond the love of excelling; and if he should once be bewitched into a mere ambition to surpass others I need not urge that the very quality of his knowledge would be materially injured, and that his character would receive a stain of a more serious description still....

And again, when Charles was leaving Richmond, he wrote:

"Be assured that I shall always feel a peculiar interest in the gentle, intelligent, and well-conducted boy who is now leaving us."

Although his father had been a Westminster boy, Charles was, for some reason or other, sent to Rugby. The great Arnold, who had, one might almost say, created Rugby School, and who certainly had done more for it than all his predecessors put together, had gone to his rest, and for four years the reins of government had been in the firm hands of Dr. Tait, afterwards Archbishop of Canterbury. He was Headmaster during the whole of the time Charles was at Rugby, except the last year, during which Dr. Goulburn held that office. Charles went up in February, 1846, and he must have found his new life a great change from his quiet experiences at Richmond. Football was in full swing, and one can imagine that to a new boy "Big-side" was not an unalloyed delight. Whether he distinguished himself as a "dropper," or ever beat the record time in the "Crick" run, I do not know. Probably not; his abilities did not lie much in the field of athletics. But he got on capitally with his work, and seldom returned home without one or more prizes. Moreover, he conducted himself so well that he never had to enter that dreaded chamber, well known to *some* Rugbeians, which is approached by a staircase that winds up a little turret, and wherein are enacted scenes better imagined than described.

A schoolboy's letter home is not, usually, remarkable for the intelligence displayed in it; as a rule it merely leads up with more or less ingenuity to the inevitable request for money contained in the postscript. Some of Charles's letters were of a different sort, as the following example shows:

Yesterday evening I was walking out with a friend of mine who attends as mathematical pupil Mr. Smythies the second mathematical master; we went up to Mr. Smythies' house, as he wanted to speak to him, and he asked us to stop and have a glass of wine and some figs. He seems as devoted to his duty as Mr. Mayor, and asked me with a smile of delight, "Well Dodgson I suppose you're getting well on with your mathematics?" He is very clever at them, though not equal to Mr. Mayor, as indeed few men are, Papa excepted.... I have read the first number of Dickens' new tale, "Davy Copperfield." It purports to be his life, and begins with his birth and childhood; it seems a poor plot, but some of the characters and scenes are good. One of the persons that amused me was a Mrs. Gummidge, a wretched melancholy person, who is always crying, happen what will, and whenever the fire smokes, or other trifling accident occurs, makes the remark with great bitterness, and many tears, that she is a "lone lorn creetur, and everything goes contrairy with her." I have not yet been able to get the second volume Macaulay's "England" to read. I have seen it however and one passage struck me when seven bishops had signed the invitation to the pretender, and King James sent for Bishop Compton (who was one of the seven) and asked him "whether he or any of his ecclesiastical brethren had anything to do with it?" He replied, after a moment's thought "I am fully persuaded your majesty, that there is not one of my brethren who is not as innocent in the matter as myself." This was certainly no actual lie, but certainly, as Macaulay says, it was very little different from one.

The Mr. Mayor who is mentioned in this letter formed a very high opinion of his pupil's ability, for in 1848 he wrote to Archdeacon Dodgson: "I have not had a more promising boy at his age since I came to Rugby."

Dr. Tait speaks no less warmly:—

My dear Sir,—I must not allow your son to leave school without expressing to you the very high opinion I entertain of him. I fully coincide in Mr. Cotton's estimate both of his abilities and upright conduct. His mathematical knowledge is great for his age, and I doubt not he will do himself credit in classics. As I believe I mentioned to you before, his examination for the Divinity prize was one of the most creditable exhibitions I have ever seen.

During the whole time of his being in my house, his conduct has been excellent.

Believe me to be, My dear Sir,

Yours very faithfully,

A.C. TAIT.

Public school life then was not what it is now; the atrocious system then in vogue of setting hundreds of lines for the most trifling offences made every day a weariness and a hopeless waste of time, while the bad discipline which was maintained in the dormitories made even the nights intolerable—especially for the small boys, whose beds in winter were denuded of blankets that the bigger ones might not feel cold.

Charles kept no diary during his time at Rugby; but, looking back upon it, he writes in 1855:—

During my stay I made I suppose some progress in learning of various kinds, but none of it was done *con amore*, and I spent an incalculable time in writing out impositions—this last I consider one of the chief faults of Rugby School. I made some friends there, the most intimate being Henry Leigh Bennett (as college acquaintances we find fewer common sympathies, and are consequently less intimate)—but I cannot say that I look back upon my life at a Public School with any sensations of pleasure, or that any earthly considerations would induce me to go through my three years again.

When, some years afterwards, he visited Radley School, he was much struck by the cubicle system which prevails in the dormitories there, and wrote in his Diary, "I can say that if I had been thus secure from annoyance at night, the hardships of the daily life would have been comparative trifles to bear."

The picture on page 32 was, I believe, drawn by Charles while he was at Rugby in illustration of a letter received from one of his sisters. Halnaby, as I have said before, was an outlying district of Croft parish.

During his holidays he used to amuse himself by editing local magazines. Indeed, they might be called *very local* magazines, as their circulation was confined to the inmates of Croft Rectory. The first of these, *Useful and Instructive Poetry*, was written about 1845. It came to an untimely end after a six months' run, and was followed at varying intervals by several other periodicals, equally short-lived.

In 1849 or 1850, *The Rectory Umbrella* began to appear. As the editor was by this time seventeen or eighteen years old, it was naturally of a more ambitious character than any of its precursors. It contained a serial story of the most thrilling interest, entitled, "The Walking-Stick of Destiny," some meritorious poetry, a few humorous essays, and several caricatures of pictures in the Vernon Gallery. Three reproductions of these pictures follow, with extracts from the *Umbrella* descriptive of them.

[Illustration: The only sister who *would* write to her brother, though the table had just "folded down"! The other sisters are depicted "sternly resolved to set off to Halnaby & the Castle," tho' it is yet "early, early morning"—Rembrondt.]

"The Scanty Meal."

We have been unusually[001] successful in our second engraving from the Vernon Gallery. The picture is intended, as our readers will perceive, to illustrate the evils of homoeopathy.[002] This idea is well carried out through the whole picture. The thin old lady at the head of the table is in the painter's best style; we almost fancy we can trace in the eye of the other lady a lurking suspicion that her glasses are not really in fault, and that the old gentleman has helped her to *nothing* instead of a nonillionth.[003] Her companion has evidently got an empty glass in his hand; the two children in front are admirably managed, and there is a sly smile on the footman's face, as if he thoroughly enjoyed either the bad news he is bringing or the wrath of his mistress. The carpet is executed with that elaborate care for which Mr. Herring is so famed, and the picture on the whole is one of his best.

"The First Ear-ring"

The scene from which this excellent picture is painted is taken from a passage in the autobiography[004] of the celebrated Sir William Smith[005] of his life when a schoolboy: we transcribe the passage: "One day Bill Tomkins[006] and I were left alone in the house, the old doctor being out; after playing a number of pranks Bill laid me a bet of sixpence that I wouldn't pour a bottle of ink over the doctor's cat. *I did it*, but at that moment old Muggles came home, and caught me by the ear as I attempted to run away. My sensations at the moment I shall never forget; *on that occasion I received my first ear-ring*.[007] The only remark Bill made to me, as he paid me the money afterwards was, 'I say, didn't you just howl jolly!'" The engraving is an excellent copy of the picture.

The best thing in the *Rectory Umbrella* was a parody on Lord Macaulay's style in the "Lays of Ancient Rome"; Charles had a special aptitude for parody, as is evidenced by several of the best-known verses in his later books.

LAYS OF SORROW.

Fair stands the ancient[1] Rectory,
The Rectory of Croft,
The sun shines bright upon it,
The breezes whisper soft.
From all the house and garden
Its inhabitants come forth,
And muster in the road without,
And pace in twos and threes about,
The children of the North.

Some are waiting in the garden,
Some are waiting at the door,
And some are following behind,
And some have gone before.
But wherefore all this mustering?

Wherefore this vast array?
A gallant feat of horsemanship
Will be performed to-day.

To eastward and to westward,
The crowd divides amain,
Two youths are leading on the steed,
Both tugging at the rein;
And sorely do they labour,
For the steed[009] is very strong,
And backward moves its stubborn feet,
And backward ever doth retreat,
And drags its guides along.

And now the knight hath mounted,
Before the admiring band,
Hath got the stirrups on his feet.
The bridle in his hand.
Yet, oh! beware, sir horseman!
And tempt thy fate no more,

For such a steed as thou hast got,
Was never rid before!

The rabbits[010] bow before thee.
And cower in the straw;
The chickens[011] are submissive,
And own thy will for law;
Bullfinches and canary
Thy bidding do obey;
And e'en the tortoise in its shell
Doth never say thee nay.

But thy steed will hear no master,
Thy steed will bear no stick,
And woe to those that beat her,
And woe to those that kick![012]
For though her rider smite her,
As hard as he can hit,
And strive to turn her from the yard,
She stands in silence, pulling hard
Against the pulling bit.

And now the road to Dalton
Hath felt their coming tread,
The crowd are speeding on before,
And all have gone ahead.
Yet often look they backward,
And cheer him on, and bawl,
For slower still, and still more slow,
That horseman and that charger go,
And scarce advance at all.

And now two roads to choose from
Are in that rider's sight:
In front the road to Dalton,

And New Croft upon the right.
"I can't get by!" he bellows,
"I really am not able!
Though I pull my shoulder out of joint,
I cannot get him past this point,
For it leads unto his stable!"

Then out spake Ulfrid Longbow,[013]
A valiant youth was he,
"Lo! I will stand on thy right hand
And guard the pass for thee!"

And out spake fair Flureeza,[014]
His sister eke was she,
"I will abide on thy other side,
And turn thy steed for thee!"

And now commenced a struggle
Between that steed and rider,
For all the strength that he hath left

Doth not suffice to guide her.
Though Ulfrid and his sister
Have kindly stopped the way,
And all the crowd have cried aloud,
"We can't wait here all day!"

Round turned he as not deigning
Their words to understand,
But he slipped the stirrups from his feet

The bridle from his hand,
And grasped the mane full lightly,
And vaulted from his seat,
And gained the road in triumph,[015]
And stood upon his feet.
All firmly till that moment
Had Ulfrid Longbow stood,
And faced the foe right valiantly,
As every warrior should.
But when safe on terra firma
His brother he did spy,
"What *did* you do that for?" he cried,
Then unconcerned he stepped aside
And let it canter by.

They gave him bread and butter,[016]

That was of public right,
As much as four strong rabbits,
Could munch from morn to night,
For he'd done a deed of daring,
And faced that savage steed,
And therefore cups of coffee sweet,
And everything that was a treat,
Were but his right and meed.

And often in the evenings,
When the fire is blazing bright,
When books bestrew the table
And moths obscure the light,
When crying children go to bed,
A struggling, kicking load;

We'll talk of Ulfrid Longbow's deed,
How, in his brother's utmost need,
Back to his aid he flew with speed,
And how he faced the fiery steed,
And kept the New Croft Road.

CHAPTER II

(1850—1860.)

Matriculation at Christ Church—Death of Mrs. Dodgson—The Great Exhibition—University and College Honours—A wonderful year—A theatrical treat—*Misch-Masch*—*The Train*—*College Rhymes*—His *nom de plume*—"Dotheboys Hall"—Alfred Tennyson—Ordination—Sermons—A visit to Farringford—"Where does the day begin?"—The Queen visits Oxford.

We have traced in the boyhood of Lewis Carroll the beginnings of those characteristic traits which afterwards, more fully developed, gave him so distinguished a position among his contemporaries. We now come to a period of his life which is in some respects necessarily less interesting. We all have to pass through that painful era of self-consciousness which prefaces manhood, that time when we feel so deeply, and are so utterly unable to express to others, or even to define clearly to ourselves, what it is we do feel. The natural freedom of childhood is dead within us; the conventional freedom of riper years is struggling to birth, and its efforts are sometimes ludicrous to an unsympathetic observer. In Lewis Carroll's mental attitude during this critical period there was always a calm dignity which saved him from these absurdities, an undercurrent of consciousness that what seemed so great to him was really very little.

On May 23, 1850, he matriculated at Christ Church, the venerable college which had numbered his father's among other illustrious names. A letter from Dr. Jelf, one of the canons of Christ Church, to Archdeacon Dodgson, written when the former heard that his old friend's son was coming up to "the House," contains the following words: "I am sure I express the common feeling of all who remember you at Christ Church when I say that we shall rejoice to see a son of yours worthy to tread in your footsteps."

Lewis Carroll came into residence on January 24, 1851. From that day to the hour of his death—a period of forty-seven years—he belonged to "the House," never leaving it for any length of time, becoming almost a part of it. I, for one, can hardly imagine it without him.

Though technically "in residence," he had not rooms of his own in College during his first term. The "House" was very full; and had it not been for one of the tutors, the Rev. J. Lew, kindly lending him one of his own rooms, he would have had to take lodgings in the town. The first set of rooms he occupied was in Peckwater Quadrangle, which is annually the scene of a great bonfire on Guy Fawkes' Day, and, generally speaking, is not the best place for a reading man to live in.

In those days the undergraduates dining in hall were divided into "messes." Each mess consisted of about half a dozen men, who had a table to themselves. Dinner was served at five, and very indifferently served, too; the dishes and plates were of pewter, and the joint was passed round, each man cutting off what he wanted for himself. In Mr. Dodgson's mess were Philip Pusey, the late Rev. G. C. Woodhouse, and, among others, one who still lives in "Alice in Wonderland" as the "Hatter."

Only a few days after term began, Mrs. Dodgson died suddenly at Croft. The shock was a terrible one to the whole family, and especially to her devoted husband. I have come across a delightful and most characteristic letter from Dr. Pusey—a letter full of the kindest and truest sympathy with the Archdeacon in his bereavement. The part of it which bears upon Mrs. Dodgson's death I give in full:—

My dear Friend, I hear and see so little and so few persons, that I had not heard of your sorrow until your to-day's letter; and now I but guess what it was: only your language is that of the very deepest. I have often thought, since I had to think of this, how, in all adversity, what God takes away He may give us back with increase. One cannot think that any holy earthly love will cease, when we shall "be like the Angels of God in Heaven." Love here must shadow our love there, deeper because spiritual, without any alloy from our sinful nature, and in the fulness of the love of God. But as we grow here by God's grace will be our capacity for endless love. So, then, if by our very sufferings we are purified, and our hearts enlarged, we shall, in that endless bliss, love more those whom we loved here, than if we had never had that sorrow, never been parted....

Lewis Carroll was summoned home to attend the funeral—a sad interlude amidst the novel experiences of a first term at College. The Oxford of 1851 was in many ways quite unlike the Oxford of 1898. The position of the undergraduates was much more similar to that of schoolboys than is now the case; they were subject to the same penalties—corporal punishment, even, had only just gone out of vogue!—and were expected to work, and to work hard.

Early rising then was strictly enforced, as the following extract from one of his letters will show:—

I am not so anxious as usual to begin my personal history, as the first thing I have to record is a very sad incident, namely, my missing morning chapel; before, however, you condemn me, you must hear how accidental it was. For some days now I have been in the habit of, I will not say getting up, but of being called at a quarter past six, and generally managing to be down soon after seven. In the present instance I had been up the night before till about half-past twelve, and consequently when I was called I fell asleep again, and was thunderstruck to find on waking that it was ten minutes past eight. I have had no imposition, nor heard anything about it. It is rather vexatious to have happened so soon, as I had intended never to be late.

It was therefore obviously his custom to have his breakfast *before* going to chapel. I wonder how many undergraduates of the present generation follow the same hardy rule! But then no "impositions" threaten the modern sluggard, even if he neglects chapel altogether.

During the Long Vacation he visited the Great Exhibition, and wrote his sister Elizabeth a long account of what he had seen:—

I think the first impression produced on you when you get inside is one of bewilderment. It looks like a sort of fairyland. As far as you can look in any direction, you see nothing but pillars hung about with shawls, carpets, &c., with long avenues of statues, fountains, canopies, etc., etc., etc. The first thing to be seen on entering is the Crystal Fountain, a most elegant one about thirty feet high at a rough guess, composed entirely of glass and pouring down jets of water from basin to basin; this is in the middle of the centre nave, and from it you can look down to either end, and up both transepts. The centre of the nave mostly consists of a long line of colossal statues, some most magnificent. The one considered the finest, I believe, is the Amazon and Tiger. She is sitting on horseback, and a tiger has fastened on the neck of the horse in front. You have to go to one side to see her face, and the other to see the horse's. The horse's face is really wonderful, expressing terror and pain so exactly, that you almost expect to hear it scream.... There are some very ingenious pieces of mechanism. A tree (in the French Compartment) with birds chirping and hopping from branch to branch exactly like life. The bird jumps across, turns round on the other branch, so as to face back again, settles its head and neck, and then in a few moments jumps back again. A bird standing at the foot of the tree trying to eat a beetle is rather a failure; it never succeeds in getting its head more than a quarter of an inch down, and that in uncomfortable little jerks, as if it was choking. I have to go to the Royal Academy, so must stop: as the subject is quite inexhaustible, there is no hope of ever coming to a regular finish.

On November 1st he won a Boulter scholarship, and at the end of the following year obtained First Class Honours in Mathematics and a Second in Classical Moderations. On Christmas Eve he was made a Student on Dr. Pusey's nomination, for at that time the Dean and Canons nominated to Studentships by turn. The only conditions on which these old Studentships were held were that the Student should remain unmarried, and should proceed to Holy Orders. No statute precisely defined what work was expected of them, that question being largely left to their own discretion.

The eight Students at the bottom of the list that is to say, the eight who had been nominated last—had to mark, by pricking on weekly papers called "the Bills," the attendance at morning and evening chapel. They were allowed to arrange this duty among themselves, and, if it was neglected, they were all punished. This long—defunct custom explains an entry in Lewis Carroll's Diary for October 15, 1853, "Found I had got the prickbills two hundred lines apiece, by not pricking in in the morning," which, I must confess, mystified me exceedingly at first. Another reference to College impositions occurs further on in his Diary, at a time when he was a Lecturer: "Spoke to the Dean about F—, who has brought an imposition which his tutor declares is not his own writing, after being expressly told to write it himself."

The following is an extract from his father's letter of congratulation, on his being nominated for the Studentship:—

My dearest Charles,—The feelings of thankfulness and delight with which I have read your letter just received, I must leave to *your conception*; for they are, I assure you, beyond *my expression*; and your affectionate heart will derive no small addition of joy from thinking of the joy which you have occasioned to me, and to all the circle of your home. I say "*you* have occasioned," because, grateful as I am to my old friend Dr. Pusey for what he has done, I cannot desire stronger evidence than his own words of the fact that you have *won*, and well won, this honour for *yourself*, and that it is bestowed as a matter of *justice* to *you*, and not of *kindness* to *me*. You will be interested in reading extracts from his two letters to me—the first written three years ago in answer to one from me, in which I distinctly told him that I neither asked nor expected that he should serve me in this matter, unless my son should fairly reach the standard of merit by which these appointments were regulated. In reply he says— "I thank you for the way in which you put the application to me. I have now, for nearly twenty years, not given a Studentship to any friend of my own, unless there was no very eligible person in the College. I have passed by or declined the sons of those to whom I was personally indebted for kindness. I can only say that I shall have *very great* pleasure, if circumstances permit me to nominate your son." In his letter received this morning he says—

"I have great pleasure in telling you that I have been enabled to recommend your son for a Studentship this Christmas. It must be so much more satisfactory to you that he should be nominated thus, in consequence of the recommendation of the College. One of the Censors brought me to-day five names; but in their minds it was plain that they thought your son on the whole the most eligible for the College. It has been very satisfactory to hear of your son's uniform steady and good conduct."

The last clause is a parallel to your own report, and I am glad that you should have had so soon an evidence so substantial of the truth of what I have so often inculcated, that it is the "steady, painstaking, likely-to-do-good" man, who in the long run wins the race against those who now and then give a brilliant flash and, as Shakespeare says, "straight are cold again."

In 1853 Archdeacon Dodgson was collated and installed as one of the Canons of Ripon Cathedral. This appointment necessitated a residence of three months in every year at Ripon, where Dr. Erskine was then Dean. A certain Miss Anderson, who used to stay at the Deanery, had very remarkable "clairvoyant" powers; she was able—it was averred—by merely holding in her hand a folded paper containing some words written by a person unknown to her, to describe his or her character. In this way, at what precise date is uncertain, she dictated the following description of Lewis Carroll: "Very clever head; a great deal of number; a great deal of imitation; he would make a good actor; diffident; rather shy in general society; comes out in the home circle; rather obstinate; very clever; a great deal of concentration; very affectionate; a great deal of wit and humour; not much eventuality (or memory of events); fond of deep reading; imaginative, fond, of reading poetry; *may* compose." Those who knew him well will agree that this was, at any rate, a remarkable coincidence.

Longley, afterwards Primate, was then Bishop of Ripon. His charming character endeared him to the Archdeacon and his family, as to every one else who saw much of him. He was one of the few men whose faces can truly be called *beautiful*; it was a veil through which a soul, all gentleness and truth, shone brightly.

In the early part of 1854 Mr. Dodgson was reading hard for "Greats." For the last three weeks before the examination he worked thirteen hours a day, spending the whole night before the *viva voce* over his books. But philosophy and history were not very congenial subjects to him, and when the list was published his name was only in the third class.

He spent the Long Vacation at Whitby, reading Mathematics with Professor Price. His work bore good fruit, for in October he obtained First Class Honours in the Final Mathematical School. "I am getting quite tired of being congratulated on various subjects," he writes; "there seems to be no end of it. If I had shot the Dean I could hardly have had more said about it."

In another letter dated December 13th, he says:

Enclosed you will find a list which I expect you to rejoice over considerably; it will take me more than a day to believe it, I expect—I feel at present very like a child with a new toy, but I daresay I shall be tired of it soon, and wish to be Pope of Rome next.... I have just been to Mr. Price to see how I did in the papers, and the result will I hope be gratifying to you. The following were the sums total for each in the First Class, as nearly as I can remember:—

```
Dodgson          ...         ...         ...    279
Bosanquet        ...         ...         ...    261
Cookson          ...         ...         ...    254
Fowler           ...         ...         ...    225
Ranken     ...   ...   ...   213
```

He also said he never remembered so good a set of men in. All this is very satisfactory. I must also add (this is a very boastful letter) that I ought to get the senior scholarship next term.... One thing more I will add, to crown all, and that is, I find I am the next First Class Mathematical Student to Faussett (with the exception of Kitchin who has given up Mathematics), so that I stand next (as Bosanquet is going to leave) for the Lectureship.

On December 18th he took the degree of Bachelor of Arts, and on October 15, 1855, he was made a "Master of the House," in honour of the appointment of the new Dean (Dr. Liddell) who succeeded Dean Gaisford. To be made Master of the House means that a man has all the privileges of a Master of Arts within the walls of Christ Church. But he must be of a certain number of terms' standing, and be admitted in due form by the Vice-Chancellor, before he is a Master of Arts of the University. In this wider sense Mr. Dodgson did not take his Master's degree until 1857.

This is anticipating events, and there is much to tell of the year 1855, which was a very eventful one for him. On February 15th he was made Sub-Librarian. "This will add £35 to my income," he writes, "not much towards independence." For he was most anxious to have a sufficient income to make him his own master, that he might enter on the literary and artistic career of which he was already dreaming. On May 14th he wrote in his Diary: "The Dean and Canons have been pleased to give me one of the Bostock scholarships, said to be worth £20 a year—this very nearly raises my income this year to independence. Courage!"

His college work, during 1855, was chiefly taking private pupils, but he had, in addition, about three and a half hours a day of lecturing during the last term of the year. He did not, however, work as one of the regular staff of lecturers until the next year. From that date his work rapidly increased, and he soon had to devote regularly as much as seven hours a day to delivering lectures, to say nothing of the time required for preparing them.

The following extract from his Journal, June 22, 1855, will serve to show his early love for the drama. The scene is laid at the Princess' Theatre, then at the height of its glory:—

The evening began with a capital farce, "Away with Melancholy," and then came the great play, "Henry VIII.," the greatest theatrical treat I ever had or ever expect to have. I had no idea that anything so superb as the scenery and dresses was ever to be seen on the stage. Kean was magnificent as Cardinal Wolsey, Mrs. Kean a worthy successor to Mrs. Siddons as Queen Catherine, and all the accessories without exception were good—but oh, that exquisite vision of Queen Catherine's! I almost held my breath to watch: the illusion is perfect, and I felt as if in a dream all the time it lasted. It was like a delicious reverie, or the most beautiful poetry. This is the true end and object of acting—to raise the mind above itself, and out of its petty cares. Never shall I forget that wonderful evening, that exquisite vision—sunbeams broke in through the roof, and gradually revealed two angel forms, floating in front of the carved work on the ceiling: the column of sunbeams shone down upon the sleeping queen, and gradually down it floated, a troop of angelic forms, transparent, and carrying palm branches in their hands: they waved these over the sleeping queen, with oh! such a sad and solemn grace. So could I fancy (if the thought be not profane) would real angels seem to our mortal vision, though doubtless our conception is poor and mean to the reality. She in an ecstasy raises her arms towards them, and to sweet slow music, they vanish as marvellously as they came. Then the profound silence of the audience burst at once into a rapture of applause; but even that scarcely marred the effect of the beautiful sad waking words of the Queen, "Spirits of peace, where are ye?" I never enjoyed anything so much in my life before; and never felt so inclined to shed tears at anything fictitious, save perhaps at that poetical gem of Dickens, the death of little Paul.

On August 21st he received a long letter from his father, full of excellent advice on the importance to a young man of saving money:—

I will just sketch for you [writes the Archdeacon] a supposed case, applicable to your own circumstances, of a young man of twenty-three, making up his mind to work for ten years, and living to do it, on an Income enabling him to save £150 a year—supposing him to appropriate it thus:—

	£	s.	d.
Invested at 4 per cent.	100	0	0
Life Insurance of £1,500 ...	29	15	0
Books, besides those bought in ordinary course	20	5	0
	£150	0	0

Suppose him at the end of the ten years to get a Living enabling him to settle, what will be the result of his savings:— 1. A nest egg of £1,220 ready money, for furnishing and other expenses. 2. A sum of £1,500 secured at his death on payment of a *very much* smaller annual Premium than if he had then begun to insure it. 3. A useful Library, worth more than £200, besides the books bought out of his current Income during the period....

The picture on the opposite page is one of Mr. Dodgson's illustrations in *Misch-Masch,* a periodical of the nature of *The Rectory Umbrella,* except that it contained printed stories and poems by the editor, cut out of the various newspapers to which he had contributed them. Of the comic papers of that day *Punch,* of course, held the foremost place, but it was not without rivals; there was a certain paper called *Diogenes,* then very near its end, which imitated *Punch's* style, and in 1853 the proprietor of *The Illustrated News*, at that time one of the most opulent publishers in London, started *The Comic Times*. A capable editor was found in Edmund Yates; "Phiz" and other well-known artists and writers joined the staff, and 100,000 copies of the first number were printed.

Among the contributors was Frank Smedley, author of "Frank Fairleigh." Though a confirmed invalid, and condemned to spend most of his days on a sofa, Mr. Smedley managed to write several fine novels, full of the joy of life, and free from the least taint of discontent or morbid feeling. He was one of those men—one meets them here and there—whose minds rise high above their bodily infirmities; at moments of depression, which come to them as frequently, if not more frequently, than to other men, they no doubt feel their weakness, and think themselves despised, little knowing that we, the stronger ones in body, feel nothing but admiration as we watch the splendid victory of the soul over its earthly companion which their lives display.

It was through Frank Smedley that Mr. Dodgson became one of the contributors to *The Comic Times*. Several of his poems appeared in it, and Mr. Yates wrote to him in the kindest manner, expressing warm approval of them. When *The Comic Times* changed hands in 1856, and was reduced to half its size, the whole staff left it and started a new venture, *The Train*. They were joined by Sala, whose stories in *Household Words* were at that time usually ascribed by the uninitiated to Charles Dickens. Mr. Dodgson's contributions to *The Train* included the following: "Solitude" (March, 1856); "Novelty and Romancement" (October, 1856); "The Three Voices" (November, 1856); "The Sailor's Wife" (May, 1857); and last, but by no means least, "Hiawatha's Photographing" (December, 1857). All of these, except "Novelty and Romancement," have since been republished in "Rhyme? and Reason?" and "Three Sunsets."

The last entry in Mr. Dodgson's Diary for this year reads as follows:—

I am sitting alone in my bedroom this last night of the old year, waiting for midnight. It has been the most eventful year of my life: I began it a poor bachelor student, with no definite plans or expectations; I end it a master and tutor in Ch. Ch., with an income of more than £300 a year, and the course of mathematical tuition marked out by God's providence for at least some years to come. Great mercies, great failings, time lost, talents misapplied—such has been the past year.

His Diary is full of such modest depreciations of himself and his work, interspersed with earnest prayers (too sacred and private to be reproduced here) that God would forgive him the past, and help him to perform His holy will in the future. And all the time that he was thus speaking of himself as a sinner, and a man who was utterly falling short of his aim, he was living a life full of good deeds and innumerable charities, a life of incessant labour and unremitting fulfilment of duty. So, I suppose, it is always with those who have a really high ideal; the harder they try to approach it the more it seems to recede from them, or rather, perhaps, it is impossible to be both "the subject and spectator" of goodness. As Coventry Patmore wrote:—

Become whatever good you see;
Nor sigh if, forthwith, fades from view
The grace of which you may not be
The Subject and spectator too.

The reading of "Alton Locke" turned his mind towards social subjects. "If the book were but a little more definite," he writes, "it might stir up many fellow-workers in the same good field of social improvement. Oh that God, in His good providence, may make me hereafter such a worker! But alas, what are the means? Each one has his own *nostrum* to propound, and in the Babel of voices nothing is done. I would thankfully spend and be spent so long as I were sure of really effecting something by the sacrifice, and not merely lying down under the wheels of some irresistible Juggernaut."

He was for some time the editor of *College Rhymes*, a Christ Church paper, in which his poem, "A Sea Dirge" (afterwards republished in "Phantasmagoria," and again in "Rhyme? and Reason?"), first appeared. The following verses were among his contributions to the same magazine:—

I painted her a gushing thing,
With years perhaps a score
I little thought to find they were
At least a dozen more;
My fancy gave her eyes of blue,
A curly auburn head:
I came to find the blue a green,
The auburn turned to red.

She boxed my ears this morning,
They tingled very much;
I own that I could wish her
A somewhat lighter touch;
And if you were to ask me how

Her charms might be improved,
I would not have them *added to*,
But just a few *removed*!

She has the bear's ethereal grace,
The bland hyena's laugh,
The footstep of the elephant,
The neck of the giraffe;
I love her still, believe me,
Though my heart its passion hides;
"She is all my fancy painted her,"
But oh! *how much besides*!

It was when writing for *The Train* that he first felt the need of a pseudonym. He suggested "Dares" (the first syllable of his birthplace) to Edmund Yates, but, as this did not meet with his editor's approval, he wrote again, giving a choice of four names, (1) Edgar Cuthwellis, (2) Edgar U. C. Westhall, (3) Louis Carroll, and (4) Lewis Carroll. The first two were formed from the letters of his two Christian names, Charles Lutwidge; the others are merely variant forms of those names—Lewis = Ludovicus = Lutwidge; Carroll = Carolus = Charles. Mr. Yates chose the last, and thenceforward it became Mr. Dodgson's ordinary *nom de plume* . The first occasion on which he used it was, I believe, when he wrote "The Path of Roses," a poem which appeared in *The Train* in May, 1856.

On June 16th he again visited the Princess's Theatre. This time the play was "A Winter's Tale," and he "especially admired the acting of the little Mamillius, Ellen Terry, a beautiful little creature, who played with remarkable ease and spirit."

During the Long Vacation he spent a few weeks in the English Lake District. In spite of the rain, of which he had his full share, he managed to see a good deal of the best scenery, and made the ascent of Gable in the face of an icy gale, which laid him up with neuralgia for some days. He and his companions returned to Croft by way of Barnard Castle, as he narrates in his Diary:—

We set out by coach for Barnard Castle at about seven, and passed over about forty miles of the dreariest hill-country I ever saw; the climax of wretchedness was reached in Bowes, where yet stands the original of "Dotheboys Hall"; it has long ceased to be used as a school, and is falling into ruin, in which the whole place seems to be following its example—the roofs are falling in, and the windows broken or barricaded—the whole town looks plague-stricken. The courtyard of the inn we stopped at was grown over with weeds, and a mouthing idiot lolled against the corner of the house, like the evil genius of the spot. Next to a prison or a lunatic asylum, preserve me from living at Bowes!

Although he was anything but a sportsman, he was interested in the subject of betting, from a mathematical standpoint solely, and in 1857 he sent a letter to *Bell's Life*, explaining a method by which a betting man might ensure winning over any race. The system was either to back *every* horse, or to lay against *every* horse, according to the way the odds added up. He showed his scheme to a sporting friend, who remarked, "An excellent system, and you're bound to win—*if only you can get people to take your bets.*"

In the same year he made the acquaintance of Tennyson, whose writings he had long intensely admired. He thus describes the poet's appearance:

A strange shaggy-looking man; his hair, moustache, and beard looked wild and neglected; these very much hid the character of the face. He was dressed in a loosely fitting morning coat, common grey flannel waistcoat and trousers, and a carelessly tied black silk neckerchief. His hair is black; I think the eyes too; they are keen and restless—nose aquiline—forehead high and broad—both face and head are fine and manly. His manner was kind and friendly from the first; there is a dry lurking humour in his style of talking. I took the opportunity [he goes on to say] of asking the meaning of two passages in his poems, which have always puzzled me: one in "Maud"—

Strange that I hear two men
Somewhere talking of me;
Well, if it prove a girl, my boy
Will have plenty; so let it be.

He said it referred to Maud, and to the two fathers arranging a match between himself and her.

The other was of the poet—

Dowered with the hate of hate, the scorn of scorn,
The love of love.

He said that he was quite willing it should bear any meaning the words would fairly bear; to the best of his recollection his meaning when he wrote it was "the hate of the quality hate, &c.," but he thought the meaning of "the quintessence of hatred" finer. He said there had never been a poem so misunderstood by the "ninnies of critics" as "Maud."

During an evening spent at Tent Lodge Tennyson remarked, on the similarity of the monkey's skull to the human, that a young monkey's skull is quite human in shape, and gradually alters—the analogy being borne out by the human skull being at first more like the statues of the gods, and gradually degenerating into human; and then, turning to Mrs. Tennyson,

"There, that's the second original remark I've made this evening!" Mr. Dodgson saw a great deal of the Tennysons after this, and photographed the poet himself and various members of his family.

In October he made the acquaintance of John Ruskin, who in after years was always willing to assist him with his valuable advice on any point of artistic criticism. Mr. Dodgson was singularly fortunate in his friends; whenever he was in difficulties on any technical matters, whether of religion, law, medicine, art, or whatever it might be, he always had some one especially distinguished in that branch of study whose aid he could seek as a friend. In particular, the names of Canon King (now Bishop of Lincoln), and Sir James Paget occur to me; to the latter Mr. Dodgson addressed many letters on questions of medicine and surgery—some of them intricate enough, but never too intricate to weary the unfailing patience of the great surgeon.

A note in Mr. Dodgson's Journal, May 9, 1857, describes his introduction to Thackeray:—

I breakfasted this morning with Fowler of Lincoln to meet Thackeray (the author), who delivered his lecture on George III. in Oxford last night. I was much pleased with what I saw of him; his manner is simple and unaffected; he shows no anxiety to shine in conversation, though full of fun and anecdote when drawn out. He seemed delighted with the reception he had met with last night: the undergraduates seem to have behaved with most unusual moderation.

The next few years of his life passed quietly, and without any unusual events to break the monotony of college routine. He spent his mornings in the lecture-rooms, his afternoons in the country or on the river—he was very fond of boating—and his evenings in his room, reading and preparing for the next day's work. But in spite of all this outward calm of life, his mind was very much exercised on the subject of taking Holy Orders. Not only was this step necessary if he wished to retain his Studentship, but also he felt that it would give him much more influence among the undergraduates, and thus increase his power of doing good. On the other hand, he was not prepared to live the life of almost puritanical strictness which was then considered essential for a clergyman, and he saw that the impediment of speech from which he suffered would greatly interfere with the proper performance of his clerical duties.

The Bishop of Oxford, Dr. Wilberforce, had expressed the opinion that the "resolution to attend theatres or operas was an absolute disqualification for Holy Orders," which discouraged him very much, until it transpired that this statement was only meant to refer to the parochial clergy. He discussed the matter with Dr. Pusey, and with Dr.

Liddon. The latter said that "he thought a deacon might lawfully, if he found himself unfit for the work, abstain from direct ministerial duty." And so, with many qualms about his own unworthiness, he at last decided to prepare definitely for ordination.

On December 22, 1861, he was ordained deacon by the Bishop of Oxford. He never proceeded to priest's orders, partly, I think, because he felt that if he were to do so it would be his duty to undertake regular parochial work, and partly on account of his stammering. He used, however, to preach not unfrequently, and his sermons were always delightful to listen to, his extreme earnestness being evident in every word.

"He knew exactly what he wished to say" (I am quoting from an article in *The Guardian*), "and completely forgot his audience in his anxiety to explain his point clearly. He thought of the subject only, and the words came of themselves. Looking straight in front of him he saw, as it were, his argument mapped out in the form of a diagram, and he set to work to prove it point by point, under its separate heads, and then summed up the whole."

One sermon which he preached in the University Church, on Eternal Punishment, is not likely to be soon forgotten by those who heard it. I, unfortunately, was not of that number, but I can well imagine how his clear-cut features would light up as he dwelt lovingly upon the mercy of that Being whose charity far exceeds "the measure of man's mind." It is hardly necessary to say that he himself did not believe in eternal punishment, or any other scholastic doctrine that contravenes the love of God.

He disliked being complimented on his sermons, but he liked to be told of any good effects that his words had had upon any member of the congregation. "Thank you for telling me that fact about my sermon," he wrote to one of his sisters, who told him of some such good fruit that one of his addresses had borne. "I have once or twice had such information volunteered; and it is a *great* comfort—and a kind of thing that is *really* good for one to know. It is *not* good to be told (and I never wish to be told), 'Your sermon was so *beautiful*.' We shall not be concerned to know, in the Great Day, whether we have preached beautiful sermons, but whether they were preached with the one object of serving God."

He was always ready and willing to preach at the special service for College servants, which used to be held at Christ Church every Sunday evening; but best of all he loved to preach to children. Some of his last sermons were delivered at Christ Church, Eastbourne (the church he regularly attended during the Long Vacation), to a congregation of children. On those occasions he told them an allegory—*Victor and Arnion,* which he intended to publish in course of time—putting all his heart into the work, and speaking with such deep feeling that at times he was almost unable to control his emotion as he told them of the love and compassion of the Good Shepherd.

I have dwelt at some length on this side of his life, for it is, I am sure, almost ignored in the popular estimate of him. He was essentially a religious man in the best sense of the term, and without any of that morbid sentimentality which is too often associated with the word; and while his religion consecrated his talents, and raised him to a height which without it he could never have reached, the example of such a man as he was, so brilliant, so witty, so successful, and yet so full of faith, consecrates the very conception of religion, and makes it yet more beautiful.

On April 13, 1859, he paid another visit to Tennyson, this time at Farringford.

After dinner we retired for about an hour to the smoking-room, where I saw the proof-sheets of the "King's Idylls," but he would not let me read them. He walked through the garden with me when I left, and made me remark an effect produced on the thin white clouds by the moon shining through, which I had not noticed—a ring of golden light at some distance off the moon, with an interval of white between—this, he says, he has alluded to in one of his early poems ("Margaret," vol. i.), "the tender amber." I asked his opinion of Sydney Dobell—he agrees with me in liking "Grass from the Battlefield," and thinks him a writer of genius and imagination, but extravagant.

On another occasion he showed the poet a photograph which he had taken of Miss Alice Liddell as a beggar-child, and which Tennyson said was the most beautiful photograph he had ever seen.

Tennyson told us he had often dreamed long passages of poetry, and believed them to be good at the time, though he could never remember them after waking, except four lines which he dreamed at ten years old:—

May a cock sparrow
Write to a barrow?
I hope you'll excuse
My infantile muse;
—which, as an unpublished fragment of the Poet Laureate, may be thought interesting, but not affording much promise of his after powers. He also told us he once dreamed an enormously long poem about fairies, which began with very long lines that gradually got shorter, and ended with fifty or sixty lines of two syllables each!

On October 17, 1859, the Prince of Wales came into residence at Christ Church. The Dean met him at the station, and all the dons assembled in

Tom Quadrangle to welcome him. Mr. Dodgson, as usual, had an eye to a photograph, in which hope, however, he was doomed to disappointment. His Royal Highness was tired of having his picture taken.

During his early college life he used often to spend a few days at Hastings, with his mother's sisters, the Misses Lutwidge. In a letter written from their house to his sister Mary, and dated April 11, 1860, he gives an

> I am just returned from a series of dissolving views on the Arctic regions, and, while the information there received is still fresh in my mind, I will try to give you some of it. In the first place, you may not know that one of the objects of the Arctic expeditions was to discover "the intensity of the magnetic needle." He [the lecturer] did not tell us, however, whether they had succeeded in discovering it, or whether that rather obscure question is still doubtful. One of the explorers, Baffin, "*though* he did not suffer all the hardships the others did, *yet* he came to an untimely end (of course one would think in the Arctic regions), *for instance* (what follows being, I suppose, one of the untimely ends he came to), being engaged in a war of the Portuguese against the Prussians, while measuring the ground in front of a fortification, a cannon-ball came against him, with the force with which cannon-balls in that day *did* come, and killed him dead on the spot." How many instances of this kind would you demand to prove that he did come to an untimely end? One of the ships was laid up three years in the ice, during which time, he told us, "Summer came and went frequently." This, I think, was the most remarkable phenomenon he mentioned in the whole lecture, and gave *me* quite a new idea of those regions.

account of a lecture he had just heard:—

On Tuesday I went to a concert at St. Leonard's. On the front seat sat a youth about twelve years of age, of whom the enclosed is a tolerably accurate sketch. He really was, I think, the ugliest boy I ever saw. I wish I could get an opportunity of photographing him.

The following note occurs in his Journal for May 6th:—

A Christ Church man, named Wilmot, who is just returned from the West Indies, dined in Hall. He told us some curious things about the insects in South America—one that he had himself seen was a spider charming a cockroach with flashes of light; they were both on the wall, the spider about a yard the highest, and the light was like a glow-worm, only that it came by flashes and did not shine continuously; the cockroach gradually crawled up to it, and allowed itself to be taken and killed.

A few months afterwards, when in town and visiting Mr. Munroe's studio, he found there two of the children of Mr. George Macdonald, whose acquaintance he had already made: "They were a girl and boy, about seven and six years old—I claimed their acquaintance, and began at once proving to the boy, Greville, that he had better take the opportunity of having his head changed for a marble one. The effect was that in about two minutes they had entirely forgotten that I was a total stranger, and were earnestly arguing the question as if we were old acquaintances." Mr. Dodgson urged that a marble head would not have to be brushed and combed. At this the boy turned to his sister with an air of great relief, saying, "Do you hear *that*, Mary? It needn't be combed!" And the narrator adds, "I have no doubt combing, with his great head of long hair, like Hallam Tennyson's, was *the* misery of his life. His final argument was that a marble head couldn't speak, and as I couldn't convince either that he would be all the better for that, I gave in."

In November he gave a lecture at a meeting of the Ashmolean Society on "Where does the Day begin?" The problem, which was one he was very fond of propounding, may be thus stated: If a man could travel round the world so fast that the sun would be always directly above his head, and if he were to start travelling at midday on Tuesday, then in twenty-four hours he would return to his original point of departure, and would find that the day was now called Wednesday—at what point of his journey would the day change its name? The difficulty of answering this apparently simple question has cast a gloom over many a pleasant party.

On December 12th he wrote in his Diary:—

Visit of the Queen to Oxford, to the great surprise of everybody, as it had been kept a secret up to the time. She arrived in Christ Church about twelve, and came into Hall with the Dean, where the Collections were still going on, about a dozen men being in Hall. The party consisted of the Queen, Prince Albert, Princess Alice and her intended husband, the Prince of Hesse-Darmstadt, the Prince of Wales, Prince Alfred, and suite. They remained a minute or two looking at the pictures, and the Sub-Dean was presented: they then visited the Cathedral and Library. Evening entertainment at the Deanery, *tableaux vivants* . I went a little after half-past eight, and found a great party assembled—the Prince had not yet come. He arrived before nine, and I found an opportunity of reminding General Bruce of his promise to introduce me to the Prince, which he did at the next break in the conversation H.R.H. was holding with Mrs. Fellowes. He shook hands very graciously, and I began with a sort of apology for having been so importunate about the photograph. He said something of the weather being against it, and I asked if the Americans had victimised him much as a sitter; he said they had, but he did not think they had succeeded well, and I told him of the new American process of taking twelve thousand photographs in an hour. Edith Liddell coming by at the moment, I remarked on the beautiful *tableau* which the children might make: he assented, and also said, in answer to my question, that he had seen and admired my photographs of them. I then said that I hoped, as I had missed the photograph, he would at least give me his autograph in my album, which he promised to do. Thinking I had better bring the talk to an end, I concluded by saying that, if he would like copies of any of my photographs, I should feel honoured by his accepting them; he thanked me for this, and I then drew back, as he did not seem inclined to pursue the conversation.

A few days afterwards the Prince gave him his autograph, and also chose a dozen or so of his photograph (sic).

CHAPTER III

(1861—1867)

Jowett—Index to "In Memoriam"—The Tennysons—The beginning of "Alice"—Tenniel—Artistic friends—"Alice's Adventures in Wonderland"—"Bruno's Revenge"—Tour with Dr. Liddon—Cologne—Berlin architecture—The "Majesty of Justice"—Peterhof—Moscow—A Russian wedding—Nijni—The Troitska Monastery—"Hieroglyphic" writing—Giessen.

It is my aim in this Memoir to let Mr. Dodgson tell his own story as much as possible. In order to effect this object I have drawn largely upon his Diary and correspondence. Very few men have left behind them such copious information about their lives as he has; unfortunately it is not equally copious throughout, and this fact must be my apology for the somewhat haphazard and disconnected way in which parts of this book are written. That it is the best which, under the circumstances, I have been able to do needs, I hope, no saying, but the circumstances have at times been too strong for me.

Though in later years Mr. Dodgson almost gave up the habit of dining out, at this time of his life he used to do it pretty frequently, and several of the notes in his Diary refer to after-dinner and Common Room stories. The two following extracts will show the sort of facts he recorded:—

January 2, 1861.—Mr. Grey (Canon) came to dine and stay the night. He told me a curious old custom of millers, that they place the sails of the mill as a Saint Andrew's Cross when work is entirely suspended, thus x, but in an upright cross, thus +, if they are just going to resume work. He also mentioned that he was at school with Dr. Tennyson (father of the poet), and was a great favourite of his. He remembers that Tennyson used to do his school-translations in rhyme.

May 9th.—Met in Common Room Rev. C.F. Knight, and the Hon'ble. F.J. Parker, both of Boston, U.S. The former gave an amusing account of having seen Oliver Wendell Holmes in a fishmonger's, lecturing *extempore* on the head of a freshly killed turtle, whose eyes and jaws still showed muscular action: the lecture of course being all "cram," but accepted as sober earnest by the mob outside.

Old Oxford men will remember the controversies that raged from about 1860 onwards over the opinions of the late Dr. Jowett. In my time the name "Jowett" only represented the brilliant translator of Plato, and the deservedly loved master of Balliol, whose sermons in the little College Chapel were often attended by other than Balliol men, and whose reputation for learning was expressed in the well-known verse of "The Masque of Balliol":—

First come I, my name is Jowett.
There's no knowledge but I know it;
I am Master of this College;
What I don't know isn't knowledge.

But in 1861 he was anything but universally popular, and I am afraid that Mr. Dodgson, nothing if not a staunch Conservative, sided with the majority against him. Thus he wrote in his Diary:—

November 20th.—Promulgation, in Congregation, of the new statute to endow Jowett. The speaking took up the whole afternoon, and the two points at issue, the endowing a *Regius* Professorship, and the countenancing Jowett's theological opinions, got so inextricably mixed up that I rose to beg that they might be kept separate. Once on my feet, I said more than I at first meant, and defied them ever to tire out the opposition by perpetually bringing the question on (*Mem.*: if I ever speak again I will try to say no more than I had resolved before rising). This was my first speech in Congregation.

At the beginning of 1862 an "Index to In Memoriam," compiled by Mr. Dodgson and his sisters, was published by Moxon. Tennyson had given his consent, and the little book proved to be very useful to his admirers.

On January 27th Morning Prayer was for the first time read in English at the Christ Church College Service. On the same day Mr. Dodgson moved over into new rooms, as the part of the College where he had formerly lived (Chaplain's Quadrangle) was to be pulled down.

During the Easter Vacation he paid another visit to the Tennysons, which he describes as follows:—

After luncheon I went to the Tennysons, and got Hallam and Lionel to sign their names in my album. Also I made a bargain with Lionel, that he was to give me some MS. of his verses, and I was to send him some of mine. It was a very difficult bargain to make; I almost despaired of it at first, he put in so many conditions—first, I was to play a game of chess with him; this, with much difficulty, was reduced to twelve moves on each side; but this made little difference, as I check-mated him at the sixth move. Second, he was to be allowed to give me one blow on the head with a mallet (this he at last consented to give up). I forget if there were others, but it ended in my getting the verses, for which I have written out "The Lonely Moor" for him.

Mr. Dodgson took a great interest in occult phenomena, and was for some time an enthusiastic member of the "Psychical Society." It was his interest in ghosts that led to his meeting with the artist Mr. Heaphy, who had painted a picture of a ghost which he himself had seen. I quote the following from a letter to his sister Mary:—

During my last visit to town, I paid a very interesting visit to a new artist, Mr. Heaphy. Do you remember that curious story of a ghost lady (in *Household Words* or *All the Year Round*), who sat to an artist for her picture; it was called "Mr. H.'s Story," and he was the writer.... He received me most kindly, and we had a very interesting talk about the ghost, which certainly is one of the most curious and inexplicable stories I ever heard. He showed me her picture (life size), and she must have been very lovely, if it is like her (or like it, which ever is the correct pronoun).... Mr. Heaphy showed me a most interesting collection of drawings he has made abroad; he has been about, hunting up the earliest and most authentic pictures of our Saviour, some merely outlines, some coloured pictures. They agree wonderfully in the character of the face, and one, he says, there is no doubt was done before the year 150.... I feel sure from his tone that he is doing this in a religious spirit, and not merely as an artist.

On July 4, 1862, there is a very important entry: "I made an expedition *up* the river to Godstow with the three Liddells; we had tea on the bank there, and did not reach Christ Church till half-past eight."

On the opposite page he added, somewhat later, "On which occasion I told them the fairy-tale of 'Alice's Adventures Underground,' which I undertook to write out for Alice."

These words need to be supplemented by the verses with which he prefaced the "Wonderland":—

All in the golden afternoon
Full leisurely we glide;
For both our oars, with little skill,
By little arms are plied,
While little hands make vain pretence
Our wanderings to guide.

Ah, cruel Three! In such an hour,
Beneath such dreamy weather,
To beg a tale of breath too weak
To stir the tiniest feather!
Yet what can one poor voice avail
Against three tongues together?

Imperious Prima flashes forth
Her edict "to begin it"—
In gentler tones Secunda hopes
"There will be nonsense in it!"
While Tertia interrupts the tale
Not *more* than once a minute.

Anon, to sudden silence won,
In fancy they pursue
The dream-child moving through a land
Of wonders wild and new,
In friendly chat with bird or beast—
And half believe it true.

And ever, as the story drained
The wells of fancy dry,
And faintly strove that weary one
To put the subject by,
"The rest next time"—"It *is* next time!"
The happy voices cry.

Thus grew the tale of Wonderland:
Thus slowly, one by one,
Its quaint events were hammered out—
And now the tale is done,
And home we steer, a merry crew,
Beneath the setting sun.

"Alice" herself (Mrs. Reginald Hargreaves) has given an account of the scene, from which what follows is quoted:—

Most of Mr. Dodgson's stories were told to us on river expeditions to Nuneham or Godstow, near Oxford. My eldest sister, now Mrs. Skene, was "Prima," I was "Secunda," and "Tertia" was my sister Edith. I believe the beginning of "Alice" was told one summer afternoon when the sun was so burning that we had landed in the meadows down the river, deserting the boat to take refuge in the only bit of shade to be found, which was under a new-made hayrick. Here from all three came the old petition of "Tell us a story," and so began the ever-delightful tale. Sometimes to tease us—and perhaps being really tired—Mr. Dodgson would stop suddenly and say, "And that's all till next time." "Ah, but it is next time," would be the exclamation from all three; and after some persuasion the story would start afresh. Another day, perhaps, the story would begin in the boat, and Mr. Dodgson, in the middle of telling a thrilling adventure, would pretend to go fast asleep, to our great dismay.

"Alice's Adventures Underground" was the original name of the story; later on it became "Alice's Hour in Elfland." It was not until June 18, 1864, that he finally decided upon "Alice's Adventures in Wonderland." The illustrating of the manuscript book gave him some trouble. He had to borrow a "Natural History" from the Deanery to learn the correct shapes of some of the strange animals with which Alice conversed; the Mock Turtle he must have evolved out of his inner consciousness, for it is, I think, a species unknown to naturalists.

He was lucky enough during the course of the year to see a ceremony which is denied to most Oxford men. When degrees are given, any tradesman who has been unable to get his due from an undergraduate about to be made a Bachelor of Arts is allowed, by custom, to pluck the Proctor's gown as he passes, and then to make his complaint. This law is more honoured in the breach than in the observance; but, on the occasion of this visit of Mr. Dodgson's to Convocation, the Proctor's gown was actually plucked—on account of an unfortunate man who had gone through the Bankruptcy Court.

When he promised to write out "Alice" for Miss Liddell he had no idea of publication; but his friend, Mr. George Macdonald, to whom he had shown the story, persuaded him to submit it to a publisher. Messrs. Macmillan agreed to produce it, and as Mr. Dodgson had not sufficient faith in his own artistic powers to venture to allow his illustrations to appear, it was necessary to find some artist who would undertake the work. By the advice of Tom Taylor he approached Mr. Tenniel, who was fortunately well disposed, and on April 5, 1864, the final arrangements were made.

The following interesting account of a meeting with Mr. Dodgson is from the pen of Mrs. Bennie, wife of the Rector of Glenfield, near Leicester:—

Some little time after the publication of "Alice's Adventures" we went for our summer holiday to Whitby. We were visiting friends, and my brother and sister went to the hotel. They soon after asked us to dine with them there at the *table d'hôte*. I had on one side of me a gentleman whom I did not know, but as I had spent a good deal of time travelling in foreign countries, I always, at once, speak to any one I am placed next. I found on this occasion I had a very agreeable neighbour, and we seemed to be much interested in the same books, and politics also were touched on. After dinner my sister and brother rather took me to task for talking so much to a complete stranger. I said. "But it was quite a treat to talk to him and to hear him talk. Of one thing I am quite sure, he is a genius." My brother and sister, who had not heard him speak, again laughed at me, and said, "You are far too easily pleased." I, however, maintained my point, and said what great delight his conversation had given me, and how remarkably clever it had been. Next morning nurse took out our two little twin daughters in front of the sea. I went out a short time afterwards, looked for them, and found them seated with my friend of the *table d'hôte* between them, and they were listening to him, open-mouthed, and in the greatest state of enjoyment, with his knee covered with minute toys. I, seeing their great delight, motioned to him to go on; this he did for some time. A most charming story he told them about sea-urchins and Ammonites. When it was over, I said, "You must be the author of 'Alice's Adventures.'" He laughed, but looked astonished, and said, "My dear Madam, my name is Dodgson, and 'Alice's Adventures' was written by Lewis Carroll." I replied, "Then you must have borrowed the name, for only he could have told a story as you have just done." After a little sparring he admitted the fact, and I went home and proudly told my sister and brother how my genius had turned out a greater one than I expected. They assured me I must be mistaken, and that, as I had suggested it to him, he had taken advantage of the idea, and said he was what I wanted him to be. A few days after some friends came to Whitby who knew his aunts, and confirmed the truth of his statement, and thus I made the acquaintance of one whose friendship has been the source of great pleasure for nearly thirty years. He has most generously sent us all his books, with kind inscriptions, to "Minnie and Doe," whom he photographed, but would not take Canon Bennie or me; he said he never took portraits of people of more than seventeen years of age until they were seventy. He visited us, and we often met him at Eastbourne, and his death was indeed a great loss after so many happy years of friendship with one we so greatly admired and loved.

He spent a part of the Long Vacation at Freshwater, taking great interest in the children who, for him, were the chief attraction of the seaside.

Every morning four little children dressed in yellow go by from the front down to the beach: they go by in a state of great excitement, brandishing wooden spades, and making strange noises; from that moment they disappear entirely—they are never to be seen *on* the beach. The only theory I can form is, that they all tumble into a hole somewhere, and continue excavating therein during the day: however that may be, I have once or twice come across them returning at night, in exactly the same state of excitement, and seemingly in quite as great a hurry to get home as they were before to get out. The evening noises they make sound to me very much like the morning noises, but I suppose they are different to them, and contain an account of the day's achievements.

His enthusiasm for photography, and his keen appreciation of the beautiful, made him prefer the society of artists to that of any other class of people. He knew the Rossettis intimately, and his Diary shows him to have been acquainted with Millais, Holman Hunt, Sant, Westmacott, Val Prinsep, Watts, and a host of others. Arthur Hughes painted a charming picture to his order ("The Lady with the Lilacs") which used to hang in his rooms at Christ Church. The Andersons were great friends of his, Mrs. Anderson being one of his favourite child-painters. Those who have visited him at Oxford will remember a beautiful girl's head, painted by her from a rough sketch she had once made in a railway carriage of a child who happened to be sitting opposite her.

His own drawings were in no way remarkable. Ruskin, whose advice he took on his artistic capabilities, told him that he had not enough talent to make it worth his while to devote much time to sketching, but every one who saw his photographs admired them. Considering the difficulties of the "wet process," and the fact that he had a conscientious horror of "touching up" his negatives, the pictures he produced are quite wonderful. Some of them were shown to the Queen, who said that she admired them very much, and that they were "such as the Prince would have appreciated very highly, and taken much pleasure in."

On July 4, 1865, exactly three years after the memorable row up the river, Miss Alice Liddell received the first presentation copy of "Alice's Adventures in Wonderland": the second was sent to Princess Beatrice.

The first edition, which consisted of two thousand copies, was condemned by both author and illustrator, for the pictures did not come out well. All purchasers were accordingly asked to return their copies, and to send their names and addresses; a new edition was prepared, and distributed to those who had sent back their old copies, which the author gave away to various homes and hospitals. The substituted edition was a complete success, "a perfect piece of artistic printing," as Mr. Dodgson called it. He hardly dared to hope that more than two thousand copies would be sold, and anticipated a considerable loss over the book. His surprise was great when edition after edition was demanded, and when he found that "Alice," far from being a monetary failure, was bringing him in a very considerable income every year.

A rough comparison between "Alice's Adventures Underground" and the book in its completed form, shows how slight were the alterations that Lewis Carroll thought it necessary to make.

The "Wonderland" is somewhat longer, but the general plan of the book, and the simplicity of diction, which is one of its principal charms, are unchanged. His memory was so good that I believe the story as he wrote it down was almost word for word the same that he had told in the boat. The whole idea came like an inspiration into his mind, and that sort of inspiration does not often come more than once in a lifetime. Nothing which he wrote afterwards had anything like the same amount of freshness, of wit, of real genius. The "Looking-Glass" most closely approached it in these qualities, but then it was only the following out of the same idea. The most ingenuous comparison of the two books I have seen was the answer of a little girl whom Lewis Carroll had asked if she had read them: "Oh yes, I've read both of them, and I think," (this more slowly and thoughtfully) "I think 'Through the Looking-Glass' is more stupid than 'Alice's Adventures.' Don't you think so?"

The critics were loud in their praises of "Alice"; there was hardly a dissentient voice among them, and the reception which the public gave the book justified their opinion. So recently as July, 1898, the *Pall Mall Gazette* conducted an inquiry into the popularity of children's books. "The verdict is so natural that it will surprise no normal person. The winner is 'Alice in Wonderland'; 'Through the Looking-Glass' is in the twenty, but much lower down."

"Alice" has been translated into French, German, Italian, and Dutch, while one poem, "Father William," has even been turned into Arabic. Several plays have been based upon it; lectures have been given, illustrated by magic-lantern slides of Tenniel's pictures, which have also adorned wall-papers and biscuit-boxes. Mr. Dodgson himself designed a very ingenious "Wonderland" stamp-case; there has been an "Alice" birthday-book; at schools, children have been taught to read out of "Alice," while the German edition, shortened and simplified for the purpose, has also been used as a lesson-book. With the exception of Shakespeare's plays, very few, if any, books are so frequently quoted in the daily Press as the two "Alices."

In 1866 Mr. Dodgson was introduced to Miss Charlotte M. Yonge, whose novels had long delighted him. "It was a pleasure I had long hoped for," he says, "and I was very much pleased with her cheerful and easy manners—the sort of person one knows in a few minutes as well as many in many years."

In 1867 he contributed a story to *Aunt Judy's Magazine* called "Bruno's Revenge," the charming little idyll out of which "Sylvie and Bruno" grew. The creation of Bruno was the only act of homage Lewis Carroll ever paid to boy-nature, for which, as a rule, he professed an aversion almost amounting to terror. Nevertheless, on the few occasions on which I have seen him in the company of boys, he seemed to be thoroughly at his ease, telling them stories and showing them puzzles.

I give an extract from Mrs. Gatty's letter, acknowledging the receipt of "Bruno's Revenge" for her magazine:—

I need hardly tell you that the story is *delicious*. It is beautiful and fantastic and childlike, and I cannot sufficiently thank you. I am so *proud* for *Aunt Judy* that you have honoured *her* by sending it here, rather than to the *Cornhill*, or one of the grander Magazines.

To-morrow I shall send the Manuscript to London probably; to-day I keep it to enjoy a little further, and that the young ladies may do so too. One word more. Make this one of a series. You may have great mathematical abilities, but so have hundreds of others. This talent is peculiarly your own, and as an Englishman you are almost unique in possessing it. If you covet fame, therefore, it will be (I think) gained by this. Some of the touches are so exquisite, one would have thought nothing short of intercourse with fairies could have put them into your head.

Somewhere about this time he was invited to witness a rehearsal of a children's play at a London theatre. As he sat in the wings, chatting to the manager, a little four-year-old girl, one of the performers, climbed up on his knee, and began talking to him. She was very anxious to be allowed to play the principal part (Mrs. Mite), which had been assigned to some other child. "I wish I might act Mrs. Mite," she said; "I know all her part, and I'd get an *encore* for every word."

During the year he published his book on "Determinants." To those accustomed to regard mathematics as the driest of dry subjects, and mathematicians as necessarily devoid of humour, it seems scarcely credible that "An Elementary Treatise on Determinants," and "Alice in Wonderland" were written by the same author, and it came quite as a revelation to the undergraduate who heard for the first time that Mr. Dodgson of Christ Church and Lewis Carroll were identical.

The book in question, admirable as it is in many ways, has not commanded a large sale. The nature of the subject would be against it, as most students whose aim is to get as good a place as possible in the class lists cannot afford the luxury of a separate work, and have to be content with the few chapters devoted to "Determinants" in works on Higher Algebra or the Theory of Equations, supplemented by references to Mr. Dodgson's work which can be found in the College libraries.

The general acceptance of the book would be rather restricted by the employment of new words and symbols, which, as the author himself felt, "are always a most unwelcome addition to a science already burdened with an enormous vocabulary." But the work itself is largely original, and its arrangement and style are, perhaps, as attractive as the nature of the subject will allow. Such a book as this has little interest for the general reader, yet, amongst the leisured few who are able to read mathematics for their own sake, the treatise has found warm admirers.

In the Summer Vacation of 1867 he went for a tour on the Continent, accompanied by Dr. Liddon, whom I have already mentioned as having been one of his most intimate friends at this time. During the whole of this tour Mr. Dodgson kept a diary, more with the idea that it would help him afterwards to remember what he had seen than with any notion of publication. However, in later years it did occur to him that others might be interested in his impressions and experiences, though he never actually took any steps towards putting them before the public. Perhaps he was wise, for a traveller's diary always contains much information that can be obtained just as well from any guide-book. In the extracts which I reproduce here, I hope that I have not retained anything which comes under that category.

July 12th.—The Sultan and I arrived in London almost at the same time, but in different quarters—*my* point of entry being Paddington, and *his* Charing Cross. I must admit that the crowd was greatest at the latter place.

Mr. Dodgson and Dr. Liddon met at Dover, and passed the night at one of the hotels there:—

July 13th.—We breakfasted, as agreed, at eight, or at least we then sat down and nibbled bread and butter till such time as the chops should be done, which great event took place about half past. We tried pathetic appeals to the wandering waiters, who told us, "They are coming, sir," in a soothing tone, and we tried stern remonstrance, and they then said, "They are coming, sir," in a more injured tone; and after all such appeals they retired into their dens, and hid themselves behind side-boards and dish-covers, and still the chops came not. We agreed that of all virtues a waiter can display, that of a retiring disposition is quite the least desirable....

The pen refuses to describe the sufferings of some of the passengers during our smooth trip of ninety minutes: my own sensations were those of extreme surprise, and a little indignation, at there being no other sensations—it was not for *that* I paid my money....

We landed at Calais in the usual swarm of friendly natives, offering services and advice of all kinds; to all such remarks I returned one simple answer, *Non!* It was probably not strictly applicable in all cases, but it answered the purpose of getting rid of them; one by one they left me, echoing the *Non!* in various tones, but all expressive of disgust.

At Cologne began that feast of beautiful things which his artistic temperament fitted him so well to enjoy. Though the churches he visited and the ceremonies he witnessed belonged to a religious system widely different from his own, the largeness and generosity of his mind always led him to insist upon that substratum of true devotion—to use a favourite word of his—which underlies all forms of Christianity.

We spent an hour in the cathedral, which I will not attempt to describe further than by saying it was the most beautiful of all churches I have ever seen or can imagine. If one could imagine the spirit of devotion embodied in any material form, it would be in such a building.

In spite of all the wealth of words that has been expended upon German art, he found something new to say on this most fertile subject:—

The amount of art lavished on the whole region of Potsdam is marvellous; some of the tops of the palaces were like forests of statues, and they were all over the gardens, set on pedestals. In fact, the two principles of Berlin architecture appear to me to be these. On the house-tops, wherever there is a convenient place, put up the figure of a man; he is best placed standing on one leg. Wherever there is room on the ground, put either a circular group of busts on pedestals, in consultation, all looking inwards—or else the colossal figure of a man killing, about to kill, or having killed (the present tense is preferred) a beast; the more pricks the beast has, the better—in fact a dragon is the correct thing, but if that is beyond the artist, he may content himself with a lion or a pig. The beast—killing principle has been carried out everywhere with a relentless monotony, which makes some parts of Berlin look like a fossil slaughter-house.

He never missed an opportunity of studying the foreign drama, which was most praiseworthy, as he knew very little German and not a word of Russ:—

At the hotel [at Danzig] was a green parrot on a stand; we addressed it as "Pretty Poll," and it put its head on one side and thought about it, but wouldn't commit itself to any statement. The waiter came up to inform us of the reason of its silence: "Er spricht nicht Englisch; er spricht nicht Deutsch." It appeared that the unfortunate bird could speak nothing but Mexican! Not knowing a word of that language, we could only pity it.

July 23rd.—We strolled about and bought a few photographs, and at 11.39 left for Königsberg. On our way to the station we came across the grandest instance of the "Majesty of Justice" that I have ever witnessed. A little boy was being taken to the magistrate, or to prison (probably for picking a pocket). The achievement of this feat had been entrusted to two soldiers in full uniform, who were solemnly marching, one in front of the poor little urchin and one behind, with bayonets fixed, of course, to be ready to charge in case he should attempt an escape.

July 25th.—In the evening I visited the theatre at Königsberg, which was fairly good in every way, and very good in the singing and some of the acting. The play was "Anno 66," but I could only catch a few words here and there, so have very little idea of the plot. One of the characters was a correspondent of an English newspaper. This singular being came on in the midst of a soldiers' bivouac before Sadowa, dressed very nearly in white—a very long frock-coat, and a tall hat on the back of his head, both nearly white. He said "Morning" as a general remark, when he first came on, but afterwards talked what I suppose was broken German. He appeared to be regarded as a butt by the soldiers, and ended his career by falling into a drum.

From Königsberg the travellers went on to St. Petersburg, where they stayed several days, exploring the wonderful city and its environs:—

There is a fine equestrian statue of Peter the Great near the Admiralty. The lower part is not a pedestal, but left shapeless and rough like a real rock. The horse is rearing, and has a serpent coiled about its hind feet, on which, I think, it is treading. If this had been put up in Berlin, Peter would no doubt have been actively engaged in killing the monster, but here he takes no notice of it; in fact, the killing theory is not recognised. We found two colossal figures of lions, which are so painfully mild that each of them is rolling a great ball about like a kitten.

Aug. 1st.—About half-past ten Mr. Merrilies called for us, and with really remarkable kindness gave up his day to taking us down to Peterhof, a distance of about twenty miles, and showing us over the place. We went by steamer down the tideless, saltless Gulf of Finland; the first peculiarity extends through the Baltic, and the second through a great part of it. The piece we crossed, some fifteen miles from shore to shore, is very shallow, in many parts only six or eight feet deep, and every winter it is entirely frozen over with ice two feet thick, and when this is covered with snow it forms a secure plain, which is regularly used for travelling on, though the immense distance, without means of food or shelter, is dangerous for poorly clad foot passengers. Mr. Merrilies told us of a friend of his who, in crossing last winter, passed the bodies of eight people who had been frozen. We had a good view, on our way, of the coast of Finland, and of Kronstadt. When we landed at Peterhof, we found Mr. Muir's carriage waiting for us, and with its assistance, getting out every now and then to walk through portions where it could not go, we went over the grounds of two imperial palaces, including many little summer-houses, each of which would make a very good residence in itself, as, though small, they were fitted up and adorned in every way that taste could suggest or wealth achieve. For varied beauty and perfect combination of nature and art, I think the gardens eclipse those of Sans Souci. At every corner, or end of an avenue or path, where a piece of statuary could be introduced with effect, there one was sure to find one, in bronze or in white marble; many of the latter had a sort of circular niche built behind, with a blue background to throw the figure into relief. Here we found a series of shelving ledges made of stone, with a sheet of water gliding down over them; here a long path, stretching down slopes and flights of steps, and arched over all the way with trellises and creepers; here a huge boulder, hewn, just as it lay, into the shape of a gigantic head and face, with mild, sphinx-like eyes, as if some buried Titan were struggling to free himself; here a fountain, so artfully formed of pipes set in circles, each set shooting the water higher than those outside, as to form a solid pyramid of glittering spray; here a lawn, seen through a break in the woods below us, with threads of scarlet geraniums running over it, and looking in the distance like a huge branch of coral; and here and there long avenues of trees, lying in all directions, sometimes three or four together side by side, and sometimes radiating like a star, and stretching away into the distance till the eye was almost weary of following them. All this will rather serve to remind me, than to convey any idea, of what we saw.

But the beauties of Peterhof were quite eclipsed by the Oriental splendours of Moscow, which naturally made a great impression upon a mind accustomed to the cold sublimity of Gothic architecture at Oxford.

We gave five or six hours to a stroll through this wonderful city, a city of white houses and green roofs, of conical towers that rise one out of another like a foreshortened telescope; of bulging gilded domes, in which you see, as in a looking-glass, distorted pictures of the city; of churches which look, outside, like bunches of variegated cactus (some branches crowned with green prickly buds, others with blue, and others with red and white) and which, inside, are hung all round with *eikons* and lamps, and lined with illuminated pictures up to the very roof; and, finally, of pavement that goes up and down like a ploughed field, and *drojky*—drivers who insist on being paid thirty per cent. extra to-day, "because it is the Empress's birthday." ...

Aug. 5th.—After dinner we went by arrangement to Mr. Penny, and accompanied him to see a Russian wedding. It was a most interesting ceremony. There was a large choir, from the cathedral, who sang a long and beautiful anthem before the service began; and the deacon (from the Church of the Assumption) delivered several recitative portions of the service in the most magnificent bass voice I ever heard, rising gradually (I should say by less than half a note at a time if that is possible), and increasing in volume of sound as he rose in the scale, until his final note rang through the building like a chorus of many voices. I could not have conceived that one voice could have produced such an effect. One part of the ceremony, the crowning the married couple, was very nearly grotesque. Two gorgeous golden crowns were brought in, which the officiating priest first waved before them, and then placed on their heads—or rather the unhappy bridegroom had to wear *his*, but the bride, having prudently arranged her hair in a rather complicated manner with a lace veil, could not have hers put on, but had it held above her by a friend. The bridegroom, in plain evening dress, crowned like a king, holding a candle, and with a face of resigned misery, would have been pitiable if he had not been so ludicrous. When the people had gone, we were invited by the priests to see the east end of the church, behind the golden gates, and were finally dismissed with a hearty shake of the hand and the "kiss of peace," of which even I, though in lay costume, came in for a share.

One of the objects of the tour was to see the fair at Nijni Novgorod, and here the travellers arrived on August 6th, after a miserable railway journey. Owing to the breaking down of a bridge, the unfortunate passengers had been compelled to walk a mile through drenching rain.

We went to the Smernovaya (or some such name) Hotel, a truly villainous place, though no doubt the best in the town. The feeding was very good, and everything else very bad. It was some consolation to find that as we sat at dinner we furnished a subject of the liveliest interest to six or seven waiters, all dressed in white tunics, belted at the waist, and white trousers, who ranged themselves in a row and gazed in a quite absorbed way at the collection of strange animals that were feeding before them. Now and then a twinge of conscience would seize them that they were, after all, not fulfilling the great object of life as waiters, and on these occasions they would all hurry to the end of the room, and refer to a great drawer which seemed to contain nothing but spoons and corks. When we asked for anything, they first looked at each other in an alarmed way; then, when they had ascertained which understood the order best, they all followed his example, which always was to refer to the big drawer. We spent most of the afternoon wandering through the fair, and buying *eikons*, &c. It was a wonderful place. Besides there being distinct quarters for the Persians, the Chinese, and others, we were constantly meeting strange beings with unwholesome complexions and unheard-of costumes. The Persians, with their gentle, intelligent faces, the long eyes set wide apart, the black hair, and yellow-brown skin, crowned with a black woollen fez something like a grenadier, were about the most picturesque we met. But all the novelties of the day were thrown into the shade by our adventure at sunset, when we came upon the Tartar mosque (the only one in Nijni) exactly as one of the officials came out on the roof to utter the muezzin cry, or call to prayers. Even if it had been in no way singular in itself, it would have been deeply interesting from its novelty and uniqueness, but the cry itself was quite unlike anything I have ever heard before. The beginning of each sentence was uttered in a rapid monotone, and towards the end it rose gradually till it ended in a prolonged, shrill wail, which floated overhead through the still air with an indescribably sad and ghostlike effect; heard at night, it would have thrilled one like the cry of the Banshee.

This reminds one of the wonderful description in Mr. Kipling's "City of Dreadful Night." It is not generally known that Mr. Dodgson was a fervent admirer of Mr. Kipling's works; indeed during the last few years of his life I think he took more pleasure in his tales than in those of any other modern author.

Dr. Liddon's fame as a preacher had reached the Russian clergy, with the result that he and Mr. Dodgson found many doors open to them which are usually closed to travellers in Russia. After their visit to Nijni Novgorod they returned to Moscow, whence, escorted by Bishop Leonide, Suffragan Bishop of Moscow, they made an expedition to the Troitska Monastery.

August 12th.—A most interesting day. We breakfasted at half-past five, and soon after seven left by railway, in company with Bishop Leonide and Mr. Penny, for Troitska Monastery. We found the Bishop, in spite of his limited knowledge of English, a very conversational and entertaining fellow-traveller. The service at the cathedral had already begun when we reached it, and the Bishop took us in with him, through a great crowd which thronged the building, into a side room which opened into the chancel, where we remained during the service, and enjoyed the unusual privilege of seeing the clergy communicate—a ceremony for which the doors of the chancel are always shut, and the curtains drawn, so that the congregation never witness it. It was a most elaborate ceremony, full of crossings, and waving of incense before everything that was going to be used, but also clearly full of much deep devotion.... In the afternoon we went down to the Archbishop's palace, and were presented to him by Bishop Leonide. The Archbishop could only talk Russian, so that the conversation between him and Liddon (a most interesting one, which lasted more than an hour) was conducted in a very original fashion—the Archbishop making a remark in Russian, which was put into English by the Bishop; Liddon then answered the remark in French, and the Bishop repeated his answer in Russian to the Archbishop. So that a conversation, entirely carried on between two people, required the use of three languages!

The Bishop had kindly got one of the theological students, who could talk French, to conduct us about, which he did most zealously, taking us, among other things, to see the subterranean cells of the hermits, in which some of them live for many years. We were shown the doors of two of the inhabited ones; it was a strange and not quite comfortable feeling, in a dark narrow passage where each had to carry a candle, to be shown the low narrow door of a little cellar, and to know that a human being was living within, with only a small lamp to give him light, in solitude and silence day and night.

His experiences with an exorbitant *drojky*—driver at St. Petersburg are worthy of record. They remind one of a story which he himself used to tell as having happened to a friend of his at Oxford. The latter had driven up in a cab to Tom Gate, and offered the cabman the proper fare, which was, however, refused with scorn. After a long altercation he left the irate cabman to be brought to reason by the porter, a one-armed giant of prodigious strength. When he was leaving college, he stopped at the gate to ask the porter how he had managed to dispose of the cabman. "Well, sir," replied that doughty champion, "I could not persuade him to go until I floored him."

After a hearty breakfast I left Liddon to rest and write letters, and went off shopping, &c., beginning with a call on Mr. Muir at No. 61, Galerne Ulitsa. I took a *drojky* to the house, having first bargained with the driver for thirty *kopecks*; he wanted forty to begin with. When we got there we had a little scene, rather a novelty in my experience of *drojky*—driving. The driver began by saying "*Sorok*" (forty) as I got out; this was a warning of the coming storm, but I took no notice of it, but quietly handed over the thirty. He received them with scorn and indignation, and holding them out in his open hand, delivered an eloquent discourse in Russian, of which *sorok* was the leading idea. A woman, who stood by with a look of amusement and curiosity, perhaps understood him. *I* didn't, but simply held out my hand for the thirty, returned them to the purse and counted out twenty-five instead. In doing this I felt something like a man pulling the string of a shower-bath—and the effect was like it—his fury boiled over directly, and quite eclipsed all the former row. I told him in very bad Russian that I had offered thirty once, but wouldn't again; but this, oddly enough, did not pacify him. Mr. Muir's servant told him the same thing at length, and finally Mr. Muir himself came out and gave him the substance of it sharply and shortly—but he failed to see it in a proper light. Some people are very hard to please.

When staying at a friend's house at Kronstadt he wrote:—

Liddon had surrendered his overcoat early in the day, and when going we found it must be recovered from the waiting-maid, who only talked Russian, and as I had left the dictionary behind, and the little vocabulary did not contain *coat*, we were in some difficulty. Liddon began by exhibiting his coat, with much gesticulation, including the taking it half-off. To our delight, she appeared to understand at once—left the room, and returned in a minute with—a large clothes-brush. On this Liddon tried a further and more energetic demonstration; he took off his coat, and laid it at her feet, pointed downwards (to intimate that in the lower regions was the object of his desire), smiled with an expression of the joy and gratitude with which he would receive it, and put the coat on again. Once more a gleam of intelligence lighted up the plain but expressive features of the young person; she was absent much longer this time, and when she returned, she brought, to our dismay, a large cushion and a pillow, and began to prepare the sofa for the nap that she now saw clearly was the thing the dumb gentleman wanted. A happy thought occurred to me, and I hastily drew a sketch representing Liddon, with one coat on, receiving a second and larger one from the hands of a benignant Russian peasant. The language of hieroglyphics succeeded where all other means had failed, and we returned to St. Petersburg with the humiliating knowledge that our standard of civilisation was now reduced to the level of ancient Nineveh.

At Warsaw they made a short stay, putting up at the Hotel d'Angleterre:—

Our passage is inhabited by a tall and very friendly grey-hound, who walks in whenever the door is opened for a second or two, and who for some time threatened to make the labour of the servant, who was bringing water for a bath, of no effect, by drinking up the water as fast as it was brought.

From Warsaw they went on to Leipzig, and thence to Giessen, where they arrived on September 4th.

We moved on to Giessen, and put up at the "Rappe Hotel" for the night, and ordered an early breakfast of an obliging waiter who talked English. "Coffee!" he exclaimed delightedly, catching at the word as if it were a really original idea, "Ah, coffee—very nice—and eggs? Ham with your eggs? Very nice—" "If we can have it broiled," I said. "Boiled?" the waiter repeated, with an incredulous smile. "No, not *boiled*," I explained—"*broiled*." The waiter put aside this distinction as trivial, "Yes, yes, ham," he repeated, reverting to his favourite idea. "Yes, ham," I said, "but how cooked?" "Yes, yes, how cooked," the waiter replied, with the careless air of one who assents to a proposition more from good nature than from a real conviction of its truth.

Sept. 5th.—At midday we reached Ems, after a journey eventless, but through a very interesting country-valleys winding away in all directions among hills clothed with trees to the very top, and white villages nestling away wherever there was a comfortable corner to hide in. The trees were so small, so uniform in colour, and so continuous, that they gave to the more distant hills something of the effect of banks covered with moss. The really unique feature of the scenery was the way in which the old castles seemed to grow, rather than to have been built, on the tops of the rocky promontories that showed their heads here and there among the trees. I have never seen architecture that seemed so entirely in harmony with the spirit of the place. By some subtle instinct the old architects seem to have chosen both form and colour, the grouping of the towers with their pointed spires, and the two neutral tints, light grey and brown, on the walls and roof, so as to produce buildings which look as naturally fitted to the spot as the heath or the harebells. And, like the flowers and the rocks, they seemed instinct with no other meaning than rest and silence.

And with these beautiful words my extracts from the Diary may well conclude. Lewis Carroll's mind was completely at one with Nature, and in her pleasant places of calm and infinite repose he sought his rest—and has found it.

CHAPTER IV

(1868—1876)

Death of Archdeacon Dodgson—Lewis Carroll's rooms at Christ Church—"Phantasmagoria"—Translations of "Alice"—"Through the Looking-Glass"—"Jabberwocky" in Latin—C.S. Calverley—"Notes by an Oxford Chiel"—Hatfield—Vivisection—"The Hunting of the Snark."

The success of "Alice in Wonderland" tempted Mr. Dodgson to make another essay in the same field of literature. His idea had not yet been plagiarised, as it was afterwards, though the book had of course been parodied, a notable instance being "Alice in Blunderland," which appeared in *Punch*. It was very different when he came to write "Sylvie and Bruno"; the countless imitations of the two "Alice" books which had been foisted upon the public forced him to strike out in a new line. Long before the publication of his second tale, people had heard that Lewis Carroll was writing again, and the editor of a well-known magazine had offered him two guineas a page, which was a high rate of pay in those days, for the story, if he would allow it to appear in serial form.

The central idea was, as every one knows, the adventures of a little girl who had somehow or other got through a looking-glass. The first difficulty, however, was to get her through, and this question exercised his ingenuity for some time, before it was satisfactorily solved. The next thing was to secure Tenniel's services again. At first it seemed that he was to be disappointed in this matter; Tenniel was so fully occupied with other work that there seemed little hope of his being able to undertake any more. He then applied to Sir Noel Paton, with whose fairy-pictures he had fallen in love; but the artist was ill, and wrote in reply, "Tenniel is *the* man." In the end Tenniel consented to undertake the work, and once more author and artist settled down to work together. Mr. Dodgson was no easy man to work with; no detail was too small for his exact criticism. "Don't give Alice so much crinoline," he would write, or "The White Knight must not have whiskers; he must not be made to look old"—such were the directions he was constantly giving.

On June 21st Archdeacon Dodgson died, after an illness of only a few days' duration. Lewis Carroll was not summoned until too late, for the illness took a sudden turn for the worse, and he was unable to reach his father's bedside before the end had come. This was a terrible shock to him;

his father had been his ideal of what a Christian gentleman should be, and it seemed to him at first as if a cloud had settled on his life which could never be dispelled. Two letters of his, both of them written long after the sad event, give one some idea of the grief which his father's death, and all that it entailed, caused him. The first was written long afterwards, to one who had suffered a similar bereavement. In this letter he said:—

We are sufficiently old friends, I feel sure, for me to have no fear that I shall seem intrusive in writing about your great sorrow. The greatest blow that has ever fallen on *my* life was the death, nearly thirty years ago, of my own dear father; so, in offering you my sincere sympathy, I write as a fellow-sufferer. And I rejoice to know that we are not only fellow-sufferers, but also fellow-believers in the blessed hope of the resurrection from the dead, which makes such a parting holy and beautiful, instead of being merely a blank despair.

The second was written to a young friend, Miss Edith Rix, who had sent him an illuminated text:

My dear Edith,—I can now tell you (what I wanted to do when you sent me that text-card, but felt I could not say it to *two* listeners, as it were) *why* that special card is one I like to have. That text is consecrated for me by the memory of one of the greatest sorrows I have known—the death of my dear father. In those solemn days, when we used to steal, one by one, into the darkened room, to take yet another look at the dear calm face, and to pray for strength, the one feature in the room that I remember was a framed text, illuminated by one of my sisters, "Then are they glad, because they are at rest; and so he bringeth them into the haven where they would be!" That text will always have, for me, a sadness and a sweetness of its own. Thank you again for sending it me. Please don't mention this when we meet. I can't *talk* about it.

Always affectionately yours,

C. L. DODGSON.

The object of his edition of Euclid Book V., published during the course of the year, was to meet the requirements of the ordinary Pass Examination, and to present the subject in as short and simple a form as possible. Hence the Theory of Incommensurable Magnitudes was omitted, though, as the author himself said in the Preface, to do so rendered the work incomplete, and, from a logical point of view, valueless. He hinted pretty plainly his own preference for an equivalent amount of Algebra, which would be complete in itself. It is easy to understand this preference in a mind so strictly logical as his.

So far as the object of the book itself is concerned, he succeeded admirably; the propositions are clearly and beautifully worked out, and the hints on proving Propositions in Euclid Book V., are most useful.

In November he again moved into new rooms at Christ Church; the suite which he occupied from this date to the end of his life was one of the best in the College. Situated at the north-west corner of Tom Quad, on the first floor of the staircase from the entrance to which the Junior Common Room is now approached, they consist of four sitting-rooms and about an equal number of bedrooms, besides rooms for lumber, &c. From the upper floor one can easily reach the flat college roof. Mr. Dodgson saw at once that here was the very place for a photographic studio, and he lost no time in obtaining the consent of the authorities to erect one. Here he took innumerable photographs of his friends and their children, as indeed he had been doing for some time under less favourable conditions. One of his earliest pictures is an excellent likeness of Professor Faraday.

His study was characteristic of the man; oil paintings by A. Hughes, Mrs. Anderson, and Heaphy proclaimed his artistic tastes; nests of pigeon-holes, each neatly labelled, showed his love of order; shelves, filled with the best books on every subject that interested him, were evidence of his wide reading. His library has now been broken up and, except for a few books retained by his nearest relatives, scattered to the winds; such dispersions are inevitable, but they are none the less regrettable. It always seems to me that one of the saddest things about the death of a literary man is the fact that the breaking-up of his collection of books almost invariably follows; the building up of a good library, the work of a lifetime, has been so much labour lost, so far as future generations are concerned. Talent, yes, and genius too, are displayed not only in writing books but also in buying them, and it is a pity that the ruthless hammer of the auctioneer should render so much energy and skill fruitless.

Lewis Carroll's dining-room has been the scene of many a pleasant little party, for he was very fond of entertaining. In his Diary, each of the dinners and luncheons that he gave is recorded by a small diagram, which shows who his guests were, and their several positions at the table. He kept a *menu* book as well, that the same people might not have the same dishes too frequently. He sometimes gave large parties, but his favourite form of social relaxation was a *dîner à deux*.

At the beginning of 1869 his "Phantasmagoria," a collection of poems grave and gay, was published by Macmillan. Upon the whole he was more successful in humorous poetry, but there is an undeniable dignity and pathos in his more serious verses. He gave a copy to Mr. Justice Denman, with whom he afterwards came to be very well acquainted, and who appreciated the gift highly. "I did not lay down the book," he wrote, "until I had read them [the poems] through; and enjoyed many a hearty laugh, and something like a cry or two. Moreover, I hope to read them through (as the *old man* said) 'again and again.'"

It had been Lewis Carroll's intention to have "Phantasmagoria" illustrated, and he had asked George du Maurier to undertake the work; but the plan fell through. In his letter to du Maurier, Mr. Dodgson had made some inquiries about Miss Florence Montgomery, the authoress of "Misunderstood." In reply du Maurier said, "Miss Florence Montgomery is a very charming and sympathetic young lady, the daughter of the admiral of that ilk. I am, like you, a very great admirer of "Misunderstood," and cried pints over it. When I was doing the last picture I had to put a long white pipe in the little boy's mouth until it was finished, so as to get rid of the horrible pathos of the situation while I was executing the work. In reading the book a second time (knowing the sad end of the dear little boy), the funny parts made me cry almost as much as the pathetic ones."

A few days after the publication of "Phantasmagoria," Lewis Carroll sent the first chapter of his new story to the press. "Behind the Looking-Glass and what Alice saw there" was his original idea for its title; it was Dr. Liddon who suggested the name finally adopted.

During this year German and French translations of "Alice in Wonderland" were published by Macmillan; the Italian edition appeared in 1872. Henri Bué, who was responsible for the French version, had no easy task to perform. In many cases the puns proved quite untranslatable; while the poems, being parodies on well-known English pieces, would have been pointless on the other side of the Channel. For instance, the lines beginning, "How doth the little crocodile" are a parody on "How doth the little busy bee," a song which a French child has, of course, never heard of. In this case Bué gave up the idea of translation altogether, and, instead, parodied La Fontaine's "Maître Corbeau" as follows:—

Maître Corbeau sur un arbre perché
Faisait son nid entre des branches;
Il avait relevé ses manches,
Car il était très affairé.
Maître Renard par là passant,
Lui dit: "Descendez donc, compère;

Venez embrasser votre frère!"
Le Corbeau, le reconnaissant,
Lui répondit en son ramage!—
"Fromage."

The dialogue in which the joke occurs about "tortoise" and "taught us" ("Wonderland," p. 142) is thus rendered:—

"La maîtresse était une vieille tortue; nous l'appelions chélonée."
"Et pourquoi l'appeliez-vous chélonée, si ce n'était pas son nom?"
"Parcequ'on ne pouvait s'empêcher de s'écrier en la voyant: Quel long nez!" dit la Fausse-Tortue d'un ton fâché; "vous êtes vraiment bien bornée!"

At two points, however, both M. Bué and Miss Antonie Zimmermann, who translated the tale into German, were fairly beaten: the reason for the whiting being so called, from its doing the boots and shoes, and for no wise fish going anywhere without a porpoise, were given up as untranslatable.

At the beginning of 1870 Lord Salisbury came up to Oxford to be installed as Chancellor of the University. Dr. Liddon introduced Mr. Dodgson to him, and thus began a very pleasant acquaintance. Of course he photographed the Chancellor and his two sons, for he never missed an opportunity of getting distinguished people into his studio.

In December, seven "Puzzles from Wonderland" appeared in Mrs. Gatty's paper, *Aunt Judy's Magazine*. They had originally been written for the Cecil children, with whom Lewis Carroll was already on the best terms. Meanwhile "Through the Looking-Glass" was steadily progressing—not, however, without many little hitches. One question which exercised Mr. Dodgson very much was whether the picture of the Jabberwock would do as a frontispiece, or whether it would be too frightening for little children. On this point he sought the advice of about thirty of his married lady friends, whose experiences with their own children would make them trustworthy advisers; and in the end he chose the picture of the White Knight on horseback. In 1871 the book appeared, and was an instantaneous success. Eight thousand of the first edition had been taken up by the booksellers before Mr. Dodgson had even received his own presentation copies. The compliments he received upon the "Looking-Glass" would have been enough to turn a lesser man's head, but he was, I think, proof against either praise or blame.

I can say with a clear head and conscience [wrote Henry Kingsley] that your new book is the finest thing we have had since "Martin Chuzzlewit." ... I can only say, in comparing the new "Alice" with the old, "this is a more excellent song than the other." It is perfectly splendid, but you have, doubtless, heard that from other quarters. I lunch with Macmillan habitually, and he was in a terrible pickle about not having printed enough copies the other day.

Jabberwocky[017] was at once recognised as the best and most original thing in the book, though one fair correspondent of *The Queen* declared that it was a translation from the German! The late Dean of Rochester, Dr. Scott, writes about it to Mr. Dodgson as follows:—

Are we to suppose, after all, that the Saga of Jabberwocky is one of the universal heirlooms which the Aryan race at its dispersion carried with it from the great cradle of the family? You must really consult Max Müller about this. It begins to be probable that the *origo originalissima* may be discovered in Sanscrit, and that we shall by and by have a *Iabrivokaveda* . The hero will turn out to be the Sungod in one of his *Avatars*; and the Tumtum tree the great Ash *Ygdrasil* of the Scandinavian mythology.

In March, 1872, the late Mr. A.A. Vansittart, of Trinity College, Cambridge, translated the poem into Latin elegiacs. His rendering was printed, for private circulation only, I believe, several years later, but will probably be new to most of my readers. A careful comparison with the original shows the wonderful fidelity of this translation:—

"MORS IABROCHII"

Coesper[018] erat: tunc lubriciles[019] ultravia circum
Urgebant gyros gimbiculosque tophi;
Moestenui visae borogovides ire meatu;
Et profugi gemitus exgrabuêre rathae.

O fuge Iabrochium, sanguis meus![020] Ille recurvis
Unguibus, estque avidis dentibus ille minax.
Ububae fuge cautus avis vim, gnate! Neque unquam
Faedarpax contra te frumiosus eat!

Vorpali gladio juvenis succingitur: hostis
Manxumus ad medium quaeritur usque diem:
Jamque via fesso, sed plurima mente prementi,
Tumtumiae frondis suaserat umbra moram.

Consilia interdum stetit egnia[021] mente revolvens:
At gravis in densa fronde susuffrus[022] erat,
Spiculaque[023] ex oculis jacientis flammea, tulscam
Per silvam venit burbur?[024] Iabrochii!

Vorpali, semel atque iterum collectus in ictum,
Persnicuit gladio persnacuitque puer:
Deinde galumphatus, spernens informe cadaver,
Horrendum monstri rettulit ipse caput.

Victor Iabrochii, spoliis insignis opimis,
Rursus in amplexus, o radiose, meos!
O frabiose dies! CALLO clamateque CALLA!
Vix potuit laetus chorticulare pater.

Coesper erat: tunc lubriciles ultravia circum
Urgebant gyros gimbiculosque tophi;
Moestenui visae borogovides ire meatu;
Et profugi gemitus exgrabuêre rathae.

A.A.V.

JABBERWOCKY.

'Twas brillig, and the slithy toves
Did gyre and gimble in the wabe;
All mimsy were the borogroves,
And the mome raths outgrabe.

"Beware the Jabberwock, my son!
The jaws that bite, the claws that scratch!
Beware the Jubjub bird, and shun
The frumious Bandersnatch!"

He took his vorpal sword in hand:
Long time the manxome foe he sought—
So rested he by the Tumtum tree,
And stood awhile in thought.

And as in uffish thought he stood,
The Jabberwock, with eyes of flame,
Came whiffling through the tulgey wood
And burbled as it came!

One, two! One, two! And through and through
The vorpal blade went snicker-snack!
He left it dead, and with its head
He went galumphing back.

"And hast thou slain the Jabberwock?
Come to my arms, my beamish boy!
O frabjous day! Callooh! Callay!"
He chortled in his joy.

'Twas brillig, and the slithy toves

Did gyre and gimble in the wabe;
All mimsy were the borogroves,
And the mome raths outgrabe.

The story, as originally written, contained thirteen chapters, but the published book consisted of twelve only. The omitted chapter introduced a wasp, in the character of a judge or barrister, I suppose, since Mr. Tenniel wrote that "a *wasp* in a *wig* is altogether beyond the appliances of art." Apart from difficulties of illustration, the "wasp" chapter was not considered to be up to the level of the rest of the book, and this was probably the principal reason of its being left out.

"It is a curious fact," wrote Mr. Tenniel some years later, when replying to a request of Lewis Carroll's that he would illustrate another of his books, "that with 'Through the Looking-Glass' the faculty of making drawings for book illustration departed from me, and, notwithstanding all sorts of tempting inducements, I have done nothing in that direction since."

"Through the Looking Glass" has recently appeared in a solemn judgment of the House of Lords. In *Eastman Photographic Materials Company v. Comptroller General of Patents, Designs, and Trademarks* (1898), the question for decision was, What constitutes an invented word? A trademark that consists of or contains an invented word or words is capable of registration. "Solio" was the word in issue in the case. Lord Macnaghten in his judgment said, when alluding to the distinguishing characteristics of an invented word:

I do not think that it is necessary that it should be wholly meaningless. To give an illustration: your lordships may remember that in a book of striking humour and fancy, which was in everybody's hands when it was first published, there is a collection of strange words where "there are" (to use the language of the author) "two meanings packed up into one word." No one would say that those were not invented words. Still they contain a meaning—a meaning is wrapped up in them if you can only find it out.

Before I leave the subject of the "Looking-Glass," I should like to mention one or two circumstances in connection with it which illustrate his reverence for sacred things. In his original manuscript the bad-tempered flower (pp. 28—33) was the passion-flower; the sacred origin of the name never struck him, until it was pointed out to him by a friend, when he at once changed it into the tiger-lily. Another friend asked him if the final scene was based upon the triumphal conclusion of "Pilgrim's Progress." He repudiated the idea, saying that he would consider such trespassing on holy ground as highly irreverent.

He seemed never to be satisfied with the amount of work he had on hand, and in 1872 he determined to add to his other labours by studying anatomy and physiology. Professor Barclay Thompson supplied him with a set of bones, and, having purchased the needful books, he set to work in good earnest. His mind was first turned to acquiring medical knowledge by his happening to be at hand when a man was seized with an epileptic fit. He had prevented the poor creature from falling, but was utterly at a loss what to do next. To be better prepared on any future occasion, he bought a little manual called "What to do in Emergencies." In later years he was constantly buying medical and surgical works, and by the end of his life he had a library of which no doctor need have been ashamed. There were only two special bequests in his will, one of some small keepsakes to his landlady at Eastbourne, Mrs. Dyer, and the other of his medical books to my brother.

Whenever a new idea presented itself to his mind he used to make a note of it; he even invented a system by which he could take notes in the dark, if some happy thought or ingenious problem suggested itself to him during a sleepless night. Like most men who systematically overtax their brains, he was a poor sleeper. He would sometimes go through a whole book of Euclid in bed; he was so familiar with the bookwork that he could actually see the figures before him in the dark, and did not confuse the letters, which is perhaps even more remarkable.

Most of his ideas were ingenious, though many were entirely useless from a practical point of view. For instance, he has an entry in his Diary on November 8, 1872: "I wrote to Calverley, suggesting an idea (which I think occurred to me yesterday) of guessing well-known poems as acrostics, and making a collection of them to hoax the public." Calverley's reply to this letter was as follows:—

My dear Sir,—I have been laid up (or laid down) for the last few days by acute lumbago, or I would have written before. It is rather absurd that I was on the point of propounding to you this identical idea. I realised, and I regret to add revealed to two girls, a fortnight ago, the truth that all existing poems were in fact acrostics; and I offered a small pecuniary reward to whichever would find out Gray's "Elegy" within half an hour! But it never occurred to me to utilise the discovery, as it did to you. I see that it might be utilised, now you mention it— and I shall instruct these two young women not to publish the notion among their friends.

This is the way Mr. Calverley treated Kirke White's poem "To an early Primrose." "The title," writes C.S.C. "might either be ignored or omitted. Possibly carpers might say that a primrose was not a rose."

    Mild offspring of a dark and sullen sire!

  Whose modest form, so delicately fine,   Wild

     Was nursed in whistling storms   Rose

     And cradled in the winds!

  Thee, when young Spring first questioned Winter's sway,

   And dared the sturdy blusterer to the fight,   W   a

R

    Thee on this bank he threw

    To mark his victory.

  In this low vale, the promise of the year,

  Serene thou openest to the nipping gale,

    Unnoticed and alone   I
ncognit O

    Thy tender elegance.

  So Virtue blooms, brought forth amid the storms

  Of chill adversity, in some lone walk

    Of life she rears her head   L
owlines S

    Obscure and unobserved.

  While every bleaching breeze that on her blows

  Chastens her spotless purity of breast,

    And hardens her to bear   D
isciplin E

    Serene the ills of life.

In the course of their correspondence Mr. Calverley wrote a Shakespearian sonnet, the initial letters of which form the name of William Herbert; and a parody entitled "The New Hat." I reproduce them both.

When o'er the world Night spreads her mantle dun,
In dreams, my love, I see those stars, thine eyes,
Lighting the dark: but when the royal sun
Looks o'er the pines and fires the orient skies,
I bask no longer in thy beauty's ray,
And lo! my world is bankrupt of delight.
Murk night seemed lately fair-complexioned day;
Hope-bringing day now seems most doleful night.
End, weary day, that art no day to me!
Return, fair night, to me the best of days!
But O my rose, whom in my dreams I see,
Enkindle with like bliss my waking gaze!
Replete with thee, e'en hideous night grows fair:
Then what would sweet morn be, if thou wert there?

THE NEW HAT.

My boots had been wash'd, well wash'd, by a shower;
But little I car'd about that:
What I felt was the havoc a single half-hour
Had made with my beautiful Hat.

For the Boot, tho' its lustre be dimm'd, shall assume
New comeliness after a while;
But no art may restore its original bloom,
When once it hath fled, to the Tile.

I clomb to my perch, and the horses (a bay
And a brown) trotted off with a clatter;
The driver look'd round in his humorous way,
And said huskily, "Who is your hatter?"

I was pleased that he'd noticed its shape and its shine;
And, as soon as we reached the "Old Druid,"
I begged him to drink to its welfare and mine
In a glass of my favourite fluid.

A gratified smile sat, I own, on my lips
When the barmaid exclaimed to the master,
(He was standing inside with his hands on his hips),
"Just look at that gentleman's castor."

I laughed, when an organman paus'd in mid-air—
('Twas an air that I happened to know,
By a great foreign *maestro*)—expressly to stare
At ze gent wiz *ze joli chapeau* .

Yet how swift is the transit from laughter to tears!
How rife with results is a day!
That Hat might, with care, have adorned me for years;
But one show'r wash'd its beauty away.

How I lov'd thee, my Bright One! I pluck in remorse
My hands from my pockets and wring 'em:
Oh, why did not I, dear, as a matter of course,
Ere I purchas'd thee purchase a gingham?

C.S. CALVERLEY.

Mr. Dodgson spent the last night of the old year (1872) at Hatfield, where he was the guest of Lord Salisbury. There was a large party of children in the house, one of them being Princess Alice, to whom he told as much of the story of "Sylvie and Bruno" as he had then composed. While the tale was in progress Lady Salisbury entered the room, bringing in some new toy or game to amuse her little guests, who, with the usual thoughtlessness of children, all rushed off and left Mr. Dodgson. But the little Princess, suddenly appearing to remember that to do so might perhaps hurt his feelings, sat down again by his side. He read the kind thought which prompted her action, and was much pleased by it.

As Mr. Dodgson knew several members of the *Punch* staff, he used to send up any little incidents or remarks that particularly amused him to that paper. He even went so far as to suggest subjects for cartoons, though I do not know if his ideas were ever carried out. One of the anecdotes he sent to *Punch* was that of a little boy, aged four, who after having listened with much attention to the story of Lot's wife, asked ingenuously, "Where does salt come from that's *not* made of ladies?" This appeared on January 3, 1874.

The following is one of several such little anecdotes jotted down by Lewis Carroll for future use: Dr. Paget was conducting a school examination, and in the course of his questions he happened to ask a small child the meaning of "Average." He was utterly bewildered by the reply, "The thing that hens lay on," until the child explained that he had read in a book that hens lay *on an average* so many eggs a year.

Among the notable people whom he photographed was John Ruskin, and, as several friends begged him for copies, he wrote to ask Mr. Ruskin's leave. The reply was, "Buy Number 5 of *Fors Clavigera* for 1871, which will give you your answer." This was not what Mr. Dodgson wanted, so he wrote back, "Can't afford ten-pence!" Finally Mr. Ruskin gave his consent.

About this time came the anonymous publication of "Notes by an Oxford Chiel," a collection of papers written on various occasions, and all of them dealing with Oxford controversies. Taking them in order, we have first "The New Method of Evaluation as applied to *pi*," first published by Messrs. Parker in 1865, which had for its subject the controversy about the Regius Professorship of Greek. One extract will be sufficient to show the way in which the affair was treated: "Let U = the University, G = Greek, and P = Professor. Then G P = Greek Professor; let this be reduced to its lowest terms and call the result J [i.e., Jowett]."

The second paper is called "The Dynamics of a Parti-cle," and is quite the best of the series; it is a geometrical treatment of the contest between Mr. Gathorne Hardy and Mr. Gladstone for the representation of the University. Here are some of the "Definitions" with which the subject was introduced:—

Plain Superficiality is the character of a speech, in which any two points being taken, the speaker is found to lie wholly with regard to those two points.

Plain Anger is the inclination of two voters to one another, who meet together, but whose views are not in the same direction.

When two parties, coming together, feel a Right Anger, each is *said* to be *complimentary* to the other, though, strictly speaking, this is very seldom the case.

A *surd* is a radical whose meaning cannot be exactly ascertained.

As the "Notes of an Oxford Chiel" has been long out of print, I will give a few more extracts from this paper:—

On Differentiation.

The effect of Differentiation on a Particle is very remarkable, the first differential being frequently of greater value than the original particle, and the second of less enlightenment.

For example, let L = "Leader", S = "Saturday", and then LS = "Leader in the Saturday" (a particle of no assignable value). Differentiating once, we get L.S.D., a function of great value. Similarly it will be found that, by taking the second

Differential of an enlightened Particle (*i.e.,* raising it to the Degree D.D.), the enlightenment becomes rapidly less. The effect is much increased by the addition of a C: in this case the enlightenment often vanishes altogether, and the Particle becomes Conservative.

PROPOSITIONS.

PROP. I. PR.

To find the value of a given Examiner.

Example.—A takes in ten books in the Final Examination and gets a 3rd class; B takes in the Examiners, and gets a 2nd. Find the value of the Examiners in terms of books. Find also their value in terms in which no Examination is held.

PROP. II. PR.

To estimate Profit and Loss.

Example.—Given a Derby Prophet, who has sent three different winners to three different betting-men, and given that none of the three horses are placed. Find the total loss incurred by the three men (*a*) in money, (*b*) in temper. Find also the Prophet. Is this latter usually possible?

PROP. IV. TH.

The end (i.e., *"the product of the extremes") justifies* (i.e., *"is equal to"*—*see Latin "aequus") the means.*

No example is appended to this Proposition, for obvious reasons.

PROP. V. PR.

To continue a given series.

Example.—A and B, who are respectively addicted to Fours and Fives, occupy the same set of rooms, which is always at Sixes and Sevens. Find the probable amount of reading done by A and B while the Eights are on.

The third paper was entitled "Facts, Figures, and Fancies." The best thing in it was a parody on "The Deserted Village," from which an extract will be found in a later chapter. There was also a letter to the Senior Censor of Christ Church, in burlesque of a similar letter in which the Professor of Physics met an offer of the Clarendon Trustees by a detailed enumeration of the requirements in his own department of Natural Science. Mr. Dodgson's letter deals with the imaginary requirements of the Mathematical school:—

Dear Senior Censor,—In a desultory conversation on a point connected with the dinner at our high table, you incidentally remarked to me that lobster-sauce, "though a necessary adjunct to turbot, was not entirely wholesome!"

It is entirely unwholesome. I never ask for it without reluctance: I never take a second spoonful without a feeling of apprehension on the subject of a possible nightmare. This naturally brings me to the subject of Mathematics, and of the accommodation provided by the University for carrying on the calculations necessary in that important branch of Science.

As Members of Convocation are called upon (whether personally, or, as is less exasperating, by letter) to consider the offer of the Clarendon Trustees, as well as every other subject of human, or inhuman, interest, capable of consideration, it has occurred to me to suggest for your consideration how desirable roofed buildings are for carrying on mathematical calculations: in fact, the variable character of the weather in Oxford renders it highly inexpedient to attempt much occupation, of a sedentary nature, in the open air.

Again, it is often impossible for students to carry on accurate mathematical calculations in close contiguity to one another, owing to their mutual conversation; consequently these processes require different rooms in which irrepressible conversationalists, who are found to occur in every branch of Society, might be carefully and permanently fixed.

It may be sufficient for the present to enumerate the following requisites—others might be added as funds permit:—

A. A very large room for calculating Greatest Common Measure. To this a small one might be attached for Least Common Multiple: this, however, might be dispensed with.

B. A piece of open ground for keeping Roots and practising their extraction: it would be advisable to keep Square Roots by themselves, as their corners are apt to damage others.

C. A room for reducing Fractions to their Lowest Terms. This should be provided with a cellar for keeping the Lowest Terms when found, which might also be available to the general body of Undergraduates, for the purpose of "keeping Terms."

D. A large room, which might be darkened, and fitted up with a magic lantern, for the purpose of exhibiting circulating Decimals in the act of circulation. This might also contain cupboards, fitted with glass doors, for keeping the various Scales of Notation.

E. A narrow strip of ground, railed off and carefully levelled, for investigating the properties of Asymptotes, and testing practically whether Parallel Lines meet or not: for this purpose it should reach, to use the expressive language of Euclid, "ever so far."

This last process of "continually producing the lines," may require centuries or more; but such a period, though long in the life of an individual, is as nothing in the life of the University.

As Photography is now very much employed in recording human expressions, and might possibly be adapted to Algebraical Expressions, a small photographic room would be desirable, both for general use and for representing the various phenomena of Gravity, Disturbance of Equilibrium, Resolution, &c., which affect the features during severe mathematical operations.

May I trust that you will give your immediate attention to this most important subject?

Believe me,

Sincerely yours,

Mathematicus.

Next came "The New Belfry of Christ Church, Oxford; a Monograph by D.C.L." On the title-page was a neatly drawn square—the figure of Euclid I. 46—below which was written "East view of the New Belfry, Christ Church, as seen from the meadow." The new belfry is fortunately a thing of the past, and its insolent hideousness no longer defaces Christ Church, but while it lasted it was no doubt an excellent target for Lewis Carroll's sarcasm. His article on it is divided into thirteen chapters. Three of them are perhaps worth quoting:—

§1. *On the etymological significance of the new Belfry, Ch. Ch.*

The word "Belfry" is derived from the French *bel*, "beautiful, becoming, meet," and from the German *frei*, "free unfettered, secure, safe." Thus, the word is strictly equivalent to "meat-safe," to which the new Belfry bears a resemblance so perfect as almost to amount to coincidence.

§4. *On the chief architectural merit of the new Belfry, Ch. Ch.*

Its chief merit is its simplicity—a simplicity so pure, so profound, in a word, so *simple*, that no other word will fitly describe it. The meagre outline, and baldness of detail, of the present Chapter, are adopted in humble imitation of this great feature.

§5. *On the other architectural merits of the new Belfry, Ch. Ch.*

The Belfry has no other architectural merits.

"The Vision of the Three T's" followed. It also was an attack on architectural changes in Christ Church; the general style was a parody of the "Compleat Angler." Last of all came "The Blank Cheque, a Fable," in reference to the building of the New Schools, for the expenses of which it was actually proposed (in 1874), to sign a blank cheque before any estimate had been made, or any plan laid before the University, and even before a committee had been elected to appoint an architect for the work.

At the end of 1874 Mr. Dodgson was again at Hatfield, where he told the children the story of Prince Uggug, which was afterwards made a part of "Sylvie and Bruno," though at that time it seems to have been a separate tale. But "Sylvie and Bruno," in this respect entirely unlike "Alice in Wonderland," was the result of notes taken during many years; for while he was thinking out the book he never neglected any amusing scraps of childish conversation or funny anecdotes about children which came to his notice. It is this fact which gives such verisimilitude to the prattle of Bruno; childish talk is a thing which a grown-up person cannot possibly *invent*. He can only listen to the actual things the children say, and then combine what he has heard into a connected narrative.

During 1875 Mr. Dodgson wrote an article on "Some Popular Fallacies about Vivisection," which was refused by the *Pall Mall Gazette*, the editor saying that he had never heard of most of them; on which Mr. Dodgson plaintively notes in his Diary that seven out of the thirteen fallacies dealt with in his essay had appeared in the columns of the *Pall Mall Gazette*. Ultimately it was accepted by the editor of *The Fortnightly Review*. Mr. Dodgson had a peculiar horror of vivisection. I was once walking in Oxford with him when a certain well-known professor passed us. "I am afraid that man vivisects," he said, in his gravest tone. Every year he used to get a friend to recommend him a list of suitable charities to which he should subscribe. Once the name of some Lost Dogs' Home appeared in this list. Before Mr. Dodgson sent his guinea he wrote to the secretary to ask whether the manager of the Home was in the habit of sending dogs that had to be killed to physiological laboratories for vivisection. The answer was in the negative, so the institution got the cheque. He did not, however, advocate the total abolition of vivisection—what reasonable man could?—but he would have liked to see it much more carefully restricted by law. An earlier letter of his to the *Pall Mall Gazette* on the same subject is sufficiently characteristic to deserve a place here. Be it noted that he signed it "Lewis Carroll," in order that whatever influence or power his writings had gained him might tell in the controversy.

VIVISECTION AS A SIGN OF THE TIMES.

Sir,—The letter which appeared in last week's *Spectator*, and which must have saddened the heart of every one who read it, seems to suggest a question which has not yet been asked or answered with sufficient clearness, and that is, How far may vivisection be regarded as a sign of the times, and a fair specimen of that higher civilisation which a purely secular State education is to give us? In that much-vaunted panacea for all human ills we are promised not only increase of knowledge, but also a higher moral character; any momentary doubt on this point which we may feel is set at rest at once by quoting the great crucial instance of Germany. The syllogism, if it deserves the name, is usually stated thus: Germany has a higher scientific education than England; Germany has a lower average of crime than England; *ergo*, a scientific education tends to improve moral conduct. Some old-fashioned logician might perhaps whisper to himself, "Praemissis particularibus nihil probatur," but such a remark, now that Aldrich is out of date, would only excite a pitying smile. May we, then, regard the practice of vivisection as a legitimate fruit, or as an abnormal development, of this higher moral character? Is the anatomist, who can contemplate unmoved the agonies he is inflicting for no higher purpose than to gratify a scientific curiosity, or to illustrate some well-established truth, a being higher or lower, in the scale of humanity, than the ignorant boor whose very soul would sicken at the horrid sight? For if ever there was an argument in favour of purely scientific education more cogent than another, it is surely this (a few years back it might have been put into the mouth of any advocate of science; now it reads like the merest mockery): "What can teach the noble quality of mercy, of sensitiveness to all forms of suffering, so powerfully as the knowledge of what suffering really is? Can the man who has once realised by minute study what the nerves are, what the brain is, and what waves of agony the one can convey to the other, go forth and wantonly inflict pain on any sentient being?" A little while ago we should have confidently replied, "He cannot do it"; in the light of modern revelations we must sorrowfully confess "He can." And let it never be said that this is done with serious forethought of the balance of pain and gain; that the operator has pleaded with himself, "Pain is indeed an evil, but so much suffering may fitly be endured to purchase so much knowledge." When I hear of one of these ardent searchers after truth giving, not a helpless dumb animal, to whom he says in effect, "*You* shall suffer that *I* may know," but his own person to the probe and to the scalpel, I will believe in him as recognising a principle of justice, and I will honour him as acting up to his principles. "But the thing cannot be!" cries some amiable reader, fresh from an interview with that most charming of men, a London physician. "What! Is it possible that one so gentle in manner, so full of noble sentiments, can be hardhearted? The very idea is an outrage to common sense!" And thus we are duped every day of our lives. Is it possible that that bank director, with his broad honest face, can be meditating a fraud? That the chairman of that meeting of shareholders, whose every tone has the ring of truth in it, can hold in his hand a "cooked" schedule of accounts? That my wine merchant, so outspoken, so confiding, can be supplying me with an adulterated article? That the schoolmaster, to whom I have entrusted my little boy, can starve or neglect him? How well I remember his words to the dear child when last we parted. "You are leaving your friends," he said, "but you will have a father in me, my dear, and a mother in Mrs. Squeers!" For all such rose-coloured dreams of the necessary immunity from human vices of educated men the facts in last week's *Spectator* have a terrible significance. "Trust no man further than you can see him," they seem to say. "Qui vult decipi, decipiatur."

Allow me to quote from a modern writer a few sentences bearing on this subject:—
"We are at present, legislature and nation together, eagerly pushing forward schemes which proceed on the postulate that conduct is determined, not by feelings, but by cognitions. For what else is the assumption underlying this anxious urging-on of organisations for teaching? What is the root-notion common to Secularists and Denominationalists but the notion that spread of knowledge is the one thing needful for bettering behaviour? Having both swallowed certain statistical fallacies, there has grown up in them the belief that State education will check ill-doing.... This belief in the moralising effects of intellectual culture, flatly contradicted by facts, is absurd *a priori*.... This faith in lesson-books and readings is one of the superstitions of the age.... Not by precept, though heard daily; not by example, unless it is followed; but only by action, often caused by the related feeling, can a moral habit be formed. And yet this truth, which mental science clearly teaches, and which is in harmony with familiar sayings, is a truth wholly ignored in current educational fanaticisms."

There need no praises of mine to commend to the consideration of all thoughtful readers these words of Herbert Spencer. They are to be found in "The Study of Sociology"
Let us, however, do justice to science. It is not so wholly wanting as Mr. Herbert Spencer would have us believe in principles of action—principles by which we

may regulate our conduct in life. I myself once heard an accomplished man of science declare that his labours had taught him one special personal lesson which, above all others, he had laid to heart. A minute study of the nervous system, and of the various forms of pain produced by wounds had inspired in him one profound resolution; and that was—what think you?—never, under any circumstances, to adventure his own person into the field of battle! I have somewhere read in a book—a rather antiquated book, I fear, and one much discredited by modern lights—the words, "the whole creation groaneth and travaileth in pain together until now." Truly we read these words with a new meaning in the present day! "Groan and travail" it undoubtedly does still (more than ever, so far as the brute creation is concerned); but to what end? Some higher and more glorious state? So one might have said a few years back. Not so in these days. The *telos teleion* of secular education, when divorced from religious or moral training, is—I say it deliberately—the purest and most unmitigated selfishness. The world has seen and tired of the worship of Nature, of Reason, of Humanity; for this nineteenth century has been reserved the development of the most refined religion of all—the worship of Self. For that, indeed, is the upshot of it all. The enslavement of his weaker brethren—"the labour of those who do not enjoy, for the enjoyment of those who do not labour"—the degradation of woman—the torture of the animal world—these are the steps of the ladder by which man is ascending to his higher civilisation. Selfishness is the key-note of all purely secular education; and I take vivisection to be a glaring, a wholly unmistakable case in point. And let it not be thought that this is an evil that we can hope to see produce the good for which we are asked to tolerate it, and then pass away. It is one that tends continually to spread. And if it be tolerated or even ignored now, the age of universal education, when the sciences, and anatomy among them, shall be the heritage of all, will be heralded by a cry of anguish from the brute creation that will ring through the length and breadth of the land! This, then, is the glorious future to which the advocate of secular education may look forward: the dawn that gilds the horizon of his hopes! An age when all forms of religious thought shall be things of the past; when chemistry and biology shall be the ABC of a State education enforced on all; when vivisection shall be practised in every college and school; and when the man of science, looking forth over a world which will then own no other sway than his, shall exult in the thought that he has made of this fair green earth, if not a heaven for man, at least a hell for animals.

I am, sir,

Your obedient servant,

Lewis Carroll.

February 10th.

On March 29, 1876, "The Hunting of the Snark" was published. Mr. Dodgson gives some interesting particulars of its evolution. The first idea for the poem was the line "For the Snark *was* a Boojum, you see," which came into his mind, apparently without any cause, while he was taking a country walk. The first complete verse which he composed was the one which stands last in the poem:—

In the midst of the word he was trying to say,
In the midst of his laughter and glee,
He had softly and suddenly vanished away—
For the Snark *was* a Boojum, you see.

The illustrations were the work of Mr. Henry Holiday, and they are thoroughly in keeping with the spirit of the poem. Many people have tried to show that "The Hunting of the Snark" was an allegory; some regarding it as being a burlesque upon the Tichborne case, and others taking the Snark as a personification of popularity. Lewis Carroll always protested that the poem had no meaning at all.

As to the meaning of the Snark [he wrote to a friend in America], I'm very much afraid I didn't mean anything but nonsense. Still, you know, words mean more than we mean to express when we use them; so a whole book ought to mean a great deal more than the writer means. So, whatever good meanings are in the book, I'm glad to accept as the meaning of the book. The best that I've seen is by a lady (she published it in a letter to a newspaper), that the whole book is an allegory on the search after happiness. I think this fits in beautifully in many ways—particularly about the bathing-machines: when the people get weary of life, and can't find happiness in towns or in books, then they rush off to the seaside, to see what bathing-machines will do for them.

Mr. H. Holiday, in a very interesting article on "The Snark's Significance" (*Academy,* January 29, 1898), quoted the inscription which Mr. Dodgson had written in a vellum-bound, presentation-copy of the book. It is so characteristic that I take the liberty of reproducing it here:—

Presented to Henry Holiday, most patient of artists, by Charles L. Dodgson, most exacting, but not most ungrateful of authors, March 29, 1876.

A little girl, to whom Mr. Dodgson had given a copy of the "Snark," managed to get the whole poem off by heart, and insisted on reciting, it from beginning to end during a long carriage-drive. Her friends, who, from the nature of the case, were unable to escape, no doubt wished that she, too, was a Boojum.

During the year, the first public dramatic representation of "Alice in Wonderland" was given at the Polytechnic, the entertainment taking the form of a series of *tableaux,* interspersed with appropriate readings and songs. Mr. Dodgson exercised a rigid censorship over all the extraneous matter introduced into the performance, and put his veto upon a verse in one of the songs, in which the drowning of kittens was treated from the humorous point of view, lest the children in the audience might learn to think lightly of death in the case of the lower animals.

CHAPTER V

(1877—1883)

Dramatic tastes—Miss Ellen Terry—"Natural Science at Oxford"—Mr. Dodgson as an artist—Miss E. G. Thomson—The drawing of children—A curious dream—"The Deserted Parks"—"Syzygies"—Circus children—Row-loving undergraduates—A letter to *The Observer*—Resignation of the Lectureship—He is elected Curator of the Common Room—Dream-music.

Mr. Dodgson's love of the drama was not, as I have shown, a taste which he acquired in later years. From early college days he never missed anything which he considered worth seeing at the London theatres. I believe he used to reproach himself—unfairly, I think—with spending too much time on such recreations. For a man who worked so hard and so incessantly as he did; for a man to whom vacations meant rather a variation of mental employment than absolute rest of mind, the drama afforded just the sort of relief that was wanted. His vivid imagination, the very earnestness and intensity of his character enabled him to throw himself utterly into the spirit of what he saw upon the stage, and to forget in it all the petty worries and disappointments of life. The old adage says that a man cannot burn the candle at both ends; like most proverbs, it is only partially true, for often the hardest worker is the man who enters with most zest into his recreations, and this was emphatically the case with Mr. Dodgson.

Walter Pater, in his book on the Renaissance, says (I quote from rough notes only), "A counted number of pulses only is given to us of a variegated dramatic life. How may we see in them all that is to be seen in them by the finest senses? How shall we pass most swiftly from point to point, and be present always at the focus where the greatest number of vital forces unite in their purest energy? To burn always with this hard gem-like flame, to maintain this ecstasy, is success in life." Here we have the truer philosophy, here we have the secret of Lewis Carroll's life. He never wasted time on social formalities; he refused to fulfil any of those (so called) duties which involve ineffable boredom, and so his mind was always fresh and ready. He said in one of his letters that he hoped that in the next world all knowledge would not be given to us suddenly, but that we should gradually grow wiser, for the *acquiring* knowledge was to him the real pleasure. What is this but a paraphrase of another of Pater's thoughts, "Not the fruit of experience, but experience itself is the end."

And so, times without number, he allowed himself to be carried away by emotion as he saw life in the mirror of the stage; but, best of all, he loved to see the acting of children, and he generally gave copies of his books to any of the little performers who specially pleased him. On January 13, 1877, he wrote in his Diary:—

Went up to town for the day, and took E— with me to the afternoon pantomime at the Adelphi, "Goody Two-Shoes," acted entirely by children. It was a really charming performance. Little Bertie Coote, aged ten, was clown—a wonderfully clever little fellow; and Carrie Coote, about eight, was Columbine, a very pretty graceful little thing. In a few years' time she will be just *the* child to act "Alice," if it is ever dramatised. The harlequin was a little girl named Gilchrist, one of the most beautiful children, in face and figure, that I have ever seen. I must get an opportunity of photographing her. Little Bertie Coote, singing "Hot Codlings," was curiously like the pictures of Grimaldi.

It need hardly be said that the little girl was Miss Constance Gilchrist. Mr. Dodgson sent her a copy of "Alice in Wonderland," with a set of verses on her name.

Many people object altogether to children appearing on the stage; it is said to be bad for their morals as well as for their health. A letter which Mr. Dodgson once wrote in the *St. James's Gazette* contains a sufficient refutation of the latter fancy:—

I spent yesterday afternoon at Brighton, where for five hours I enjoyed the society of three exceedingly happy and healthy little girls, aged twelve, ten, and seven. I think that any one who could have seen the vigour of life in those three children—the intensity with which they enjoyed everything, great or small, that came in their way—who could have watched the younger two running races on the Pier, or have heard the fervent exclamation of the eldest at the end of the afternoon, "We *have* enjoyed ourselves!" would have agreed with me that here, at least, there was no excessive "physical strain," nor any *imminent* danger of "fatal results"! A drama, written by Mr. Savile Clarke, is now being played at Brighton, and in this (it is called "Alice in Wonderland") all three children have been engaged. They had been acting every night this week, and *twice* on the day before I met them, the second performance lasting till half-past ten at night, after which they got up at seven next morning to bathe! That such (apparently) severe work should co-exist with blooming health and buoyant spirits seems at first sight a paradox; but I appeal to any one who has ever worked *con amore* at any subject whatever to support me in the assertion that, when you really love the subject you are working at, the "physical strain" is absolutely *nil*; it is only when working "against the grain" that any strain is felt, and I believe the apparent paradox is to be explained by the fact that a taste for *acting* is one of the strongest passions of human nature, that stage-children show it nearly from infancy, and that, instead of being miserable drudges who ought to be celebrated in a new "Cry of the Children," they simply *rejoice* in their work "even as a giant rejoiceth to run his course."

Mr. Dodgson's general views on the mission of the drama are well shown by an extract from a circular which he sent to many of his friends in 1882:—

The stage (as every playgoer can testify) is an engine of incalculable power for influencing society; and every effort to purify and ennoble its aims seems to me to deserve all the countenance that the great, and all the material help that the wealthy, can give it; while even those who are neither great nor wealthy may yet do their part, and help to—
"Ring out the darkness of the land, Ring in the Christ that is to be."

I do not know if Mr. Dodgson's suggested amendment of some lines in the "Merchant of Venice" was ever carried out, but it further illustrates the serious view he took of this subject. The hint occurs in a letter to Miss Ellen Terry, which runs as follows:—

You gave me a treat on Saturday such as I have very seldom had in my life. You must be weary by this time of hearing your own praises, so I will only say that Portia was all I could have imagined, and more. And Shylock is superb—especially in the trial-scene.

Now I am going to be very bold, and make a suggestion, which I do hope you will think well enough of to lay it before Mr. Irving. I want to see that clause omitted (in the sentence on Shylock)—

That, for this favour, He presently become a Christian;
It is a sentiment that is entirely horrible and revolting to the feelings of all who believe in the Gospel of Love. Why should our ears be shocked by such words merely because they are Shakespeare's? In his day, when it was held to be a Christian's duty to force his belief on others by fire and sword—to burn man's body in order to save his soul—the words probably conveyed no shock. To all Christians now (except perhaps extreme Calvinists) the idea of forcing a man to abjure his religion, whatever that religion may be, is (as I have said) simply horrible.

I have spoken of it as a needless outrage on religious feeling: but surely, being so, it is a great artistic mistake. Its tendency is directly contrary to the spirit of the scene. We have despised Shylock for his avarice, and we rejoice to see him lose his wealth: we have abhorred him for his bloodthirsty cruelty, and we rejoice to see him baffled. And now, in the very fulness of our joy at the triumph of right over wrong, we are suddenly called on to see in him the victim of a cruelty a thousand times worse than his own, and to honour him as a martyr. This, I am sure, Shakespeare never meant. Two touches only of sympathy does he allow us, that we may realise him as a man, and not as a demon incarnate. "I will not pray with you"; "I had it of Leah, when I was a bachelor." But I am sure he never meant our sympathies to be roused in the supreme moment of his downfall, and, if he were alive now, I believe he would cut out those lines about becoming a Christian.

No interpolation is needed—(I should not like to suggest the putting in a single word that is not Shakespeare's)—I would read the speech thus:—

That lately stole his daughter:
Provided that he do record a gift,
Here in the court, &c.
And I would omit Gratiano's three lines at Shylock's exit, and let the text stand:—
Duke: "Get thee gone, but do it." (*Exit Shylock*.)
The exit, in solemn silence, would be, if possible, even grander than it now is, and would lose nothing by the omission of Gratiano's flippant jest....

On January 16th he saw "New Men and Old Acres" at the Court Theatre. The two authors of the pieces, Dubourg and Tom Taylor, were great friends of his. "It was a real treat," he writes, "being well acted in every detail. Ellen Terry was wonderful, and I should think unsurpassable in all but the lighter parts." Mr. Dodgson himself had a strong wish to become a dramatic author, but, after one or two unsuccessful attempts to get his plays produced, he wisely gave up the idea, realising that he had not the necessary constructive powers. The above reference to Miss Ellen Terry's acting is only one out of a countless number; the great actress and he were excellent friends, and she did him many a kindness in helping on young friends of his who had taken up the stage as a profession.

She and her sister, Miss Kate Terry, were among the distinguished people whom he photographed. The first time he saw the latter actress was, I think, in 1858, when she was playing in "The Tempest" at the Princess's. "The gem of the piece," he writes, "was the exquisitely graceful and beautiful Ariel, Miss Kate Terry. Her appearance as a sea-nymph was one of the most beautiful living pictures I ever saw, but this, and every other one in my recollection (except Queen Katherine's dream), were all outdone by the concluding scene, where Ariel is left alone, hovering over the wide ocean, watching the retreating ship. It is an innovation on Shakespeare, but a worthy one, and the conception of a true poet."

Mr. Dodgson was a frequent contributor to the daily Press. As a rule his letters appeared in the *St. James's Gazette*, for the editor, Mr. Greenwood, was a friend of his, but the following sarcastic epistle was an exception:—

NATURAL SCIENCE AT OXFORD.

Sir,—There is no one of the many ingenious appliances of mechanical science that is more appreciated or more successfully employed than the wedge; so subtle and imperceptible are the forces needed for the insertion of its "thin end," so astounding the results which its "thick end" may ultimately produce. Of the former process we shall see a beautiful illustration in a Congregation to be holden at Oxford on the 24th inst., when it will be proposed to grant, to those who have taken the degrees of bachelor and master in Natural Science only, the same voting powers as in the case of the "M.A." degree. This means the omission of one of the two classical languages, Latin and Greek, from what has been hitherto understood as the curriculum of an Oxford education. It is to this "thin end" of the wedge that I would call the attention of our non-residents, and of all interested in Oxford education, while the "thick end" is still looming in the distance. But why fear a "thick end" at all? I shall be asked. Has Natural Science shown any such tendency, or given any reason to fear that such a concession would lead to further demands? In answer to that question, let me sketch, in dramatic fashion, the history of her recent career in Oxford. In the dark ages of our University (some five-and-twenty years ago), while we still believed in classics and mathematics as constituting a liberal education, Natural Science sat weeping at our gates. "Ah, let me in!" she moaned; "why cram reluctant youth with your unsatisfying lore? Are they not hungering for bones; yea, panting for sulphuretted hydrogen?" We heard and we pitied. We let her in and housed her royally; we adorned her palace with re-agents and retorts, and made it a very charnel-house of bones, and we cried to our undergraduates, "The feast of Science is spread! Eat, drink, and be happy!" But they would not. They fingered the bones, and thought them dry. They sniffed at the hydrogen, and turned away. Yet for all that Science ceased not to cry, "More gold, more gold!" And her three fair daughters, Chemistry, Biology, and Physics (for the modern horse-leech is more prolific than in the days of Solomon), ceased not to plead, "Give, give!" And we gave; we poured forth our wealth like water (I beg her pardon, like H_2O), and we could not help thinking there was something weird and uncanny in the ghoul-like facility with which she absorbed it.

The curtain rises on the second act of the drama. Science is still weeping, but this time it is for lack of pupils, not of teachers or machinery. "We are unfairly handicapped!" she cries. "You have prizes and scholarships for classics and mathematics, and you bribe your best students to desert us. Buy us some bright, clever boys to teach, and then see what we can do!" Once more we heard and pitied. We had bought her bones; we bought her boys. And now at last her halls were filled—not only with teachers paid to teach, but also with learners paid to learn. And we have not much to complain of in results, except that perhaps she is a little too ready to return on our hands all but the "honour-men"—all, in fact, who really need the helping hand of an educator. "Here, take back your stupid ones!" she cries. "Except as subjects for the scalpel (and we have not yet got the Human Vivisection Act through Parliament) we can do nothing with them!"

The third act of the drama is yet under rehearsal; the actors are still running in and out of the green-room, and hastily shuffling on their new and ill-fitting dresses; but its general scope is not far to seek. At no distant day our once timid and tearful guest will be turning up her nose at the fare provided for her. "Give me no more youths to teach," she will say; "but pay me handsomely, and let me think. Plato and Aristotle were all very well in their way; Diogenes and his tub for me!" The allusion is not inappropriate. There can be little doubt that some of the researches conducted by that retiring philosopher in the recesses of that humble edifice were strictly scientific, embracing several distinct branches of entomology. I do not mean, of course, that "research" is a new idea in Oxford. From time immemorial we have had our own chosen band of researchers (here called "professors"), who have advanced the boundaries of human knowledge in many directions. True, they are not left so wholly to themselves as some of these modern thinkers would wish to be, but are expected to give some few lectures, as the outcome of their "research" and the evidence of its reality, but even that condition has not always been enforced—for instance, in the case of the late Professor of Greek, Dr. Gaisford, the University was too conscious of the really valuable work he was doing in philological research to complain that he ignored the usual duties of the chair and delivered no lectures.

And, now, what is the "thick end" of the wedge? It is that Latin and Greek may *both* vanish from our curriculum; that logic, philosophy, and history may follow; and that the destinies of Oxford may some day be in the hands of those who have had no education other than "scientific." And why not? I shall be asked. Is it not as high a form of education as any other? That is a matter to be settled by facts. I can but offer my own little item of evidence, and leave it to others to confirm or to refute. It used once to be thought indispensable for an educated man that he should be able to write his own language correctly, if not elegantly; it seems doubtful how much longer this will be taken as a criterion. Not so many years ago I had the honour of assisting in correcting for the press some pages of the *Anthropological Review*, or some such periodical. I doubt not that the writers were eminent men in their own line; that each could triumphantly prove, to his own satisfaction, the unsoundness of what the others had advanced; and that all would unite in declaring that the theories of a year ago were entirely exploded by the latest German treatise; but they were not able to set forth these thoughts, however consoling in themselves, in anything resembling the language of educated society. In all my experience, I have never read, even in the "local news" of a country paper, such slipshod, such deplorable English.

I shall be told that I am ungenerous in thus picking out a few unfavourable cases, and that some of the greatest minds of the day are to be found in the ranks of science. I freely admit that such may be found, but my contention is that *they* made the science, not the science them; and that in any line of thought they would have been equally distinguished. As a general principle, I do not think that the exclusive study of any *one* subject is really education; and my experience as a teacher has shown me that even a considerable proficiency in Natural Science, taken alone, is so far from proving a high degree of cultivation and great natural ability that it is fully compatible with general ignorance and an intellect quite below par. Therefore it is that I seek to rouse an interest, beyond the limits of Oxford, in preserving classics as an essential feature of a University education. Nor is it as a classical tutor (who might be suspected of a bias in favour of his own subject) that I write this. On the contrary, it is as one who has taught science here for more than twenty years (for mathematics, though good-humouredly scorned by the biologists on account of the abnormal certainty of its conclusions, is still reckoned among the sciences) that I beg to sign myself,—Your obedient servant,

Charles L. Dodgson,

Mathematical Lecturer of Christ Church, Oxford.

May 17th.

I give the above letter because I think it amusing; it must not be supposed that the writer's views on the subject remained the same all through his life. He was a thorough Conservative, and it took a long time to reconcile him to any new departure. In a political discussion with a friend he once said that he was "first an Englishman, and then a Conservative," but however much a man may try to put patriotism before party, the result will be but partially successful, if patriotism would lead him into opposition to the mental bias which has originally made him either a Conservative or a Radical.

He took, of course, great pleasure in the success of his books, as every author must; but the greatest pleasure of all to him was to know that they had pleased others. Notes like the following are frequent in his Diary: "*June 25th.*—Spent the afternoon in sending off seventy circulars to Hospitals, offering copies of 'Alice' and the 'Looking-Glass' for sick children." He well deserved the name which one of his admirers gave him—"The man who loved little children."

In April, 1878, he saw a performance of "Olivia" at the Court Theatre. "The gem of the piece is Olivia herself, acted by Ellen Terry with a sweetness and pathos that moved some of the audience (nearly including myself) to tears. Her leave-taking was exquisite; and when, in her exile, she hears that her little brother had cried at the mention of her name, her exclamation 'Pet!' was tenderness itself. Altogether, I have not had a greater dramatic treat for a long time. *Dies cretâ notandus*."

I see that I have marked for quotation the following brief entries in the Diary:—

Aug. 4th (at Eastbourne).—Went, morning and evening, to the new chapel-of-ease belonging to S. Saviour's. It has the immense advantage of *not* being crowded; but this scarcely compensates for the vile Gregorian chants, which vex and weary one's ear.

Aug. 17th.—A very inquisitive person, who had some children with her, found out my name, and then asked me to shake hands with her child, as an admirer of my books: this I did, unwisely perhaps, as I have no intention of continuing the acquaintance of a "Mrs. Leo Hunter."

Dec. 23rd.—I have been making a plan for work next term, of this kind: Choose a subject (*e.g.*, "Circulation," "Journeys of S. Paul," "English Counties") for each week. On Monday write what I know about it; during week get up subject; on Saturday write again; put the two papers away, and six months afterwards write again and compare.

As an artist, Mr. Dodgson possessed an intense natural appreciation of the beautiful, an abhorrence of all that is coarse and unseemly which might almost be called hyper-refinement, a wonderfully good eye for form, and last, but not least, the most scrupulous conscientiousness about detail. On the other hand his sense of colour was somewhat imperfect, and his hand was almost totally untrained, so that while he had all the enthusiasm of the true artist, his work always had the defects of an amateur.

In 1878 some drawings of Miss E. Gertrude Thomson's excited his keen admiration, and he exerted himself to make her acquaintance. Their first meeting is described so well by Miss Thomson herself in *The Gentlewoman* for January 29, 1898, that I cannot do better than quote the description of the scene as given there:—

It was at the end of December, 1878, that a letter, written in a singularly legible and rather boyish-looking hand, came to me from Christ Church, Oxford, signed "C. L. Dodgson." The writer said that he had come across some fairy designs of mine, and he should like to see some more of my work. By the same post came a letter from my London publisher (who had supplied my address) telling me that the "Rev. C. L. Dodgson" was "Lewis Carroll."

"Alice in Wonderland" had long been one of my pet books, and as one regards a favourite author as almost a personal friend, I felt less restraint than one usually feels in writing to a stranger, though I carefully concealed my knowledge of his identity, as he had not chosen to reveal it.

This was the beginning of a frequent and delightful correspondence, and as I confessed to a great love for fairy lore of every description, he asked me if I would accept a child's fairy-tale book he had written, called "Alice in Wonderland." I replied that I knew it nearly all off by heart, but that I should greatly prize a copy given to me by himself. By return came "Alice," and "Through the Looking-Glass," bound most luxuriously in white calf and gold.

And this is the graceful and kindly note that came with them: "I am now sending you 'Alice,' and the 'Looking-Glass' as well. There is an incompleteness about giving only one, and besides, the one you bought was probably in red and would not match these. If you are at all in doubt as to what to do with the (now) superfluous copy, let me suggest your giving it to some poor sick child. I have been distributing copies to all the hospitals and convalescent homes I can hear of, where there are sick children capable of reading them, and though, of course, one takes some pleasure in the popularity of the books elsewhere, it is not nearly so pleasant a thought to me as that they may be a comfort and relief to children in hours of pain and weariness. Still, no recipient *can* be more appropriate than one who seems to have been in fairyland herself, and to have seen, like the 'weary mariners' of old—

'Between the green brink and the running foam
White limbs unrobed in a crystal air,
Sweet faces, rounded arms, and bosoms prest
To little harps of gold.'"

"Do you ever come to London?" he asked in another letter; "if so, will you allow me to call upon you?"

Early in the summer I came up to study, and I sent him word that I was in town. One night, coming into my room, after a long day spent at the British Museum, in the half-light I saw a card lying on the table. "Rev. C. L. Dodgson." Bitter, indeed, was my disappointment at having missed him, but just as I was laying it sadly down I spied a small T.O. in the corner. On the back I read that he couldn't get up to my rooms early or late enough to find me, so would I arrange to meet him at some museum or gallery the day but one following? I fixed on South Kensington Museum, by the "Schliemann" collection, at twelve o'clock.

A little before twelve I was at the rendezvous, and then the humour of the situation suddenly struck me, that *I* had not the ghost of an idea what *he* was like, nor would *he* have any better chance of discovering *me!* The room was fairly full of all sorts and conditions, as usual, and I glanced at each masculine figure in turn, only to reject it as a possibility of the one I sought. Just as the big clock had clanged out twelve, I heard the high vivacious voices and laughter of children sounding down the corridor.

At that moment a gentleman entered, two little girls clinging to his hands, and as I caught sight of the tall slim figure, with the clean-shaven, delicate, refined face, I said to myself, "*That's* Lewis Carroll." He stood for a moment, head erect, glancing swiftly over the room, then, bending down, whispered something to one of the children; she, after a moment's pause, pointed straight at me.

Dropping their hands he came forward, and with that winning smile of his that utterly banished the oppressive sense of the Oxford don, said simply, "I am Mr. Dodgson; I was to meet you, I think?" To which I as frankly smiled, and said, "How did you know me so soon?"

"My little friend found you. I told her I had come to meet a young lady who knew fairies, and she fixed on you at once. But *I* knew you before she spoke."

This acquaintance ripened into a true, artistic friendship, which lasted till Mr. Dodgson's death. In his first letter to Miss Thomson he speaks of himself as one who for twenty years had found his one amusement in photographing from life—especially photographing children; he also said that he had made attempts ("most unsuccessfully") at drawing them. When he got to know her more intimately, he asked her to criticise his work, and when she wrote expressing her willingness to do so, he sent her a pile of sketch-books, through which she went most carefully, marking the mistakes, and criticising, wherever criticism seemed to be necessary.

After this he might often have been seen in her studio, lying flat on his face, and drawing some child-model who had been engaged for his especial benefit. "I *love* the effort to draw," he wrote in one of his letters to her, "but I utterly fail to please even my own eye—tho' now and then I seem to get somewhere *near* a right line or two, when I have a live child to draw from. But I have no time left now for such things. In the next life, I do *hope* we shall not only *see* lovely forms, such as this world does not contain, but also be able to *draw* them."

But while he fully recognised the limits of his powers, he had great faith in his own critical judgment; and with good reason, for his perception of the beautiful in contour and attitude and grouping was almost unerring. All the drawings which Miss Thomson made for his "Three Sunsets" were submitted to his criticism, which descended to the smallest details. He concludes a letter to her, which contained the most elaborate and minute suggestions for the improvement of one of these pictures, with the following words: "I make all these suggestions with diffidence, feeling that

I have *really no* right at all, as an amateur, to criticise the work of a real artist."

The following extract from another letter to Miss Thomson shows that seeking after perfection, that discontent with everything short of the best, which was so marked a feature of his character. She had sent him two drawings of the head of some child-friend of his:—

Your note is a puzzle—you say that "No. 2 would have been still more like if the paper had been exactly the same shade—but I'd no more at hand of the darker colour." Had I given you the impression that I was in a *hurry*, and was willing to have No. 2 *less* good than it *might* be made, so long as I could have it *quick?* If I did, I'm very sorry: I never *meant* to say a word like it: and, if you had written "I could make it still more like, on darker paper; but I've no more at hand. How long can you wait for me to get some?" I should have replied, "Six weeks, or six *months*, if you prefer it!"

I have already spoken of his love of nature, as opposed to the admiration for the morbid and abnormal. "I want you," he writes to Miss Thomson, "to do my fairy drawings from *life*. They would be very pretty, no doubt, done out of your own head, but they will be ten times as valuable if done from life. Mr. Furniss drew the pictures of 'Sylvie' from life. Mr. Tenniel is the only artist, who has drawn for me, who resolutely refused to use a model, and declared he no more needed one than I should need a multiplication-table to work a mathematical problem!" On another occasion he urges the importance of using models, in order to avoid the similarity of features which would otherwise spoil the pictures: "Cruikshank's splendid illustrations were terribly spoiled by his having only *one* pretty female face in them all. Leech settled down into *two* female faces. Du Maurier, I think, has only *one*, now. All the ladies, and all the little girls in his pictures look like twin sisters."

It is interesting to know that Sir Noel Paton and Mr. Walter Crane were, in Lewis Carroll's opinion, the most successful drawers of children: "There are but few artists who seem to draw the forms of children *con amore*. Walter Crane is perhaps the best (always excepting Sir Noel Paton): but the thick outlines, which he insists on using, seem to take off a good deal from the beauty of the result."

He held that no artist can hope to effect a higher type of beauty than that which life itself exhibits, as the following words show:—

I don't quite understand about fairies losing "grace," if too like human children. Of course I grant that to be like some *actual* child is to lose grace, because no living child is perfect in form: many causes have lowered the race from what God made it. But the *perfect* human form, free from these faults, is surely equally applicable to men, and fairies, and angels? Perhaps that is what you mean—that the Artist can imagine, and design, more perfect forms than we ever find in life?

I have already referred several times to Miss Ellen Terry as having been one of Mr. Dodgson's friends, but he was intimate with the whole family, and used often to pay them a visit when he was in town. On May 15, 1879, he records a very curious dream which he had about Miss Marion ("Polly") Terry:—

Last night I had a dream which I record as a curiosity, so far as I know, in the literature of dreams. I was staying, with my sisters, in some suburb of London, and had heard that the Terrys were staying near us, so went to call, and found Mrs. Terry at home, who told us that Marion and Florence were at the theatre, "the Walter House," where they had a good engagement. "In that case," I said, "I'll go on there at once, and see the performance—and may I take Polly with me?" "Certainly," said Mrs. Terry. And there was Polly, the child, seated in the room, and looking about nine or ten years old: and I was distinctly conscious of the fact, yet without any feeling of surprise at its incongruity, that I was going to take the *child* Polly with me to the theatre, to see the *grown-up* Polly act! Both pictures—Polly as a child, and Polly as a woman, are, I suppose, equally clear in my ordinary waking memory: and it seems that in sleep I had contrived to give the two pictures separate individualities.

Of all the mathematical books which Mr. Dodgson wrote, by far the most elaborate, if not the most original, was "Euclid and His Modern Rivals." The first edition was issued in 1879, and a supplement, afterwards incorporated into the second edition, appeared in 1885.

This book, as the author says, has for its object

to furnish evidence (1) that it is essential for the purposes of teaching or examining in Elementary Geometry to employ one text—book only; (2) that there are strong *a priori* reasons for retaining in all its main features, and especially in its sequence and numbering of Propositions, and in its treatment of Parallels, the Manual of Euclid; and (3) that no sufficient reasons have yet been shown for abandoning it in favour of any one of the modern Manuals which have been offered as substitutes.

The book is written in dramatic form, and relieved throughout by many touches in the author's happiest vein, which make it delightful not only to the scientific reader, but also to any one of average intelligence with the slightest sense of humour.

Whether the conclusions are accepted in their entirety or not, it is certain that the arguments are far more effective than if the writer had presented them in the form of an essay. Mr. Dodgson had a wide experience as a teacher and examiner, so that he knew well what he was writing about, and undoubtedly the appearance of this book has done very much to stay the hand of the innovator.

The scene opens in a College study-time, midnight. Minos, an examiner, is discovered seated between two immense piles of manuscripts. He is driven almost to distraction in his efforts to mark fairly the papers sent up, by reason of the confusion caused through the candidates offering various substitutes for Euclid. Rhadamanthus, another equally distracted examiner, comes to his room.

The two men consult together for a time, and then Rhadamanthus retires, and Minos falls asleep. Hereupon the Ghost of Euclid appears, and discusses with Minos the reasons for retaining his Manual as a whole, in its present order and arrangement. As they are mainly concerned with the wants of beginners, their attention is confined to Books I. and II.

We must be content with one short extract from the dialogue:—

Euclid.—It is, I think, a friend of yours who has amused himself by tabulating the various Theorems which might be enunciated on the single subject of Pairs of Lines. How many did he make them out to be?

Minos.—About two hundred and fifty, I believe.

Euclid.—At that rate there would probably be within the limit of my First Book—how many?

Minos.—A thousand at least.

Euclid.—What a popular school-book it will be! How boys will bless the name of the writer who first brings out the complete thousand!

With a view to discussing and criticising his various modern rivals, Euclid promises to send to Minos the ghost of a German Professor (Herr Niemand) who "has read all books, and is ready to defend any thesis, true or untrue."

"A charming companion!" as Minos drily remarks.

This brings us to Act II., in which the Manuals which reject Euclid's treatment of Parallels are dealt with one by one. Those Manuals which adopt it are reserved for Act III., Scene i.; while in Scene ii., "The Syllabus of the Association for the Improvement of Geometrical Teaching," and Wilson's "Syllabus," come under review.

Only one or two extracts need be given, which, it is hoped, will suffice to illustrate the character and style of the book:

Act II., Scene v.—Niemand and Minos are arguing for and against Henrici's "Elementary Geometry."

Minos.—I haven't quite done with points yet. I find an assertion that they never jump. Do you think that arises from their having "position," which they feel might be compromised by such conduct?

Niemand.—I cannot tell without hearing the passage read.

Minos.—It is this: "A point, in changing its position on a curve, passes in moving from one position to another through all intermediate positions. It does not move by jumps."

Niemand.—That is quite true.

Minos.—Tell me then—is every centre of gravity a point?

Niemand.—Certainly.

Minos.—Let us now consider the centre of gravity of a flea. Does it—

Niemand (indignantly).—Another word, and I shall vanish! I cannot waste a night on such trivialities.

Minos.—I can't resist giving you just *one* more tit-bit—the definition of a square at page 123: "A quadrilateral which is a kite, a symmetrical trapezium, and a parallelogram is a square!" And now, farewell, Henrici: "Euclid, with all thy faults, I love thee still!"

Again, from Act II., Scene vi.:—

Niemand.—He (Pierce, another "Modern Rival,") has a definition of direction which will, I think, be new to you. *(Reads.)*

"The *direction of a line* in any part is the direction of a point at that part from the next preceding point of the line!"

Minos.—That sounds mysterious. Which way along a line are "preceding" points to be found?

Niemand.—Both ways. He adds, directly afterwards, "A line has two different directions," &c.

Minos.—So your definition needs a postscript.... But there is yet another difficulty. How far from a point is the "next" point?

Niemand.—At an infinitely small distance, of course. You will find the matter fully discussed in my work on the Infinitesimal Calculus.

Minos.—A most satisfactory answer for a teacher to make to a pupil just beginning Geometry!

In Act IV. Euclid reappears to Minos, "followed by the ghosts of Archimedes, Pythagoras, &c., who have come to see fair play." Euclid thus sums up his case:—

"'The cock doth craw, the day doth daw,' and all respectable ghosts ought to be going home. Let me carry with me the hope that I have convinced you of the necessity of retaining my order and numbering, and my method of treating Straight Lines, Angles, Right Angles, and (most especially) Parallels. Leave me these untouched, and I shall look on with great contentment while other changes are made—while my proofs are abridged and improved—while alternative proofs are appended to mine—and while new Problems and Theorems are interpolated. In all these matters my Manual is capable of almost unlimited improvement."

In Appendices I. and II. Mr. Dodgson quotes the opinions of two eminent mathematical teachers, Mr. Todhunter and Professor De Morgan, in support of his argument.

Before leaving this subject I should like to refer to a very novel use of Mr. Dodgson's book—its employment in a school. Mr. G. Hopkins, Mathematical Master in the High School at Manchester, U.S., and himself the author of a "Manual of Plane Geometry," has so employed it in a class of boys aged from fourteen or fifteen upwards. He first called their attention to some of the more prominent difficulties relating to the question of Parallels, put a copy of Euclid in their hands, and let them see his treatment of them, and after some discussion placed before them Mr. Dodgson's "Euclid and His Modern Rivals" and "New Theory of Parallels."

Perhaps it is the fact that American boys are sharper than English, but at any rate the youngsters are reported to have read the two books with an earnestness and a persistency that were as gratifying to their instructor as they were complimentary to Mr. Dodgson.

In June of the same year an entry in the Diary refers to a proposal in Convocation to allow the University Club to have a cricket-ground in the Parks. This had been proposed in 1867, and then rejected. Mr. Dodgson sent round to the Common Rooms copies of a poem on "The Deserted Parks," which had been published by Messrs. Parker in 1867, and which was afterwards included in "Notes by an Oxford Chiel." I quote the first few lines:—

Museum! loveliest building of the plain
Where Cherwell winds towards the distant main;

How often have I loitered o'er thy green,
Where humble happiness endeared the scene!
How often have I paused on every charm,—
The rustic couple walking arm in arm,
The groups of trees, with seats beneath the shade
For prattling babes and whisp'ring lovers made,
The never-failing brawl, the busy mill,
Where tiny urchins vied in fistic skill.
(Two phrases only have that dusky race
Caught from the learned influence of the place;
Phrases in their simplicity sublime,
"Scramble a copper!" "Please, sir, what's the time?")
These round thy walks their cheerful influence shed;
These were thy charms—but all these charms are fled,
Amidst thy bowers the tyrant's hand is seen,
And rude pavilions sadden all thy green;
One selfish pastime grasps the whole domain,
And half a faction swallows up the plain;
Adown thy glades, all sacrificed to cricket,
The hollow-sounding bat now guards the wicket;
Sunk are thy mounds in shapeless level all,
Lest aught impede the swiftly rolling ball;
And trembling, shrinking from the fatal blow,
Far, far away thy hapless children go.
Ill fares the place, to luxury a prey,
Where wealth accumulates, and minds decay:
Athletic sports may flourish or may fade,
Fashion may make them, even as it has made;
But the broad Parks, the city's joy and pride,
When once destroyed can never be supplied!

Readers of "Sylvie and Bruno" will remember the way in which the invisible fairy-children save the drunkard from his evil life, and I have always felt that Mr. Dodgson meant Sylvie to be something more than a fairy—a sort of guardian angel. That such an idea would not have been inconsistent with his way of looking at things is shown by the following

Ch. Ch., *July,* 1879.

My dear Ethel,—I have been long intending to answer your letter of April 11th, chiefly as to your question in reference to Mrs. N—'s letter about the little S—s [whose mother had recently died]. You say you don't see "how they can be guided aright by their dead mother, or how light can come from her." Many people believe that our friends in the other world can and do influence us in some way, and perhaps even "guide" us and give us light to show us our duty. My own feeling is, it *may* be so: but nothing has been revealed about it. That the angels do so *is* revealed, and we may feel sure of *that*; and there is a beautiful fancy (for I don't think one can call it more) that "a mother who has died leaving a child behind her in this world, is allowed to be a sort of guardian angel to that child." Perhaps Mrs. N— believes that.

Here are two other entries in the Diary:—

Aug. 26th.—Worked from about 9.45 to 6.45, and again from 10.15 to 11.45 (making 10 1/2 hours altogether) at an idea which occurred to me of finding limits for *pi* by elementary trigonometry, for the benefit of the circle-squarers.

Dec. 12th.—Invented a new way of working one word into another. I think of calling the puzzle "syzygies."

I give the first three specimens:—

```
      MAN }
permanent }
   entice } Send MAN on ICE.
     ICE. }

     ACRE }
   sacred }
credentials } RELY on ACRE.
 entirely }
     RELY }

    PRISM }
prismatic }
 dramatic } Prove PRISM to be ODIOUS.
melodrama }
melodious }
   ODIOUS. }
```

In February, 1880, Mr. Dodgson proposed to the Christ Church "Staff-salaries Board," that as his tutorial work was lighter he should have £200 instead of £300 a year. It is not often that a man proposes to cut down *his own* salary, but the suggestion in this case was intended to help the College authorities in the policy of retrenchment which they were trying to carry out.

May 24th.—Percival, President of Trin. Coll., who has Cardinal Newman as his guest, wrote to say that the Cardinal would sit for a photo, to me, at Trinity. But I could not take my photography there and he couldn't come to me: so nothing came of it.

Aug. 19th. [At Eastbourne].—Took Ruth and Maud to the Circus (Hutchinson and Tayleure's—from America). I made friends with Mr. Tayleure, who took me to the tents of horses, and the caravan he lived in. And I added to my theatrical experiences by a chat with a couple of circus children—Ada Costello, aged 9, and Polly (Evans, I think), aged 13. I found Ada in the outer tent, with the pony on which she was to perform—practising vaulting on to it, varied with somersaults on the ground. I showed her my wire puzzle, and ultimately gave it her, promising a duplicate to Polly. Both children seemed bright and happy, and they had pleasant manners.

Sept. 2nd.—Mrs. H— took me to Dr. Bell's (the old homoeopathic doctor) to hear Lord Radstock speak about "training children." It was a curious affair. First a very long hymn; then two very long extempore prayers (not by Lord R—), which were strangely self-sufficient and wanting in reverence. Lord R—'s remarks were commonplace enough, though some of his theories were new, but, I think, not true—*e.g.,* that encouraging emulation in schoolboys, or desiring that they should make a good position in life, was un-Christian. I escaped at the first opportunity after his speech, and went down on the beach, where I made acquaintance with a family who were banking up with sand the feet and legs of a pretty little girl perched on a sand-castle. I got her father to make her stand to be drawn. Further along the beach a merry little mite began pelting me with sand; so I drew *her* too.

Nov. 16th.—Thought of a plan for simplifying money-orders, by making the sender fill up two duplicate papers, one of which he hands in to be transmitted by the postmaster—it containing a key—number which the receiver has to supply in *his* copy to get the money. I think of suggesting this, and my plan for double postage on Sunday, to the Government.

Dec. 19th.—The idea occurred to me that a game might be made of letters, to be moved about on a chess-board till they form words.

A little book, published during this year, "Alice (a dramatic version of Lewis Carroll's 'Alice'), and other Fairy Tales for Children," by Mrs. Freiligrath-Kroeker, was very successful, and, I understand, still has a regular sale. Mr. Dodgson most gladly gave his consent to the dramatisation of his story by so talented an authoress, and shortly afterwards Mrs. Kroeker brought out "Through the Looking-Glass" in a similar form.

Jan. 17, 1881.—To the Lyceum to see "The Cup" and "The Corsican Brothers." The first is exquisitely put on, and Ellen Terry as Camma is the perfection of grace, and Irving as the villain, and Mr. Terriss as the husband, were very good. But the piece wants substance.

Jan. 19th.—Tried to go to Oxford, but the line is blocked near Didcot, so stayed another night in town. The next afternoon the line was reported clear, but the journey took 5 hours! On the day before the Dean of Ch. Ch. and his family were snowed up for 21 hours near Radley.

March 27th.—Went to S. Mary's and stayed for Holy Communion, and, as Ffoulkes was alone, I mustered up courage to help him. I read the exhortation, and was pleased to find I did not once hesitate. I think I must try preaching again soon, as he has often begged me to do.

April 16th.—Mr. Greenwood approves my theory about general elections, and wants me to write on it in the *St. James's Gazette*. (The letter appeared on May 5, 1881.)

May 14th.—Took the longest walk (I believe) I have ever done—round by Dorchester, Didcot and Abingdon—27 miles—took 8 hours—no blisters, I rejoice to find, and I feel very little tired.

May 26th.—The row-loving men in College are beginning to be troublesome again, and last night some 30 or 40 of them, aided by out-College men, made a great disturbance, and regularly defied the Censors. I have just been with the other Tutors into Hall, and heard the Dean make an excellent speech to the House. Some two or three will have to go down, and twelve or fifteen others will be punished in various ways. (A later note says): The punishments had to be modified—it turned out that the disturbers were nearly all out-College men.

Mr. Dodgson sent a letter to *The Observer* on this subject:—

Sir,—Your paper of May 29th contains a leading article on Christ Church, resting on so many mis-statements of fact that I venture to appeal to your sense of justice to allow me, if no abler writer has addressed you on the subject, an opportunity of correcting them. It will, I think, be found that in so doing I shall have removed the whole foundation on which the writer has based his attack on the House, after which I may contentedly leave the superstructure to take care of itself. "Christ Church is always provoking the adverse criticism of the outer world." The writer justifies this rather broad generalisation by quoting three instances of such provocation, which I will take one by one.

At one time we are told that "The Dean ... neglects his functions, and spends the bulk of his time in Madeira." The fact is that the Dean's absence from England more than twenty years ago during two successive winters was a sad necessity, caused by the appearance of symptoms of grave disease, from which he has now, under God's blessing, perfectly recovered.

The second instance occurred eleven years ago, when some of the undergraduates destroyed some valuable statuary in the Library. Here the writer states that the Dean first announced that criminal proceedings would be taken, and then, on discovering that the offenders were "highly connected," found himself "converted to the opinion that mercy is preferable to stern justice, and charity to the strict letter of the law." The facts are that the punishment awarded to the offenders was deliberated on and determined on by the Governing Body, consisting of the Dean, the Canons, and some twenty Senior Students; that their deliberations were most assuredly in no way affected by any thoughts of the offenders being "highly connected"; and that, when all was over, we had the satisfaction of seeing ourselves roundly abused in the papers on both sides, and charged with having been too lenient, and also with having been too severe.

The third instance occurred the other night. Some undergraduates were making a disturbance, and the Junior Censor "made his appearance in person upon the scene of riot," and "was contumeliously handled." Here the only statement of any real importance, the alleged assault by Christ Church men on the Junior Censor, is untrue. The fact is that nearly all the disturbers were out-College men, and, though it is true that the Censor was struck by a stone thrown from a window, the unenviable distinction of having thrown it belongs to no member of the House. I doubt if we have one single man here who would be capable of so base and cowardly an act.

The writer then gives us a curious account of the present constitution of the House. The Dean, whom he calls "the right reverend gentleman," is, "in a kind of way, master of the College. The Canons, in a vague kind of way, are supposed to control the College." The Senior Students "dare not call their souls their own," and yet somehow dare "to vent their wrath" on the Junior Students. His hazy, mental picture of the position of the Canons may be cleared up by explaining to him that the "control" they exercise is neither more nor less than that of any other six members of the Governing Body. The description of the Students I pass over as not admitting any appeal to actual facts.

The truth is that Christ Church stands convicted of two unpardonable crimes—being great, and having a name. Such a place must always expect to find itself "a wide mark for scorn and jeers"—a target where the little and the nameless may display their skill. Only the other day an M.P., rising to ask a question about Westminster School, went on to speak of Christ Church, and wound up with a fierce attack on the ancient House. Shall we blame him? Do we blame the wanton schoolboy, with a pebble in his hand, all powerless to resist the alluring vastness of a barndoor?

The essence of the article seems to be summed up in the following sentence: "At Christ Church all attempts to preserve order by the usual means have hitherto proved uniformly unsuccessful, and apparently remain equally fruitless." It is hard for one who, like myself, has lived here most of his life, to believe that this is seriously intended as a description of the place. However, as general statements can only be met by general statements, permit me, as one who has lived here for thirty years and has taught for five-and-twenty, to say that in my experience order has been the rule, disorder the rare exception, and that, if the writer of your leading article has had an equal amount of experience in any similar place of education, and has found a set of young men more gentlemanly, more orderly, and more pleasant in every way to deal with, than I have found here, I cannot but think him an exceptionally favoured mortal.—Yours, &c.

Charles l. Dodgson,

Student and Mathematical Lecturer of Christ Church.

In July began an amusing correspondence between Mr. Dodgson and a "circle-squarer," which lasted several months. Mr. Dodgson sent the infatuated person, whom we will call Mr. B—, a proof that the area of a circle is less than 3.15 the square of the radius. Mr. B—replied, "Your proof is not in accordance with Euclid, it assumes that a circle may be considered as a rectangle, and that two right lines can enclose a space." He returned the proof, saying that he could not accept any of it as elucidating the exact area of a circle, or as Euclidean. As Mr. Dodgson's method involved a slight knowledge of trigonometry, and he had reason to suspect that Mr. B—was entirely ignorant of that subject, he thought it worth while to put him to the test by asking him a few questions upon it, but the circle-squarer, with commendable prudence, declined to discuss anything not Euclidean. Mr. Dodgson then wrote to him, "taking leave of the subject, until he should be willing to enlarge his field of knowledge to the elements of Algebraical Geometry." Mr. B—replied, with unmixed contempt, "Algebraical Geometry is all moon-shine." *He* preferred "weighing cardboard" as a means of ascertaining exact truth in mathematical research. Finally he suggested that Mr. Dodgson might care to join in a prize-competition to be got up among the followers of Euclid, and as he apparently wished him to understand that he (Mr. B—) did not think much of his chances of getting a prize, Mr. Dodgson considered that the psychological moment for putting an end to the correspondence had arrived.

Meanwhile he was beginning to feel his regular College duties a terrible clog upon his literary work. The Studentship which he held was not meant to tie him down to lectures and examinations. Such work was very well for a younger man; he could best serve "the House" by his literary fame.

July 14th.—Came to a more definite decision than I have ever yet done—that it is about time to resign the Mathematical Lectureship. My chief motive for holding on has been to provide money for others (for myself, I have been many years able to retire), but even the £300 a year I shall thus lose I may fairly hope to make by the additional time I shall have for book-writing. I think of asking the G.B. (Governing Body) next term to appoint my successor, so that I may retire at the end of the year, when I shall be close on fifty years old, and shall have held the Lectureship for exactly 26 years. (I had the Honourmen for the last two terms of 1855, but was not full Lecturer till Hilary, 1856.)

Oct. 18th.—I have just taken an important step in life, by sending to the Dean a proposal to resign the Mathematical Lectureship at the end of this year. I shall now have my whole time at my own disposal, and, if God gives me life and continued health and strength, may hope, before my powers fail, to do some worthy work in writing—partly in the cause of mathematical education, partly in the cause of innocent recreation for children, and partly, I hope (though so utterly unworthy of being allowed to take up such work) in the cause of religious thought. May God bless the new form of life that lies before me, that I may use it according to His holy will!

Oct. 21st.—I had a note in the evening from the Dean, to say that he had seen the Censors on the subject of my proposed resignation at the end of the year, and that arrangements should be made, as far as could be done, to carry out my wishes; and kindly adding an expression of regret at losing my services, but allowing that I had "earned a right to retirement." So my Lectureship seems to be near its end.

Nov. 30th.—I find by my Journal that I gave my *first* Euclid Lecture in the Lecture-room on Monday, January 28, 1856. It consisted of twelve men, of whom nine attended. This morning, I have given what is most probably my *last*: the lecture is now reduced to nine, of whom all attended on Monday: this morning being a Saint's Day, the attendance was voluntary, and only two appeared—E.H. Morris, and G. Lavie. I was Lecturer when the *father* of the latter took his degree, viz., in 1858.

There is a sadness in coming to the end of anything in life. Man's instincts cling to the Life that will never end.

May 30, 1882.—Called on Mrs. R—. During a good part of the evening I read *The Times*, while the party played a round game of spelling words—a thing I will never join in. Rational conversation and *good* music are the only things which, to me, seem worth the meeting for, for grown-up people.

June 1st.—Went out with Charsley, and did four miles on one of his velocimans, very pleasantly.

The velociman was an early and somewhat cumbrous form of tricycle; Mr. Dodgson made many suggestions for its improvement. He never attempted to ride a bicycle, however, but, in accordance with his own dictum, "In youth, try a bicycle, in age, buy a tricycle," confined himself to the three-wheeled variety.

Nov. 8th.—Whitehead, of Trinity, told us a charming story in Common Room of a father and son. They came up together: the son got into a College—the father had to go to New Inn Hall: the son passed Responsions, while his father had to put off: finally, the father failed in Mods and has gone down: the son will probably take his degree, and may then be able to prepare his father for another try.

Among the coloured cartoons in Shrimpton's window at Oxford there used to be, when I was up, a picture which I think referred to this story.

Nov. 23rd.—Spent two hours "invigilating" in the rooms of W.J. Grant (who has broken his collar-bone, and is allowed to do his Greats papers in this way) while he dictated his answers to another undergraduate, Pakenham, who acted as scribe.

Nov. 24th.—Dined with Fowler (now President of C.C.C.) in hall, to meet Ranken. Both men are now mostly bald, with quite grey hair: yet how short a time it seems since we were undergraduates together at Whitby! (in 1854).

Dec 8th.—A Common Room Meeting. Fresh powers were given to the Wine Committee, and then a new Curator elected. I was proposed by Holland, and seconded by Harcourt, and accepted office with no light heart: there will be much trouble and thought needed to work it satisfactorily, but it will take me out of myself a little, and so may be a real good—my life was tending to become too much that of a selfish recluse.

During this year he composed the words of a song, "Dreamland." The air was *dreamed* by his friend, the late Rev. C. E. Hutchinson, of Chichester. The history of the dream is here given in the words of the dreamer:—

I found myself seated, with many others, in darkness, in a large amphitheatre. Deep stillness prevailed. A kind of hushed expectancy was upon us. We sat awaiting I know not what. Before us hung a vast and dark curtain, and between it and us was a kind of stage. Suddenly an intense wish seized me to look upon the forms of some of the heroes of past days. I cannot say whom in particular I longed to behold, but, even as I wished, a faint light flickered over the stage, and I was aware of a silent procession of figures moving from right to left across the platform in front of me. As each figure approached the left-hand corner it turned and gazed at me, and I knew (by what means I cannot say) its name. One only I recall—Saint George; the light shone with a peculiar bluish lustre on his shield and helmet as he turned and slowly faced me. The figures were shadowy, and floated like mist before me; as each one disappeared an invisible choir behind the curtain sang the "Dream music." I awoke with the melody ringing in my ears, and the words of the last line complete—"I see the shadows falling, and slowly pass away." The rest I could not recall.

DREAMLAND.

Words by LEWIS CARROLL.

Music by C.E. HUTCHINSON.

When midnight mists are creeping
And all the land is sleeping
Around me tread the mighty dead,
And slowly pass away.

Lo, warriors, saints, and sages,
From out the vanished ages,
With solemn pace and reverend face
Appear and pass away.

The blaze of noonday splendour,
The twilight soft and tender,
May charm the eye: yet they shall die,
Shall die and pass away

But here, in Dreamland's centre,
No spoiler's hand may enter,
These visions fair, this radiance rare,
Shall never pass away

I see the shadows falling,
The forms of eld recalling;
Around me tread the mighty dead,
And slowly pass away

One of the best services to education which Mr. Dodgson performed was his edition of "Euclid I. and II.," which was published in 1882. In writing "Euclid and His Modern Rivals," he had criticised somewhat severely the various substitutes proposed for Euclid, so far as they concerned beginners; but at the same time he had admitted that within prescribed limits Euclid's text is capable of amendment and improvement, and this is what he attempted to do in this book. That he was fully justified is shown by the fact that during the years 1882—1889 the book ran through eight editions. In the Introduction he enumerates, under the three headings of "Additions," "Omissions," and "Alterations," the chief points of difference between his own and the ordinary editions of Euclid, with his reasons for adopting them. They are the outcome of long experience, and the most conservative of teachers would readily accept them.

The proof of I. 24, for example, is decidedly better and more satisfactory than the ordinary proof, and the introduction of the definition of "projection" certainly simplifies the cumbrous enunciations of II. 12 and 13. Again, the alternative proof of II. 8, suggested in the Introduction, is valuable, and removes all excuse for omitting this proposition, as is commonly clone.

The figures used are from the blocks prepared for the late Mr. Todhunter's well-known edition of Euclid, to which Mr. Dodgson's manual forms an excellent stepping-stone.

At the beginning of 1883 he went up to town to see the collection of D. G. Rossetti's pictures in the Burlington Gallery. He was especially struck with "Found," which he thus describes—

A picture of a man finding, in the streets of London, a girl he had loved years before in the days of her innocence. She is huddled up against the wall, dressed in gaudy colours, and trying to turn away her agonised face, while he, holding her wrists, is looking down with an expression of pain and pity, condemnation and love, which is one of the most marvellous things I have ever seen done in painting.

Jan. 27, 1883 [His birthday].—I cannot say I feel much older at 51 than at 21! Had my first "tasting-luncheon"; it seemed to give great satisfaction. [The object of the Curator's "tasting-luncheon" was, of course, to give members of Common Room an opportunity of deciding what wines should be bought.]

March 15*th.*—Went up to town to fulfil my promise to Lucy A.—: to take her for her *first* visit to the theatre. We got to the Lyceum in good time, and the play was capitally acted. I had hinted to Beatrice (Miss Ellen Terry) how much she could add to Lucy's pleasure by sending round a "carte" of herself; she sent a cabinet. She is certainly an adept in giving gifts that gratify.

April 23*d.*—Tried another long walk—22 miles, to Besilsleigh, Fyfield, Kingston, Bagpuize, Frilford, Marcham, and Abingdon. The last half of the way was in the face of wind, rain, snow, and hail. Was too lame to go into Hall.

CHAPTER VI

(1883—1887)

"The Profits of Authorship"—"Rhyme? and Reason?"—The Common Room Cat—Visit to Jersey—Purity of elections—Parliamentary Representation—Various literary projects—Letters to Miss E. Rix—Being happy—"A Tangled Tale"—Religious arguments—The "Alice" Operetta—"Alice's Adventures Underground"—"The Game of Logic"—Mr. Harry Furniss.

In 1883 Lewis Carroll was advised to make a stand against the heavy discount allowed by publishers to booksellers, and by booksellers to the public. Accordingly the following notice began to appear in all his books: "In selling Mr. Lewis Carroll's books to the Trade, Messrs. Macmillan and Co. will abate 2d. in the shilling (no odd copies), and allow 5 per cent, discount within six months, and 10 per cent, for cash. In selling them to the Public (for cash only) they will allow 10 per cent, discount."

It was a bold step to take, and elicited some loud expressions of disapproval. "Rather than buy on the terms Mr. Lewis Carroll offers," "A Firm of London Booksellers" wrote in *The Bookseller* of August 4th, "the trade will do well to refuse to take copies of his books, new or old, so long as he adheres to the terms he has just announced to the trade for their delectation and delight." On the other hand, an editorial, which appeared in the same number of *The Bookseller,* expressed warm approval of the innovation.

To avoid all possible misconceptions, the author fully explained his views in a little pamphlet on "The Profits of Authorship." He showed that the bookseller makes as much profit out of every volume he sells (assuming the buyer to pay the full published price, which he did in those days more readily than he does to-day) as author and publisher together, whereas his share in the work is very small. He does not say much about the author's part in the work—that it is a very heavy one goes without saying—but in considering the publisher's share he says:—

The publisher contributes about as much as the bookseller in time and bodily labour, but in mental toil and trouble a great deal more. I speak with some personal knowledge of the matter, having myself, for some twenty years, inflicted on that most patient and painstaking firm, Messrs. Macmillan and Co., about as much wear and worry as ever publishers have lived through. The day when they undertake a book for me is a *dies nefastus* for them. From that day till the book is out—an interval of some two or three years on an average—there is no pause in "the pelting of the pitiless storm" of directions and questions on every conceivable detail. To say that every question gets a courteous and thoughtful reply—that they are still outside a lunatic asylum—and that they still regard me with some degree of charity—is to speak volumes in praise of their good temper and of their health, bodily and mental. I think the publisher's claim on the profits is on the whole stronger than the booksellers.

"Rhyme? and Reason?" appeared at Christmas; the dedicatory verses, inscribed "To a dear child: in memory of golden summer hours and whispers of a summer sea," were addressed to a little friend of the author's, Miss Gertrude Chataway. One of the most popular poems in the book is "Hiawatha's Photographing," a delicious parody of Longfellow's "Hiawatha." "In an age of imitation," says Lewis Carroll, in a note at the head, "I can claim no special merit for this slight attempt at doing what is known to be so easy." It is not every one who has read this note who has observed that it is really in the same metre as the poem below it.

Another excellent parody, "Atalanta in Camden-Town," exactly hit off the style of that poet who stands alone and unapproached among the poets of the day, and whom Mr. Dodgson used to call "the greatest living master of language."

"Fame's Penny Trumpet," affectionately dedicated to all "original researchers" who pant for "endowment," was an attack upon the Vivisectionists,

Who preach of Justice—plead with tears
That Love and Mercy should abound—
While marking with complacent ears
The moaning of some tortured hound.

Lewis Carroll thus addresses them:—

Fill all the air with hungry wails—
"Reward us, ere we think or write!
Without your gold mere knowledge fails
To sate the swinish appetite!"

And, where great Plato paced serene,
Or Newton paused with wistful eye,
Rush to the chase with hoofs unclean
And Babel-clamour of the stye!

Be yours the pay: be theirs the praise:
We will not rob them of their due,
Nor vex the ghosts of other days
By naming them along with you.

They sought and found undying fame:
They toiled not for reward nor thanks:
Their cheeks are hot with honest shame
For you, the modern mountebanks!

"For auld lang syne" the author sent a copy of his book to Mrs. Hargreaves (Miss Alice Liddell), accompanied by a short note.

Christ Church, *December* 21, 1883.

Dear Mrs. Hargreaves,—Perhaps the shortest day in the year is not *quite* the most appropriate time for recalling the long dreamy summer afternoons of ancient times; but anyhow if this book gives you half as much pleasure to receive as it does me to send, it will be a success indeed.

Wishing you all happiness at this happy season, I am,

Sincerely yours,

C. L. Dodgson.

The beginning of 1884 was chiefly occupied in Common Room business. The Curatorship seems to have been anything but a sinecure. Besides weightier responsibilities, it involved the care of the Common Room Cat! In this case the "care" ultimately killed the cat—but not until it had passed the span of life usually allotted to those animals, and beyond which their further existence is equally a nuisance to themselves and to every one else. As to the best way of "terminating its sublunary existence," Mr. Dodgson consulted two surgeons, one of whom was Sir James Paget. I do not know what method was finally adopted, but I am sure it was one that gave no pain to pussy's nerves, and as little as possible to her feelings.

On March 11th there was a debate in Congregation on the proposed admission of women to some of the Honour Schools at Oxford. This was one of the many subjects on which Mr. Dodgson wrote a pamphlet. During the debate he made one of his few speeches, and argued strongly against the proposal, on the score of the injury to health which it would inflict upon the girl-undergraduates.

Later in the month he and the Rev. E.F. Sampson, Tutor of Christ Church, paid a visit to Jersey, seeing various friends, notably the Rev. F.H. Atkinson, an old College friend of Mr. Dodgson's, who had helped him when he was editor of *College Rhymes*. I quote a few lines from a letter of his to Mr. Atkinson, as showing his views on matrimony:—

So you have been for twelve years a married man, while I am still a lonely old bachelor! And mean to keep so, for the matter of that. College life is by no means unmixed misery, though married life has no doubt many charms to which I am a stranger.

A note in his Diary on May 5th shows one of the changes in his way of life which advancing years forced him to make:—

Wrote to—(who had invited me to dine) to beg off, on the ground that, in my old age, I find dinner parties more and more fatiguing. This is quite a new departure. I much grudge giving an evening (even if it were not tiring) to bandying small-talk with dull people.

The next extract I give does not look much like old age!

I called on Mrs. M—. She was out; and only one maid in, who, having come to the gate to answer the bell, found the door blown shut on her return. The poor thing seemed really alarmed and distressed. However, I got a man to come from a neighbouring yard with a ladder, and got in at the drawing-room window—a novel way of entering a friend's house!

Oddly enough, almost exactly the same thing happened to him in 1888: "The door blew shut, with the maid outside, and no one in the house. I got the cook of the next house to let me go through their premises, and with the help of a pair of steps got over the wall between the two back-yards."

In July there appeared an article in the *St. James's Gazette* on the subject of "Parliamentary Elections," written by Mr. Dodgson. It was a subject in which he was much interested, and a few years before he had contributed a long letter on the "Purity of Elections" to the same newspaper. I wish I had space to give both in full; as things are, a summary and a few extracts are all I dare attempt. The writer held that there are a great number of voters, and *pari passu* a great number of constituencies, that like to be on the winning side, and whose votes are chiefly influenced by that consideration. The ballot-box has made it practically impossible for the individual voter to know which is going to be the winning side, but after the first few days of a general election, one side or the other has generally got a more or less decided advantage, and a weak-kneed constituency is sorely tempted to swell the tide of victory.

But this is not all. The evil extends further than to the single constituency; nay, it extends further than to a single general election; it constitutes a feature in our national history; it is darkly ominous for the future of England. So long as general elections are conducted as at present we shall be liable to oscillations of political power, like those of 1874 and 1880, but of ever-increasing violence— one Parliament wholly at the mercy of one political party, the next wholly at the mercy of the other—while the Government of the hour, joyfully hastening to undo all that its predecessors have done, will wield a majority so immense that the fate of every question will be foredoomed, and debate will be a farce; in one word, we shall be a nation living from hand to mouth, and with no settled principle—an army, whose only marching orders will be "Right about face!"

His remedy was that the result of each single election should be kept secret till the general election is over:—

It surely would involve no practical difficulty to provide that the boxes of voting papers should be sealed up by a Government official and placed in such custody as would make it impossible to tamper with them; and that when the last election had been held they should be opened, the votes counted, and the results announced.

The article on "Parliamentary Elections" proposed much more sweeping alterations. The opening paragraph will show its general purport:—

The question, how to arrange our constituencies and conduct our Parliamentary elections so as to make the House of Commons, as far as possible, a true index of the state of opinion in the nation it professes to represent, is surely equal in importance to any that the present generation has had to settle. And the leap in the dark, which we seem about to take in a sudden and vast extension of the franchise, would be robbed of half its terrors could we feel assured that each political party will be duly represented in the next Parliament, so that every side of a question will get a fair hearing.

The axioms on which his scheme was based were as follows:—

(1) That each Member of Parliament should represent approximately the same number of electors.

(2) That the minority of the two parties into which, broadly speaking, each district may be divided, should be adequately represented.

(3) That the waste of votes, caused by accidentally giving one candidate more than he needs and leaving another of the same party with less than he needs, should be, if possible, avoided.

(4) That the process of marking a ballot-paper should be reduced to the utmost possible simplicity, to meet the case of voters of the very narrowest mental calibre.

(5) That the process of counting votes should be as simple as possible.

Then came a precise proposal. I do not pause to compare it in detail with the suggestions of Mr. Hare, Mr. Courtney, and others:—

I proceed to give a summary of rules for the method I propose. Form districts which shall return three, four, or more Members, in proportion to their size. Let each elector vote for one candidate only. When the poll is closed, divide the total number of votes by the number of Members to be returned *plus* one, and take the next greater integer as "quota." Let the returning officer publish the list of candidates, with the votes given for each, and declare as "returned" each that has obtained the quota. If there are still Members to return, let him name a time when all the candidates shall appear before him; and each returned Member may then formally assign his surplus votes to whomsoever of the other candidates he will, while the other candidates may in like manner assign their votes to one another.

This method would enable each of the two parties in a district to return as many Members as it could muster "quotas," no matter how the votes were distributed. If, for example, 10,000 were the quota, and the "reds" mustered 30,000 votes, they could return three Members; for, suppose they had four candidates, and that A had 22,000 votes, B 4,000, C 3,000, D 1,000, A would simply have to assign 6,000 votes to B and 6,000 to C; while D, being hopeless of success, would naturally let C have his 1,000 also. There would be no risk of a seat being left vacant through two candidates of the same party sharing a quota between them—an unwritten law would soon come to be recognised—that the one with fewest votes should give place to the other. And, with candidates of two opposite parties, this difficulty could not arise at all; one or the other could always be returned by the surplus votes of his party.

Some notes from the Diary for March, 1885, are worth reproducing here:—

March 1st.—Sent off two letters of literary importance, one to Mrs. Hargreaves, to ask her consent to my publishing the original MS. of "Alice" in facsimile (the idea occurred to me the other day); the other to Mr. H. Furniss, a very clever illustrator in *Punch*, asking if he is open to proposals to draw pictures for me.

The letter to Mrs. Hargreaves, which, it will be noticed, was earlier in date than the short note already quoted in this chapter, ran as follows:—

My Dear Mrs. Hargreaves,—I fancy this will come to you almost like a voice from the dead, after so many years of silence, and yet those years have made no difference that I can perceive in *my* clearness of memory of the days when we *did* correspond. I am getting to feel what an old man's failing memory is as to recent events and new friends, (for instance, I made friends, only a few weeks ago, with a very nice little maid of about twelve, and had a walk with her—and now I can't recall either of her names!), but my mental picture is as vivid as ever of one who was, through so many years, my ideal child-friend. I have had scores of child-friends since your time, but they have been quite a different thing.

However, I did not begin this letter to say all *that*. What I want to ask is, Would you have any objection to the original MS. book of "Alice's Adventures" (which I suppose you still possess) being published in facsimile? The idea of doing so occurred to me only the other day. If, on consideration, you come to the conclusion that you would rather *not* have it done, there is an end of the matter. If, however, you give a favourable reply, I would be much obliged if you would lend it me (registered post, I should think, would be safest) that I may consider the possibilities. I have not seen it for about twenty years, so am by no means sure that the illustrations may not prove to be so awfully bad that to reproduce them would be absurd.

There can be no doubt that I should incur the charge of gross egoism in publishing it. But I don't care for that in the least, knowing that I have no such motive; only I think, considering the extraordinary popularity the books have had (we have sold more than 120,000 of the two), there must be many who would like to see the original form.

Always your friend,

C.L. Dodgson.

The letter to Harry Furniss elicited a most satisfactory reply. Mr. Furniss said that he had long wished to illustrate one of Lewis Carroll's books, and that he was quite prepared to undertake the work ("Sylvie and Bruno").

Two more notes from the Diary, referring to the same month follow:—

March 10th.—A great Convocation assembled in the theatre, about a proposed grant for Physiology, opposed by many (I was one) who wish restrictions to be enacted as to the practice of vivisection for research. Liddon made an excellent speech against the grant, but it was carried by 412 to 244.

March 29th.—Never before have I had so many literary projects on hand at once. For curiosity, I will here make a list of them.

(1) Supplement to "Euclid and Modern Rivals."

(2) 2nd Edition of "Euc. and Mod. Rivals."

(3) A book of Math. curiosities, which I think of calling "Pillow Problems, and other Math. Trifles." This will contain Problems worked out in the dark, Logarithms without Tables, Sines and angles do., a paper I am now writing on "Infinities and Infinitesimals," condensed Long Multiplication, and perhaps others.

(4) Euclid V.

(5) "Plain Facts for Circle-Squarers," which is nearly complete, and gives actual proof of limits 3.14158, 3.14160.

(6) A symbolical Logic, treated by my algebraic method.

(7) "A Tangled Tale."

(8) A collection of Games and Puzzles of my devising, with fairy pictures by Miss E.G. Thomson. This might also contain my "Mem. Tech." for dates; my "Cipher-writing" scheme for Letter-registration, &c., &c.

(9) Nursery Alice.

(10) Serious poems in "Phantasmagoria."

(11) "Alice's Adventures Underground."

(12) "Girl's Own Shakespeare." I have begun on "Tempest."

(13) New edition of "Parliamentary Representation."

(14) New edition of Euc. I., II.

(15) The new child's book, which Mr. Furniss is to illustrate. I have settled on no name as yet, but it will perhaps be "Sylvie and Bruno."

I have other shadowy ideas, *e.g.*, a Geometry for Boys, a vol. of Essays on theological points freely and plainly treated, and a drama on "Alice" (for which Mr. Mackenzie would write music): but the above is a fair example of "too many irons in the fire!"

A letter written about this time to his friend, Miss Edith Rix, gives some very good hints about how to work, all the more valuable because he had himself successfully carried them out. The first hint was as follows:—

When you have made a thorough and reasonably long effort, to understand a thing, and still feel puzzled by it, *stop*, you will only hurt yourself by going on. Put it aside till the next morning; and if *then* you can't make it out, and have no one to explain it to you, put it aside entirely, and go back to that part of the subject which you *do* understand. When I was reading Mathematics for University honours, I would sometimes, after working a week or two at some new book, and mastering ten or twenty pages, get into a hopeless muddle, and find it just as bad the next morning. My rule was *to begin the book again*. And perhaps in another fortnight I had come to the old difficulty with impetus enough to get over it. Or perhaps not. I have several books that I have begun over and over again.

My second hint shall be—Never leave an unsolved difficulty *behind*. I mean, don't go any further in that book till the difficulty is conquered. In this point, Mathematics differs entirely from most other subjects. Suppose you are reading an Italian book, and come to a hopelessly obscure sentence—don't waste too much time on it, skip it, and go on; you will do very well without it. But if you skip a *mathematical* difficulty, it is sure to crop up again: you will find some other proof depending on it, and you will only get deeper and deeper into the mud.

My third hint is, only go on working so long as the brain is *quite* clear. The moment you feel the ideas getting confused leave off and rest, or your penalty will be that you will never learn Mathematics *at all!*

Two more letters to the same friend are, I think, deserving of a place here:—

Eastbourne, *Sept.* 25, 1885.

My dear Edith,—One subject you touch on—"the Resurrection of the Body"—is very interesting to me, and I have given it much thought (I mean long ago). *My* conclusion was to give up the *literal* meaning of the *material* body altogether. *Identity*, in some mysterious way, there evidently is; but there is no resisting the scientific fact that the actual *material* usable for *physical* bodies has been used over and over again—so that each atom would have several owners. The mere solitary fact of the existence of *cannibalism* is to my mind a sufficient *reductio ad absurdum* of the theory that the particular set of atoms I shall happen to own at death (changed every seven years, they say) will be mine in the next life—and all the other insuperable difficulties (such as people born with bodily defects) are swept away at once if we accept S. Paul's "spiritual body," and his simile of the grain of corn. I have read very little of "Sartor Resartus," and don't know the passage you quote: but I accept the idea of the material body being the "dress" of the spiritual—a dress needed for material life.

Ch. Ch., *Dec.* 13, 1885.

Dear Edith,—I have been a severe sufferer from *Logical* puzzles of late. I got into a regular tangle about the "import of propositions," as the ordinary logical books declare that "all x is z" doesn't even *hint* that any x's exist, but merely that the qualities are so inseparable that, if ever x occurs, z must occur also. As to "some x is z" they are discreetly silent; and the living authorities I have appealed to, including our Professor of Logic, take opposite sides! Some say it means that the qualities are so connected that, if any x's *did* exist, some *must* be z—others that it only means compatibility, *i.e.,* that some *might* be z, and they would go on asserting, with perfect belief in their truthfulness, "some boots are made of brass," even if they had all the boots in the world before them, and knew that *none* were so made, merely because there is no inherent impossibility in making boots of brass! Isn't it bewildering? I shall have to mention all this in my great work on Logic—but *I* shall take the line "any writer may mean exactly what he pleases by a phrase so long as he explains it beforehand." But I shall not venture to assert "some boots are made of brass" till I have found a pair! The Professor of Logic came over one day to talk about it, and we had a long and exciting argument, the result of which was "$x - x$"—a magnitude which you will be able to evaluate for yourself.

C. L. Dodgson.

As an example of the good advice Mr. Dodgson used to give his young friends, the following letter to Miss Isabel Standen will serve excellently:—

Eastbourne, *Aug.* 4, 1885.

I can quite understand, and much sympathise with, what you say of your feeling lonely, and not what you can honestly call "happy." Now I am going to give you a bit of philosophy about that—my own experience is, that *every* new form of life we try is, just at first, irksome rather than pleasant. My first day or two at the sea is a little depressing; I miss the Christ Church interests, and haven't taken up the threads of interest here; and, just in the same way, my first day or two, when I get back to Christ Church, I miss the seaside pleasures, and feel with unusual clearness the bothers of business-routine. In all such cases, the true philosophy, I believe, is "*wait* a bit." Our mental nerves seem to be so adjusted that we feel *first* and most keenly, the *dis*—comforts of any new form of life; but, after a bit, we get used to them, and cease to notice them; and *then* we have time to realise the enjoyable features, which at first we were too much worried to be conscious of.

Suppose you hurt your arm, and had to wear it in a sling for a month. For the first two or three days the discomfort of the bandage, the pressure of the sling on the neck and shoulder, the being unable to use the arm, would be a constant worry. You would feel as if all comfort in life were gone; after a couple of days you would be used to the new sensations, after a week you perhaps wouldn't notice them at all; and life would seem just as comfortable as ever.

So my advice is, don't think about loneliness, or happiness, or unhappiness, for a week or two. Then "take stock" again, and compare your feelings with what they were two weeks previously. If they have changed, even a little, for the better you are on the right track; if not, we may begin to suspect the life does not suit you. But what I want *specially* to urge is that there's no use in comparing one's feelings between one day and the next; you must allow a reasonable interval, for the direction of change to show itself.

Sit on the beach, and watch the waves for a few seconds; you say "the tide is coming in "; watch half a dozen successive waves, and you may say "the last is the lowest; it is going out." Wait a quarter of an hour, and compare its *average* place with what it was at first, and you will say "No, it is coming in after all." ...

With love, I am always affectionately yours,

C. L. Dodgson.

The next event to chronicle in Lewis Carroll's Life is the publication, by Messrs. Macmillan, of "A Tangled Tale," a series of mathematical problems which had originally appeared in the *Monthly Packet*. In addition to the problems themselves, the author added their correct solutions, with criticisms on the solutions, correct or otherwise, which the readers of the *Monthly Packet* had sent in to him. With some people this is the most popular of all his books; it is certainly the most successful attempt he ever made to combine mathematics and humour. The book was illustrated by Mr. A.B. Frost, who entered most thoroughly into the spirit of the thing. One of his pictures, "Balbus was assisting his mother-in-law to convince the dragon," is irresistibly comic. A short quotation will better enable the reader to understand the point of the joke:—

Balbus was waiting for them at the hotel; the journey down had tried him, he said; so his two pupils had been the round of the place, in search of lodgings, without the old tutor who had been their inseparable companion from their childhood. They had named him after the hero of their Latin exercise-book, which overflowed with anecdotes about that versatile genius—anecdotes whose vagueness in detail was more than compensated by their sensational brilliance. "Balbus has overcome all his enemies" had been marked by their tutor, in the margin of the book, "Successful Bravery." In this way he had tried to extract a moral from every anecdote about Balbus—sometimes one of warning, as in "Balbus had borrowed a healthy dragon," against which he had written, "Rashness in Speculation "—sometimes of encouragement, as in the words, "Influence of Sympathy in United Action," which stood opposite to the anecdote "Balbus was assisting his mother-in-law to convince the dragon"—and sometimes it dwindled down to a single word, such as "Prudence," which was all he could extract from the touching record that "Balbus, having scorched the tail of the dragon, went away." His pupils liked the short morals best, as it left them more room for marginal illustrations, and in this instance they required all the space they could get to exhibit the rapidity of the hero's departure.

Balbus and his pupils go in search of lodgings, which are only to be found in a certain square; at No. 52, one of the pupils supplements the usual questions by asking the landlady if the cat scratches:—

The landlady looked round suspiciously, as if to make sure the cat was not listening. "I will not deceive you, gentlemen," she said. "It *do* scratch, but not without you pulls its whiskers! It'll never do it," she repeated slowly, with a visible effort to recall the exact words of some written agreement between herself and the cat, "without you pulls its whiskers!"

"Much may be excused in a cat so treated," said Balbus as they left the house and crossed to No. 70, leaving the landlady curtesying on the doorstep, and still murmuring to herself her parting words, as if they were a form of blessing—"Not without you pulls its whiskers!"

They secure one room at each of the following numbers—the square contains 20 doors on each side—Nine, Twenty-five, Fifty-two, and Seventy-three. They require three bedrooms and one day-room, and decide to take as day—room the one that gives them the least walking to do to get to it. The problem, of course, is to discover which room they adopted as the day-room. There are ten such "knots" in the book, and few, if any of them, can be untied without a good deal of thought.

Owing, probably, to the strain of incessant work, Mr. Dodgson about this period began to be subject to a very peculiar, yet not very uncommon, optical delusion, which takes the form of seeing moving fortifications. Considering the fact that he spent a good twelve hours out of every twenty-four in reading and writing, and that he was now well over fifty years old, it was not surprising that nature should begin to rebel at last, and warn him of the necessity of occasional rest.

Some verses on "Wonderland" by "One who loves Alice," appeared in the Christmas number of *Sylvia's Home Journal*, 1885. They were written by Miss M.E. Manners, and, as Lewis Carroll himself admired them, they will, I think, be read with interest:—

WONDERLAND.

How sweet those happy days gone by,
Those days of sunny weather,
When Alice fair, with golden hair,
And we—were young together;—
When first with eager gaze we scann'd
The page which told of Wonderland.

On hearthrug in the winter-time
We lay and read it over;
We read it in the summer's prime,
Amidst the hay and clover.
The trees, by evening breezes fann'd,
Murmured sweet tales of Wonderland.

We climbed the mantelpiece, and broke
The jars of Dresden china;
In Jabberwocky tongue we spoke,
We called the kitten "Dinah!"
And, oh! how earnestly we planned
To go ourselves to Wonderland.

The path was fringed with flowers rare,
With rainbow colours tinted;
The way was "up a winding stair,"
Our elders wisely hinted.
We did not wish to understand
Bed was the road to Wonderland.

We thought we'd wait till we should grow
Stronger as well as bolder,
But now, alas! full well we know
We're only growing older.
The key held by a childish hand,
Fits best the door of Wonderland.

Yet still the Hatter drinks his tea,

The Duchess finds a moral,
And Tweedledum and Tweedledee
Forget in fright their quarrel.
The Walrus still weeps on the sand,
That strews the shores of Wonderland.

And other children feel the spell
Which once we felt before them,
And while the well-known tale we tell,
We watch it stealing o'er them:
Before their dazzled eyes expand
The glorious realms of Wonderland.

Yes, "time is fleet," and we have gained
Years more than twice eleven;
Alice, dear child, hast thou remained
"Exactually" seven?
With "proper aid," "two" could command
Time to go back in Wonderland.

Or have the years (untouched by charms),
With joy and sorrow laden,
Rolled by, and brought unto thy arms
A dainty little maiden?
Another Alice, who shall stand
By thee to hear of Wonderland.

Carroll! accept the heartfelt thanks
Of children of all ages,
Of those who long have left their ranks,
Yet still must love the pages
Written by him whose magic wand
Called up the scenes of Wonderland.

Long mayst thou live, the sound to hear
Which most thy heart rejoices,
Of children's laughter ringing clear,
And children's merry voices,
Until for thee an angel-hand
Draws back the veil of Wonderland.

One Who Loves "Alice."

Three letters, written at the beginning of 1886 to Miss Edith Rix, to whom he had dedicated "A Tangled Tale," are interesting as showing the deeper side of his character:—

Guildford, *Jan.* 15, 1886.

My dear Edith,—I have been meaning for some time to write to you about agnosticism, and other matters in your letter which I have left unnoticed. And yet I do not know, much as what you say interests me, and much as I should like to be of use to any wandering seeker after truth, that I am at all likely to say anything that will be new to you and of any practical use.

The Moral Science student you describe must be a beautiful character, and if, as you say, she lives a noble life, then, even though she does not, as yet, see any God, for whose sake she can do things, I don't think you need be unhappy about her. "When thou wast under the fig tree, I saw thee," is often supposed to mean that Nathanael had been *praying*, praying no doubt ignorantly and imperfectly, but yet using the light he had: and it seems to have been accepted as faith in the Messiah. More and more it seems to me (I hope you won't be *very* much shocked at me as an ultra "Broad" Churchman) that what a person *is* is of more importance in God's sight than merely what propositions he affirms or denies. *You*, at any rate, can do more good among those new friends of yours by showing them what a Christian *is*, than by telling them what a Christian *believes*....

I have a deep dread of argument on religious topics: it has many risks, and little chance of doing good. You and I will never *argue*, I hope, on any controverted religious question: though I do hope we may see the day when we may freely *speak* of such things, even where we happen to hold different views. But even then I should have no inclination, if we did differ, to conclude that my view was the right one, and to try to convert you to it....

Now I come to your letter dated Dec. 22nd, and must scold you for saying that my solution of the problem was "quite different *to* all common ways of doing it": if *you* think that's good English, well and good; but *I* must beg to differ to you, and to hope you will *never* write me a sentence similar from this again. However, "worse remains behind"; and if you deliberately intend in future, when writing to me about one of England's greatest poets, to call him "Shelly," then all I can say is, that you and I will have to quarrel! Be warned in time.

C. L. Dodgson.

Ch. Ch., *Jan.* 26, 1886.

My Dear Edith,—I am interested by what you say of Miss—. You will know, without my saying it, that if she, or any other friend of yours with any troubles, were to like to write to me, I would *very* gladly try to help: with all my ignorance and weakness, God has, I think, blessed my efforts in that way: but then His strength is made perfect in weakness....

Ch. Ch., *Feb*. 14, 1886.

My Dear Edith,... I think I've already noticed, in a way, most of the rest of that letter—except what you say about learning more things "after we are dead." *I* certainly like to think that may be so. But I have heard the other view strongly urged, a good deal based on "then shall we know even as we are known." But I can't believe that that means we shall have *all* knowledge given us in a moment—nor can I fancy it would make me any happier: it is the *learning* that is the chief joy, here, at any rate....

I find another remark anent "pupils"—a bold speculation that my 1,000 pupils may really "go on" in the future life, till they *have* really outstripped Euclid. And, please, what is *Euclid* to be doing all that time? ...

One of the most dreadful things you have ever told me is your students' theory of going and speaking to any one they are interested in, without any introductions. This, joined with what you say of some of them being interested in "Alice," suggests the horrid idea of their some day walking into this room and beginning a conversation. It is enough to make one shiver, even to think of it!

Never mind if people do say "Good gracious!" when you help old women: it *is* being, in some degree, both "good" *and* "gracious," one may hope. So the remark wasn't so inappropriate.

I fear I agree with your friend in not liking all sermons. Some of them, one has to confess, are rubbish: but then I release my attention from the preacher, and go ahead in any line of thought he may have started: and his after-eloquence acts as a kind of accompaniment—like music while one is reading poetry, which often, to me, adds to the effect.

C. L. Dodgson.

The "Alice" operetta, which Mr. Dodgson had despaired of, was at last to become a reality. Mr. Savile Clarke wrote on August 28th to ask his leave to dramatise the two books, and he gladly assented. He only made one condition, which was very characteristic of him, that there should be "no *suggestion* even of coarseness in libretto or in stage business." The hint was hardly necessary, for Mr. Savile Clarke was not the sort of man to spoil his work, or to allow others to spoil it, by vulgarity. Several alterations were made in the books before they were suitable for a dramatic performance; Mr. Dodgson had to write a song for the ghosts of the oysters, which the Walrus and the Carpenter had devoured. He also completed "Tis the voice of the lobster," so as to make it into a song. It ran as follows:—

Tis the voice of the lobster; I heard him declare
"You have baked me too brown: I must sugar my hair."
As a duck with its eyelids, so he with his nose
Trims his belt and his buttons, and turns out his toes.
When the sands are all dry, he is gay as a lark,
And talks with the utmost contempt of the shark;
But when the tide rises, and sharks are around,
His words have a timid and tremulous sound.

I passed by his garden, and marked, with one eye,
How the owl and the panther were sharing a pie:
The panther took pie-crust, and gravy, and meat,
And the owl had the dish for his share of the treat.
When the plate was divided, the owl, as a boon,
Was kindly permitted to pocket the spoon:
But the panther obtained both the fork and the knife,
So, when *he* lost his temper, the owl lost its life.

The play, for the first few weeks at least, was a great success. Some notes in Mr. Dodgson's Diary which relate to it, show how he appreciated Mr. Savile Clarke's venture:—

Dec. 30th.—To London with M—, and took her to "Alice in Wonderland," Mr. Savile Clarke's play at the Prince of Wales's Theatre. The first act (Wonderland) goes well, specially the Mad Tea Party. Mr. Sydney Harcourt is a capital Hatter, and little Dorothy d'Alcourt (æt. 6 1/2) a delicious Dormouse. Phoebe Carlo is a splendid Alice. Her song and dance with the Cheshire Cat (Master C. Adeson, who played the Pirate King in "Pirates of Penzance") was a gem. As a whole the play seems a success.

Feb. 11, 1887.—Went to the "Alice" play, where we sat next a chatty old gentleman, who told me that the author of "Alice" had sent Phoebe Carlo a book, and that she had written to him to say that she would do her very best, and further, that he is "an Oxford man"—all which I hope I received with a sufficient expression of pleased interest.

Shortly before the production of the play, a Miss Whitehead had drawn a very clever medley-picture, in which nearly all Tenniel's wonderful creations—the Dormouse, the White Knight, the Mad Hatter, &c.— appeared. This design was most useful as a "poster" to advertise the play. After the London run was over, the company made a tour of the provinces, where it met with a fair amount of success.

At the end of 1886, "Alice's Adventures Underground," a facsimile of the original MS. book, afterwards developed into "Alice's Adventures in Wonderland," with thirty-seven illustrations by the author, was published by Macmillan & Co. A postscript to the Preface stated that any profits that might arise from the book would be given to Children's Hospitals and Convalescent Homes for Sick Children. Shortly before the book came out, Lewis Carroll wrote to Mrs. Hargreaves, giving a description of the difficulties that he had encountered in producing it:—

Christ Church, Oxford,

November 11, 1886.

My Dear Mrs. Hargreaves,—Many thanks for your permission to insert "Hospitals" in the Preface to your book. I have had almost as many adventures in getting that unfortunate facsimile finished, *Above* ground, as your namesake had *Under* it!

First, the zincographer in London, recommended to me for photographing the book, page by page, and preparing the zinc-blocks, declined to undertake it unless I would entrust the book to *him*, which I entirely refused to do. I felt that it was only due to you, in return for your great kindness in lending so unique a book, to be scrupulous in not letting it be even *touched* by the workmen's hands. In vain I offered to come and reside in London with the book, and to attend daily in the studio, to place it in position to be photographed, and turn over the pages as required. He said that could not be done because "other authors' works were being photographed there, which must on no account be seen by the public." I undertook not to look at *anything* but my own book; but it was no use: we could not come to terms.

Then — recommended me a certain Mr. X—, an excellent photographer, but in so small a way of business that I should have to *prepay* him, bit by bit, for the zinc-blocks: and *he* was willing to come to Oxford, and do it here. So it was all done in my studio, I remaining in waiting all the time, to turn over the pages.

But I daresay I have told you so much of the story already.

Mr. X— did a first-rate set of negatives, and took them away with him to get the zinc-blocks made. These he delivered pretty regularly at first, and there seemed to be every prospect of getting the book out by Christmas, 1885.

On October 18, 1885, I sent your book to Mrs. Liddell, who had told me your sisters were going to visit you and would take it with them. I trust it reached you safely?

Soon after this—I having prepaid for the whole of the zinc-blocks—the supply suddenly ceased, while twenty-two pages were still due, and Mr. X— disappeared!

My belief is that he was in hiding from his creditors. We sought him in vain. So things went on for months. At one time I thought of employing a detective to find him, but was assured that "all detectives are scoundrels." The alternative seemed to be to ask you to lend the book again, and get the missing pages re-photographed. But I was most unwilling to rob you of it again, and also afraid of the risk of loss of the book, if sent by post—for even "registered post" does not seem *absolutely* safe.

In April he called at Macmillan's and left *eight* blocks, and again vanished into obscurity.

This left us with fourteen pages (dotted up and down the book) still missing. I waited awhile longer, and then put the thing into the hands of a solicitor, who soon found the man, but could get nothing but promises from him. "You will never get the blocks," said the solicitor, "unless you frighten him by a summons before a magistrate." To this at last I unwillingly consented: the summons had to be taken out at — (that is where this aggravating man is living), and this entailed two journeys from Eastbourne—one to get the summons (my *personal* presence being necessary), and the other to attend in court with the solicitor on the day fixed for hearing the case. The defendant didn't appear; so the magistrate said he would take the case in his absence. Then I had the new and exciting experience of being put into the witness-box, and sworn, and cross-examined by a rather savage magistrate's clerk, who seemed to think that, if he only bullied me enough, he would soon catch me out in a falsehood! I had to give the magistrate a little lecture on photo-zincography, and the poor man declared the case was so complicated he must adjourn it for another week. But this time, in order to secure the presence of our slippery defendant, he issued a warrant for his apprehension, and the constable had orders to take him into custody and lodge him in prison, the night before the day when the case was to come on. The news of *this* effectually frightened him, and he delivered up the fourteen negatives (he hadn't done the blocks) before the fatal day arrived. I was rejoiced to get them, even though it entailed the paying a second time for getting the fourteen blocks done, and withdrew the action.

The fourteen blocks were quickly done and put into the printer's hands; and all is going on smoothly at last: and I quite hope to have the book completed, and to be able to send you a very special copy (bound in white vellum, unless you would prefer some other style of binding) by the end of the month.

Believe me always,

Sincerely yours,

C. L. Dodgson.

"The Game of Logic" was Lewis Carroll's next book; it appeared about the end of February, 1887. As a method of teaching the first principles of Logic to children it has proved most useful; the subject, usually considered very difficult to a beginner, is made extremely easy by simplification of method, and both interesting and amusing by the quaint syllogisms that the author devised, such as—

No bald person needs a hair-brush;
No lizards have hair;
Therefore[1] No lizard needs a hair brush.

Caterpillars are not eloquent;
Jones is eloquent;
Jones is not a caterpillar.

Meanwhile, with much interchange of correspondence between author and artist, the pictures for the new fairy tale, "Sylvie and Bruno," were being gradually evolved. Each of them was subjected by Lewis Carroll to the most minute criticism—hyper-criticism, perhaps, occasionally. A few instances of the sort of criticisms he used to make upon Mr. Furniss's work may be interesting; I have extracted them from a letter dated September 1, 1887. It will be seen that when he really admired a sketch he did not stint his praise:—

(1) "Sylvie helping beetle" [p. 193]. A quite charming composition.

(3) "The Doctor" and "Eric." (Mr. Furniss's idea of their appearance). No! The Doctor won't do *at all!* He is a smug London man, a great "ladies' man," who would hardly talk anything but medical "shop." He is forty at least, and can have had no love-affair for the last fifteen years. I want him to be about twenty-five, powerful in frame, poetical in face: capable of intelligent interest in any subject, and of being a passionate lover. How would you draw King Arthur when he first met Guinevere? Try *that* type.

Eric's attitude is capital: but his face is a little too near to the ordinary "masher." Please avoid *that* inane creature; and please don't cut his hair short. That fashion will be "out" directly.

(4) "Lady Muriel" (head); ditto (full length); "Earl."

I don't like *either* face of Lady Muriel. I don't think I could talk to her; and I'm quite sure I couldn't fall in love with her. Her dress ("evening," of course) is very pretty, I think.

I don't like the Earl's face either. He is proud of his title, very formal, and one who would keep one "at arm's length" always. And he is too prodigiously tall. I want a gentle, genial old man; with whom one would feel at one's ease in a moment.

(8) "Uggug becoming Porcupine" ("Sylvie and Bruno, Concluded," page 388), is

exactly my conception of it. I expect this will be one of the most effective pictures in the book. The faces of the people should express intense *terror*.

(9) "The Professor" is altogether *delightful*. When you get the text, you will see that you have hit the very centre of the bull's-eye.

[A sketch of "Bruno"]. No, no! Please don't give us the (to my mind) very ugly, quite modern costume, which shows with such cruel distinctness a podgy, pot-bellied (excuse the vulgarism) boy, who couldn't run a mile to save his life. I want Bruno to be *strong*, but at the same time light and active—with the figure of one of the little acrobats one sees at the circus—not "Master Tommy," who habitually gorges himself with pudding. Also that dress I dislike very much. Please give him a short tunic, and *real* knickerbockers—not the tight knee-breeches they are rapidly shrinking to.

Very truly yours,

C. L. Dodgson.

By Mr. Furniss's kind permission I am enabled to give an example of the other side of the correspondence, one of his letters to Mr. Dodgson, all the more interesting for the charming little sketch which it contains.

With respect to the spider, Mr. Dodgson had written: "Some writer says that the full face of a spider, as seen under a magnifying-glass, is very striking."

CHAPTER VII

(1888—1891)

A systematic life—"Memoria Technica"—Mr. Dodgson's shyness—"A Lesson in Latin"—The "Wonderland" Stamp-Case—"Wise Words about Letter-Writing"—Princess Alice—"Sylvie and Bruno"—"The night cometh"—"The Nursery 'Alice'"—Coventry Patmore—Telepathy—Resignation of Dr. Liddell—A letter about Logic.

An old bachelor is generally very precise and exact in his habits. He has no one but himself to look after, nothing to distract his attention from his own affairs; and Mr. Dodgson was the most precise and exact of old bachelors. He made a précis of every letter he wrote or received from the 1st of January, 1861, to the 8th of the same month, 1898. These précis were all numbered and entered in reference-books, and by an ingenious system of cross-numbering he was able to trace a whole correspondence, which might extend through several volumes. The last number entered in his book is 98,721.

He had scores of green cardboard boxes, all neatly labelled, in which he kept his various papers. These boxes formed quite a feature of his study at Oxford, a large number of them being arranged upon a revolving bookstand. The lists, of various sorts, which he kept were innumerable; one of them, that of unanswered correspondents, generally held seventy or eighty names at a time, exclusive of autograph-hunters, whom he did not answer on principle. He seemed to delight in being arithmetically accurate about every detail of life.

He always rose at the same early hour, and, if he was in residence at Christ Church, attended College Service. He spent the day according to a prescribed routine, which usually included a long walk into the country, very often alone, but sometimes with another Don, or perhaps, if the walk was not to be as long as usual, with some little girl-friend at his side. When he had a companion with him, he would talk the whole time, telling delightful stories, or explaining some new logical problem; if he was alone, he used to think out his books, as probably many another author has done and will do, in the course of a lonely walk. The only irregularity noticeable in his mode of life was the hour of retiring, which varied from 11 p.m. to four o'clock in the morning, according to the amount of work which he felt himself in the mood for.

He had a wonderfully good memory, except for faces and dates. The former were always a stumbling-block to him, and people used to say (most unjustly) that he was intentionally short-sighted. One night he went up to London to dine with a friend, whom he had only recently met. The next morning a gentleman greeted him as he was walking. "I beg your pardon," said Mr. Dodgson, "but you have the advantage of me. I have no remembrance of having ever seen you before this moment." "That is very strange," the other replied, "for I was your host last night!" Such little incidents as this happened more than once. To help himself to remember dates, he devised a system of mnemonics, which he circulated among his friends. As it has never been published, and as some of my readers may find it useful, I reproduce it here.

My "Memoria Technica" is a modification of Gray's; but, whereas he used both consonants and vowels to represent digits, and had to content himself with a syllable of gibberish to represent the date or whatever other number was required, I use only consonants, and fill in with vowels *ad libitum,* and thus can always manage to make a real word of whatever has to be represented.

The principles on which the necessary 20 consonants have been chosen are as follows:—

1. "b" and "c," the first two consonants in the alphabet.

2. "d" from "duo," "w" from "two."

3. "t" from "tres," the other may wait awhile.

4. "f" from "four," "q" from "quattuor."

5. "l" and "v," because "l" and "v" are the Roman symbols for "fifty" and "five."

6. "s" and "x" from "six."

7. "p" and "m" from "septem."

8. "h" from "huit," and "k" from the Greek "okto."

9. "n" from "nine"; and "g" because it is so like a "9."

0. "z" and "r" from "zero."

There is now one consonant still waiting for its digit, viz., "j," and one digit waiting for its consonant, viz., "3," the conclusion is obvious.

The result may be tabulated thus:—

1	2	3	4	5	6	7	8	9	0
b	d	t	f	l	s	p	h	n	z
c	w	j	q	v	x	m	k	g	r

When a word has been found, whose last consonants represent the number required, the best plan is to put it as the last word of a rhymed couplet, so that, whatever other words in it are forgotten, the rhyme will secure the only really important word.

Now suppose you wish to remember the date of the discovery of America, which is 1492; the "1" may be left out as obvious; all we need is "492."

Write it thus:—

4	9	2
f	n	d
q	g	w

and try to find a word that contains "f" or "q," "n" or "g," "d" or "w." A word soon suggests itself—"found."

The poetic faculty must now be brought into play, and the following couplet will soon be evolved:—

"Columbus sailed the world around,
Until America was F O U N D."

If possible, invent the couplets for yourself; you will remember them better than any others.

June, 1888.

The inventor found this "Memoria Technica" very useful in helping him to remember the dates of the different Colleges. He often, of course, had to show his friends the sights of Oxford, and the easy way in which, asked or unasked, he could embellish his descriptions with dates used to surprise those who did not know how the thing was done. The couplet for St. John's College ran as follows:—

"They must have a bevel
To keep them so LEVEL."

The allusion is to the beautiful lawns, for which St. John's is famous.

In his power of remembering anecdotes, and bringing them out just at the right moment, Mr. Dodgson was unsurpassed. A guest brought into Christ Church Common Room was usually handed over to him to be amused. He was not a good man to tell a story to—he had always heard it before; but as a *raconteur* I never met his equal. And the best of it was that his stories never grew—except in number.

One would have expected that a mind so clear and logical and definite would have fought shy of the feminine intellect, which is generally supposed to be deficient in those qualities; and so it is somewhat surprising to find that by far the greater number of his friends were ladies. He was quite prepared to correct them, however, when they were guilty of what seemed to him unreasoning conduct, as is shown by the following extract from a letter of his to a young lady who had asked him to try and find a place for a governess, without giving the latter's address:—

Some of my friends are business-men, and it is pleasant to see how methodical and careful they are in transacting any business-matter. If, for instance, one of them were to write to me, asking me to look out for a place for a French governess in whom he was interested, I should be sure to admire the care with which he would give me *her name in full*—(in extra-legible writing if it were an unusual name)—as well as her address. Some of my friends are not men of business.

So many such requests were addressed to him that at one time he had a circular letter printed, with a list of people requiring various appointments or assistants, which he sent round to his friends.

In one respect Lewis Carroll resembled the stoic philosophers, for no outward circumstance could upset the tranquillity of his mind. He lived, in fact, the life which Marcus Aurelius commends so highly, the life of calm contentment, based on the assurance that so long as we are faithful to ourselves, no seeming evils can really harm us. But in him there was one exception to this rule. During an argument he was often excited. The war of words, the keen and subtle conflict between trained minds—in this his soul took delight, in this he sought and found the joy of battle and of victory. Yet he would not allow his serenity to be ruffled by any foe whom he considered unworthy of his steel; he refused to argue with people whom he knew to be hopelessly illogical—definitely refused, though with such tact that no wound was given, even to the most sensitive.

He was modest in the true sense of the term, neither overestimating nor underrating his own mental powers, and preferring to follow his own course without regarding outside criticism. "I never read anything about myself or my books," he writes in a letter to a friend; and the reason he used to give was that if the critics praised him he might become conceited, while, if they found fault, he would only feel hurt and angry. On October 25, 1888, he wrote in his Diary: "I see there is a leader in to-day's *Standard* on myself as a writer; but I do not mean to read it. It is not healthy reading, I think."

He hated publicity, and tried to avoid it in every way. "Do not tell any one, if you see me in the theatre," he wrote once to Miss Marion Terry. On another occasion, when he was dining out at Oxford, and some one, who did not know that it was a forbidden subject, turned the conversation on "Alice in Wonderland," he rose suddenly and fled from the house. I could multiply instances of this sort, but it would be unjust to his memory to insist upon the morbid way in which he regarded personal popularity. As compared with self-advertisement, it is certainly the lesser evil; but that it *is* an evil, and a very painful one to its possessor, Mr. Dodgson fully saw. Of course it had its humorous side, as, for instance, when he was brought into contact with lion-hunters, autograph-collectors, *et hoc genus omne*. He was very suspicious of unknown correspondents who addressed questions to him; in later years he either did not answer them at all, or used a typewriter. Before he bought his typewriter, he would get some friend to write for him, and even to sign "Lewis Carroll" at the end of the letter. It used to give him great amusement to picture the astonishment of the recipients of these letters, if by any chance they ever came to compare his "autographs."

On one occasion the secretary of a "Young Ladies' Academy" in the United States asked him to present some of his works to the School Library. The envelope was addressed to "Lewis Carroll, Christ Church," an incongruity which always annoyed him intensely. He replied to the Secretary, "As Mr. Dodgson's books are all on Mathematical subjects, he fears that they would not be very acceptable in a school library."

Some fourteen or fifteen years ago, the Fourth-class of the Girl's Latin School at Boston, U.S., started a magazine, and asked him if they might call it *The Jabberwock*. He wrote in reply:—

Mr. Lewis Carroll has much pleasure in giving to the editors of the proposed magazine permission to use the title they wish for. He finds that the Anglo-Saxon word "wocer" or "wocor" signifies "offspring" or "fruit." Taking "jabber" in its ordinary acceptation of "excited and voluble discussion," this would give the meaning of "the result of much excited discussion." Whether this phrase will have any application to the projected periodical, it will be for the future historian of American literature to determine. Mr. Carroll wishes all success to the forthcoming magazine.

From that time forward he took a great interest in the magazine, and thought very well of it. It used, I believe, to be regularly supplied to him. Only once did he express disapproval of anything it contained, and that was in 1888, when he felt it necessary to administer a rebuke for what he thought to be an irreverent joke. The sequel is given in the following extract from *The Jabberwock* for June, 1888:—

A FRIEND WORTH HAVING.

The Jabberwock has many friends, and perhaps a few (very few, let us hope) enemies. But, of the former, the friend who has helped us most on the road to success is Mr. Lewis Carroll, the author of "Alice in Wonderland," &c. Our readers will remember his kind letter granting us permission to use the name "Jabberwock," and also giving the meaning of that word. Since then we have received another letter from him, in which he expresses both surprise and regret at an anecdote which we published in an early number of our little paper. We would assure Mr. Carroll, as well as our other friends, that we had no intention of making light of a serious matter, but merely quoted the anecdote to show what sort of a book Washington's diary was.

But now a third letter from our kind friend has come, enclosing, to our delight, a poem, "A Lesson in Latin," the pleasantest Latin lesson we have had this year.

The first two letters from Mr. Carroll were in a beautiful literary hand, whereas the third is written with a typewriter. It is to this fact that he refers in his letter, which is as follows:—

"29, Bedford Street,
Covent Garden, LONDON,

May 16, 1888.

Dear Young Friends,—After the Black Draught of serious remonstrance which I ventured to send to you the other day, surely a Lump of Sugar will not be unacceptable? The enclosed I wrote this afternoon on purpose for you.

I hope you will grant it admission to the columns of *The Jabberwock*, and not scorn it as a mere play upon words.

This mode of writing, is, of course, an American invention. We never invent new machinery here; we do but use, to the best of our ability, the machines you send us. For the one I am now using, I beg you to accept my best thanks, and to believe me

Your sincere friend,

Lewis Carroll."

Surely we can patiently swallow many Black Draughts, if we are to be rewarded with   so   sweet   a   Lump   of   Sugar!

The enclosed poem, which has since been republished in "Three Sunsets," runs as follows:

A LESSON IN LATIN.

Our Latin books, in motley row,
Invite us to the task—
Gay Horace, stately Cicero;
Yet there's one verb, when once we know,
No higher skill we ask:
This ranks all other lore above—
We've learned "amare" means "to love"!

So hour by hour, from flower to flower,
We sip the sweets of life:
Till ah! too soon the clouds arise,
And knitted brows and angry eyes
Proclaim the dawn of strife.
With half a smile and half a sigh,
"Amare! Bitter One!" we cry.

Last night we owned, with looks forlorn,
"Too well the scholar knows
There is no rose without a thorn "—
But peace is made! we sing, this morn,
"No thorn without a rose!"
Our Latin lesson is complete:
We've learned that Love is "Bitter-sweet"

Lewis Carroll.

In October Mr. Dodgson invented a very ingenious little stamp-case, decorated with two "Pictorial Surprises," representing the "Cheshire Cat" vanishing till nothing but the grin was left, and the baby turning into a pig in "Alice's" arms. The invention was entered at Stationers' Hall, and published by Messrs. Emberlin and Son, of Oxford. As an appropriate accompaniment, he wrote "Eight or Nine Wise Words on Letter-Writing," a little booklet which is still sold along with the case. The "Wise Words," as the following extracts show, have the true "Carrollian" ring about them:—

Some American writer has said "the snakes in this district may be divided into one species—the venomous." The same principle applies here. Postage-stamp-cases may be divided into one species—the "Wonderland."

Since I have possessed a "Wonderland-Stamp-Case," Life has been bright and peaceful, and I have used no other. I believe the Queen's Laundress uses no other.

My fifth Rule is, if your friend makes a severe remark, either leave it unnoticed or make your reply distinctly less severe: and, if he makes a friendly remark, tending towards "making up" the little difference that has arisen between you, let your reply be distinctly *more* friendly. If, in picking a quarrel, each party declined to go more than *three-eighths* of the way, and if, in making friends, each was ready to go *five-eighths* of the way—why, there would be more reconciliations than quarrels! Which is like the Irishman's remonstrance to his gad-about daughter: "Shure, you're *always* goin' out! You go out *three* times for wanst that you come in!"

My sixth Rule is, *don't try to have the last word!* How many a controversy would be nipped in the bud, if each was anxious to let the *other* have the last word! Never mind how telling a rejoinder you leave unuttered: never mind your friend's supposing that you are silent from lack of anything to say: let the thing drop, as soon as it is possible without discourtesy: remember "Speech is silvern, but silence is golden"! (N.B. If you are a gentleman, and your friend a lady, this Rule is superfluous: *you won't get the last word!*)

Remember the old proverb, "Cross-writing makes cross-reading." "The *old* proverb?" you say inquiringly. "*How* old?" Well, not so *very* ancient, I must confess. In fact, I invented it while writing this paragraph. Still, you know, "old" is a *comparative* term. I think you would be *quite* justified in addressing a chicken, just out of the shell, as "old boy!" *when compared* with another chicken that was only half-out!

The pamphlet ends with an explanation of Lewis Carroll's method of using a correspondence-book, illustrated by a few imaginary pages from such a compilation, which are very humorous.

At the end of the year the "Alice" operetta was again produced at the Globe Theatre, with Miss Isa Bowman as the heroine. "Isa makes a delightful Alice," Mr. Dodgson writes, "and Emsie [a younger sister] is wonderfully good as Dormouse and as Second Ghost [of an oyster!], when she sings a verse, and dances the Sailor's Hornpipe."

The first of an incomplete series, "Curiosa Mathematica," was published for Mr. Dodgson by Messrs. Macmillan during the year. It was entitled "A New Theory of Parallels," and any one taking it up for the first time might be tempted to ask, Is the author serious, or is he simply giving us some *jeu d'esprit?* A closer inspection, however, soon settles the question, and the reader, if mathematics be his hobby, is carried irresistibly along till he reaches the last page.

The object which Mr. Dodgson set himself to accomplish was to prove Euclid I. 32 without assuming the celebrated 12th Axiom, a feat which calls up visions of the "Circle-Squarers."

The work is divided into two parts: Book I. contains certain Propositions which require no disputable Axiom for their proof, and when once the few Definitions of "amount," &c., have become familiar it is easy reading. In Book II. the author introduces a new Axiom, or rather "Quasi-Axiom"—for it's *self-evident* character is open to dispute. This Axiom is as follows:—

In any Circle the inscribed equilateral Tetragon (Hexagon in editions 1st and 2nd) is greater than any one of the Segments which lie outside it.

Assuming the truth of this Axiom, Mr. Dodgson proves a series of Propositions, which lead up to and enable him to accomplish the feat referred to above.

At the end of Book II. he places a proof (so far as finite magnitudes are concerned) of Euclid's Axiom, preceded by and dependent on the Axiom that "If two homogeneous magnitudes be both of them finite, the lesser may be so multiplied by a finite number as to exceed the greater." This Axiom, he says, he believes to be assumed by every writer who has attempted to prove Euclid's 12th Axiom. The proof itself is borrowed, with slight alterations, from Cuthbertson's "Euclidean Geometry."

In Appendix I. there is an alternative Axiom which may be substituted for that which introduces Book II., and which will probably commend itself to many minds as being more truly axiomatic. To substitute this, however, involves some additions and alterations, which the author appends.

Appendix II. is headed by the somewhat startling question, "Is Euclid's Axiom true?" and though true for finite magnitudes—the sense in which, no doubt, Euclid meant it to be taken—it is shown to be not universally true. In Appendix III. he propounds the question, "How should Parallels be defined?"

Appendix IV., which deals with the theory of Parallels as it stands to-day, concludes with the following words:—

I am inclined to believe that if ever Euclid I. 32 is proved without a new Axiom, it will be by some new and ampler definition of the *Right Line*—some definition which shall connote that mysterious property, which it must somehow possess, which causes Euclid I. 32 to be true. Try *that* track, my gentle reader! It is not much trodden as yet. And may success attend your search!

In the Introduction, which, as is frequently the case, ought to be read *last* in order to be appreciated properly, he relates his experiences with two of those "misguided visionaries," the circle-squarers. One of them had selected 3.2 as the value for "*pi*," and the other proved, to his own satisfaction at least, that it is correctly represented by 3! The Rev. Watson Hagger, to whose kindness, as I have already stated in my Preface, my readers are indebted for the several accounts of Mr. Dodgson's books on mathematics which appear in this Memoir, had a similar experience with one of these "cranks." This circle-squarer selected 3.125 as the value for "*pi*," and Mr. Hagger, who was fired with Mr. Dodgson's ambition to convince his correspondent of his error, failed as signally as Mr. Dodgson did.

The following letter is interesting as showing that, strict Conservative though he was, he was not in religious matters narrow-minded; he held his own opinions strongly, but he would never condemn those of other people. He saw "good in everything," and there was but little exaggeration, be it said in all reverence, in the phrase which an old friend of his used in speaking of him to me: "Mr. Dodgson was as broad—as broad as *Christ*."

Christ Church, Oxford, *May* 4, 1889.

Dear Miss Manners,—I hope to have a new book out very soon, and had entered your name on the list of friends to whom copies are to go; but, on second thoughts, perhaps you might prefer that I should send it to your little sister (?) (niece) Rachel, whom you mentioned in one of your letters. It is to be called "The Nursery Alice," and is meant for very young children, consisting of coloured enlargements of twenty of the pictures in "Alice," with explanations such as one would give in showing them to a little child.

I was much interested by your letter, telling me you belong to the Society of Friends. Please do not think of *me* as one to whom a "difference of creed" is a bar to friendship. My sense of brother— and sisterhood is at least broad enough to include *Christians* of all denominations; in fact, I have one valued friend (a lady who seems to live to do good kind things) who is a Unitarian.

Shall I put "Rachel Manners" in the book?

Believe me, very sincerely yours,

C. L. Dodgson.

From June 7th to June 10th he stayed at Hatfield.

Once at luncheon [he writes] I had the Duchess (of Albany) as neighbour and once at breakfast, and had several other chats with her, and found her very pleasant indeed. Princess Alice is a sweet little girl. Her little brother (the Duke of Albany) was entirely fascinating, a perfect little prince, and the picture of good-humour. On Sunday afternoon I had a pleasant half-hour with the children [Princess Alice, the Duke of Albany, Honorable Mabel Palmer, Lady Victoria Manners, and Lord Haddon], telling them "Bruno's Picnic" and folding a fishing-boat for them. I got the Duchess's leave to send the little Alice a copy of the "Nursery Alice," and mean to send it with "Alice Underground" for herself.

Towards the end of the year Lewis Carroll had tremendously hard work, completing "Sylvie and Bruno." For several days on end he worked from breakfast until nearly ten in the evening without a rest. At last it was off his hands, and for a month or so he was (comparatively) an idle man. Some notes from his Diary, written during this period, follow:—

Nov. 17th.—Met, for first time, an actual believer in the "craze" that buying and selling are wrong (!) (he is rather 'out of his mind'). The most curious thing was his declaration that he himself *lives* on that theory, and never buys anything, and has no money! I thought of railway travelling, and ventured to ask how he got from London to Oxford? "On a bicycle!" And how he got the bicycle? "It was given him!" So I was floored, and there was no time to think of any other instances. The whole thing was so new to me that, when he declared it to be *un-Christian*, I quite forgot the text, "He that hath no sword, let him sell his garment, and buy one."

Dec. 19th.—Went over to Birmingham to see a performance of "Alice" (Mrs. Freiligrath Kroeker's version) at the High School. I rashly offered to tell "Bruno's Picnic" afterwards to the little children, thinking I should have an audience of 40 or 50, mostly children, instead of which I had to tell it from the stage to an audience of about 280, mostly older girls and grown-up people! However, I got some of the children to come on the stage with me, and the little Alice (Muriel Howard-Smith, æt. 11) stood by me, which made it less awful. The evening began with some of "Julius Caesar" in German. This and "Alice" were really capitally acted, the White Queen being quite the best I have seen (Miss B. Lloyd Owen). I was introduced to Alice and a few more, and was quite sorry to hear afterwards that the other performers wanted to shake hands.

The publication of "Sylvie and Bruno" marks an epoch in its author's life, for it was the publication of all the ideals and sentiments which he held most dear. It was a book with a definite purpose; it would be more true to say with several definite purposes. For this very reason it is not an artistic triumph as the two "Alice" books undoubtedly are; it is on a lower literary level, there is no unity in the story. But from a higher standpoint, that of the Christian and the philanthropist, the book is the best thing he ever wrote. It is a noble effort to uphold the right, or what he thought to be the right, without fear of contempt or unpopularity. The influence which his earlier books had given him he was determined to use in asserting neglected truths.

Of course the story has other features, delightful nonsense not surpassed by anything in "Wonderland," childish prattle with all the charm of reality about it, and pictures which may fairly be said to rival those of Sir John Tenniel. Had these been all, the book would have been a great success. As things are, there are probably hundreds of readers who have been scared by the religious arguments and political discussions which make up a large part of it, and who have never discovered that Sylvie is just as entrancing a personage as Alice when you get to know her.

Perhaps the sentiment of the following poem, sent to Lewis Carroll by an anonymous correspondent, may also explain why some of "Alice's" lovers have given "Sylvie" a less warm welcome:—

TO SYLVIE.

Ah! Sylvie, winsome, wise and good!
Fain would I love thee as I should.
But, to tell the truth, my dear,—
And Sylvie loves the truth to hear,—
Though fair and pure and sweet thou art,
Thine elder sister has my heart!
I gave it her long, long ago
To have and hold; and well I know,
Brave Lady Sylvie, thou wouldst scorn
To accept a heart foresworn.

Lovers thou wilt have enow
Under many a greening bough—
Lovers yet unborn galore,
Like Alice all the wide world o'er;
But, darling, I am now too old
To change. And though I still shall hold
Thee, and that puckling sprite, thy brother,
Dear, I cannot *love* another:
In this heart of mine I own
She must ever reign alone!

March, 1890.

N.P.

I do not know N.P.'s name and address, or I should have asked leave before giving publicity to the above verses. If these words meet his eye, I hope he will accept my most humble apologies for the liberty I have taken.

At the beginning of 1894 a Baptist minister, preaching on the text, "No man liveth to himself," made use of "Sylvie and Bruno" to enforce his argument. After saying that he had been reading that book, he proceeded as follows:

A child was asked to define charity. He said it was "givin' away what yer didn't want yerself." This was some people's idea of self-sacrifice; but it was not Christ's. Then as to serving others in view of reward: Mr. Lewis Carroll put this view of the subject very forcibly in his "Sylvie and Bruno"—an excellent book for youth; indeed, for men and women too. He first criticised Archdeacon Paley's definition of virtue (which was said to be "the doing good to mankind, in obedience to the will of God, and for the sake of everlasting happiness,") and then turned to such hymns as the following:—

Whatever, Lord, we lend to Thee,
Repaid a thousandfold shall be,
Then gladly will we give to Thee,
Giver of all!

Mr. Carroll's comment was brief and to the point. He said: "Talk of Original *Sin*! Can you have a stronger proof of the Original Goodness there must be in this nation than the fact that Religion has been preached to us, as a commercial speculation, for a century, and that we still believe in a God?" ["Sylvie and Bruno," Part i., pp. 276, 277.] Of course it was quite true, as Mr. Carroll pointed out, that our good deeds would be rewarded; but we ought to do them because they were *good*, and not because the reward was great.

In the Preface to "Sylvie and Bruno," Lewis Carroll alluded to certain editions of Shakespeare which seemed to him unsuitable for children; it never seemed to strike him that his words might be read by children, and that thus his object very probably would be defeated, until this fact was pointed out to him in a letter from an unknown correspondent, Mr. J.C. Cropper, of Hampstead. Mr. Dodgson replied as follows:—

Dear Sir,—Accept my best thanks for your thoughtful and valuable suggestion about the Preface to "Sylvie and Bruno." The danger you point out had not occurred to me (I suppose I had not thought of *children* reading the Preface): but it is a very real one, and I am very glad to have had my attention called to it.

Believe me, truly yours,

Lewis Carroll.

Mathematical controversy carried on by correspondence was a favourite recreation of Mr. Dodgson's, and on February 20, 1890, he wrote:—

I've just concluded a correspondence with a Cambridge man, who is writing a Geometry on the "Direction" theory (Wilson's plan), and thinks he has avoided Wilson's (what *I* think) fallacies. He *hasn't*, but I can't convince him! My view of life is, that it's next to impossible to convince *anybody* of *anything*.

The following letter is very characteristic. "Whatsoever thy hand findeth to do, do it with all thy might," was Mr. Dodgson's rule of life, and, as the end drew near, he only worked the harder:—

Christ Church, Oxford, *April* 10, 1890.

My dear Atkinson,—Many and sincere thanks for your most hospitable invitation, and for the very interesting photo of the family group. The former I fear I must ask you to let me defer *sine die*, and regard it as a pleasant dream, not *quite* hopeless of being some day realised. I keep a list of such pleasant possibilities, and yours is now one of ten similar kind offers of hospitality. But as life shortens in, and the evening shadows loom in sight, one gets to *grudge any* time given to mere pleasure, which might entail the leaving work half finished that one is longing to do before the end comes.

There are several books I *greatly* desire to get finished for children. I am glad to find my working powers are as good as they ever were. Even with the mathematical book (a third edition) which I am now getting through the press, I think nothing of working six hours at a stretch.

There is one text that often occurs to me, "The night cometh, when no man can work." Kindest regards to Mrs. Atkinson, and love to Gertrude.

Always sincerely yours,

C. L. Dodgson.

For the benefit of children aged "from nought to five," as he himself phrased it, Lewis Carroll prepared a nursery edition of "Alice." He shortened the text considerably, and altered it so much that only the plot of the story remained unchanged. It was illustrated by the old pictures, coloured by Tenniel, and the cover was adorned by a picture designed by Miss E. Gertrude Thomson. As usual, the Dedication takes the form of an anagram, the solution of which is the name of one of his later child-friends. "*The Nursery 'Alice,'*" was published by Macmillan and Co., in March, 1890.

On August 18th the following letter on the "Eight Hours Movement" appeared in *The Standard:*—

Sir,—Supposing it were the custom, in a certain town, to sell eggs in paper bags at so much per bag, and that a fierce dispute had arisen between the egg vendors and the public as to how many eggs each bag should be understood to contain, the vendors wishing to be allowed to make up smaller bags; and supposing the public were to say, "In future we will pay you so much per egg, and you can make up bags as you please," would any ground remain for further dispute?

Supposing that employers of labour, when threatened with a "strike" in case they should decline to reduce the number of hours in a working day, were to reply, "In future we will pay you so much per hour, and you can make up days as you please," it does appear to me—being, as I confess, an ignorant outsider—that the dispute would die out for want of a *raison d'être*, and that these disastrous strikes, inflicting such heavy loss on employers and employed alike, would become things of the past.

I am, Sir, your obedient servant,

Lewis Carroll.

The remainder of the year was uneventful; a few notes from his Diary must represent it here:—

Oct. 4th.—Called on Mr. Coventry Patmore (at Hastings), and was very kindly received by him, and stayed for afternoon tea and dinner. He showed me some interesting pictures, including a charming little drawing, by Holman Hunt, of one of his daughters when three years old. He gave me an interesting account of his going, by Tennyson's request, to his lodging to look for the MS. of "In Memoriam," which he had left behind, and only finding it by insisting on going upstairs, in spite of the landlady's opposition, to search for it. Also he told me the story (I think I have heard it before) of what Wordsworth told his friends as the "one joke" of his life, in answer to a passing carter who asked if he had seen his wife. "My good friend, I didn't even know you had a wife!" He seems a very hale and vigorous old man for nearly seventy, which I think he gave as his age in writing to me.

Oct. 31st.—This morning, thinking over the problem of finding two squares whose sum is a square, I chanced on a theorem (which seems *true*, though I cannot prove it), that if $x^2 + y^2$ be even, its half is the sum of two squares. A kindred theorem, that $2(x^2 + y^2)$ is always the sum of two squares, also seems true and unprovable.

Nov. 5th.—I have now proved the above two theorems. Another pretty deduction from the theory of square numbers is, that any number whose square is the sum of two squares, is itself the sum of two squares.

I have already mentioned Mr. Dodgson's habit of thinking out problems at night. Often new ideas would occur to him during hours of sleeplessness, and he had long wanted to hear of or invent some easy method of taking notes in the dark. At first he tried writing within oblongs cut out of cardboard, but the result was apt to be illegible. In 1891 he conceived the device of having a series of squares cut out in card, and inventing an alphabet, of which each letter was made of lines, which could be written along the edges of the squares, and dots, which could be marked at the corners. The thing worked well, and he named it the "Typhlograph," but, at the suggestion of one of his brother-students, this was subsequently changed into "Nyctograph."

He spent the Long Vacation at Eastbourne, attending service every Sunday at Christ Church, according to his usual rule.

Sept. 6, 1891.—At the evening service at Christ Church a curious thing happened, suggestive of telepathy. Before giving out the second hymn the curate read out some notices. Meanwhile I took my hymn-book, and said to myself (I have no idea *why*), "It will be hymn 416," and I turned to it. It was not one I recognised as having ever heard; and, on looking at it, I said, "It is very prosaic; it is a very unlikely one"—and it was really startling, the next minute, to hear the curate announce "Hymn 416."

In October it became generally known that Dean Liddell was going to resign at Christmas. This was a great blow to Mr. Dodgson, but little mitigated by the fact that the very man whom he himself would have chosen, Dr. Paget, was appointed to fill the vacant place. The old Dean was very popular in College; even the undergraduates, with whom he was seldom brought into contact, felt the magic of his commanding personality and the charm of his gracious, old-world manner. He was a man whom, once seen, it was almost impossible to forget.

Shortly before the resignation of Dr. Liddell, the Duchess of Albany spent a few days at the Deanery. Mr. Dodgson was asked to meet her Royal Highness at luncheon, but was unable to go. Princess Alice and the little Duke of Albany, however, paid him a visit, and were initiated in the art of making paper pistols. He promised to send the Princess a copy of a book called "The Fairies," and the children, having spent a happy half-hour in his rooms, returned to the Deanery. This was one of the days which he "marked with a white stone." He sent a copy of "The Nursery 'Alice'" to the little Princess Alice, and received a note of thanks from her, and also a letter from her mother, in which she said that the book had taught the Princess to like reading, and to do it out of lesson-time. To the Duke he gave a copy of a book entitled "The Merry Elves." In his little note of thanks for this gift, the boy said, "Alice and I want you to love us both." Mr. Dodgson sent Princess Alice a puzzle, promising that if she found it out, he would give her a "golden chair from Wonderland."

At the close of the year he wrote me a long letter, which I think worthy of reproducing here, for he spent a long time over it, and it contains excellent examples of his clear way of putting things.

To S.D. Collingwood.

Ch. Ch., Oxford, *Dec.* 29, 1891.

My Dear Stuart,—(Rather a large note—sheet, isn't it? But they do differ in size, you know.) I fancy this book of science (which I have had a good while, without making any use of it), may prove of some use to you, with your boys. [I was a schoolmaster at that time.] Also this cycling-book (or whatever it is to be called) may be useful in putting down engagements, &c., besides telling you a lot about cycles. There was no use in sending it to *me; my* cycling days are over.

You ask me if your last piece of "Meritt" printing is dark enough. I think not. I should say the rollers want fresh inking. As to the *matter* of your specimen—[it was a poor little essay on killing animals for the purpose of scientific recreations, *e.g.*, collecting butterflies]—I think you *cannot* spend your time better than in trying to set down clearly, in that essay-form, your ideas on any subject that chances to interest you; and *specially* any theological subject that strikes you in the course of your reading for Holy Orders.

It will be most *excellent* practice for you, against the time when you try to compose sermons, to try thus to realise exactly what it is you mean, and to express it clearly, and (a much harder matter) to get into proper shape the *reasons* of your opinions, and to see whether they do, or do not, tend to prove the conclusions you come to. You have never studied technical Logic, at all, I fancy. [I *had*, but I freely admit that the essay in question proved that I had not then learnt to apply my principles to practice.] It would have been a great help: but still it is not indispensable: after all, it is only the putting into rules of the way in which *every* mind proceeds, when it draws valid conclusions; and, by practice in careful thinking, you may get to know "fallacies" when you meet with them, without knowing the formal *rules*.

At present, when you try to give *reasons*, you are in considerable danger of propounding fallacies. Instances occur in this little essay of yours; and I hope it won't offend your *amour propre* very much, if an old uncle, who has studied Logic for forty years, makes a few remarks on it.

I am not going to enter *at all* on the subject-matter itself, or to say whether I agree, or not, with your *conclusions* : but merely to examine, from a logic-lecturer's point of view, your *premisses* as relating to them.

(1) "As the lower animals do not appear to have personality or individual existence, I cannot see that any particular one's life can be very important," &c. The word "personality" is very vague: I don't know what you mean by it. If you were to ask yourself, "What test should I use in distinguishing what *has*, from what has *not*, personality?" you might perhaps be able to express your meaning more clearly. The phrase "individual existence" is clear enough, and is in direct logical contradiction to the phrase "particular one." To say, of anything, that it has *not* "individual existence," and yet that it *is* a "particular one," involves the logical fallacy called a "contradiction in terms."

(2) "In both cases" (animal and plant) "death is only the conversion of matter

from one form to another." The word "form" is very vague—I fancy you use it in a sort of *chemical* sense (like saying "sugar is starch in another form," where the change in nature is generally believed to be a rearrangement of the very same atoms). If you mean to assert that the difference between a live animal and a dead animal, *i.e.*, between animate and sensitive matter, and the same matter when it becomes inanimate and insensitive, is a mere rearrangement of the same atoms, your premiss is intelligible. (It is a bolder one than any biologists have yet advanced. The most sceptical of them admits, I believe, that "vitality" is a thing *per se*. However, that is beside my present scope.) But this premiss is advanced to prove that it is of no "consequence" to kill an animal. But, granting that the conversion of sensitive into insensitive matter (and of course *vice versa*) is a mere change of "form," and *therefore* of no "consequence"; granting this, we cannot escape the including under this rule all similar cases. If the *power* of feeling pain, and the *absence* of that power, are only a difference of "form," the conclusion is inevitable that the *feeling* pain, and the *not* feeling it, are *also* only a difference in form, *i.e.*, to convert matter, which is *not* feeling pain, into matter *feeling* pain, is only to change its "form," and, if the process of "changing form" is of no "consequence" in the case of sensitive and insensitive matter, we must admit that it is *also* of no "consequence" in the case of pain-feeling and *not* pain-feeling matter. This conclusion, I imagine, you neither intended nor foresaw. The premiss, which you use, involves the fallacy called "proving too much."

The best advice that could be given to you, when you begin to compose sermons, would be what an old friend once gave to a young man who was going out to be an Indian judge (in India, it seems, the judge decides things, without a jury, like our County Court judges). "Give *your decisions* boldly and clearly; they will probably be *right*. But do *not* give your *reasons: they* will probably be *wrong*" If your lot in life is to be in a *country* parish, it will perhaps not matter *much* whether the reasons given in your sermons do or do not prove your conclusions. But even there you *might* meet, and in a town congregation you would be *sure* to meet, clever sceptics, who know well how to argue, who will detect your fallacies and point them out to those who are *not* yet troubled with doubts, and thus undermine *all* their confidence in your teaching.

At Eastbourne, last summer, I heard a preacher advance the astounding argument, "We believe that the Bible is true, because our holy Mother, the Church, tells us it is." I pity that unfortunate clergyman if ever he is bold enough to enter any Young Men's Debating Club where there is some clear-headed sceptic who has heard, or heard of, that sermon. I can fancy how the young man would rub his hands, in delight, and would say to himself, "Just see me get him into a corner, and convict him of arguing in a circle!"

The bad logic that occurs in many and many a well-meant sermon, is a real danger to modern Christianity. When detected, it may seriously injure many believers, and fill them with miserable doubts. So my advice to you, as a young theological student, is "Sift your reasons *well* , and, before you offer them to others, make sure that they prove your conclusions."

I hope you won't give this letter of mine (which it has cost me some time and thought to write) just a single reading and then burn it; but that you will lay it aside. Perhaps, even years hence, it may be of some use to you to read it again.

Believe me always

Your affectionate Uncle,

C. L. Dodgson.

CHAPTER VIII

(1892—1896)

Mr. Dodgson resigns the Curatorship—Bazaars—He lectures to children—A mechanical "Humpty Dumpty"—A logical controversy—Albert Chevalier—"Sylvie and Bruno Concluded"—"Pillow Problems"—Mr. Dodgson's generosity—College services—Religious difficulties—A village sermon—Plans for the future—Reverence—"Symbolic Logic."

At Christ Church, as at other Colleges, the Common Room is an important feature. Open from eight in the morning until ten at night, it takes the place of a club, where the "dons" may see the newspapers, talk, write letters, or enjoy a cup of tea. After dinner, members of High Table, with their guests if any are present, usually adjourn to the Common Room for wine and dessert, while there is a smoking-room hard by for those who do not despise the harmless but unnecessary weed, and below are cellars, with a goodly store of choice old wines.

The Curator's duties were therefore sufficiently onerous. They were doubly so in Mr. Dodgson's case, for his love of minute accuracy greatly increased the amount of work he had to do. It was his office to select and purchase wines, to keep accounts, to adjust selling price to cost price, to see that the two Common Room servants performed their duties, and generally to look after the comfort and convenience of the members.

"Having heard," he wrote near the end of the year 1892, "that Strong was willing to be elected (as Curator), and Common Room willing to elect him, I most gladly resigned. The sense of relief at being free from the burdensome office, which has cost me a large amount of time and trouble, is very delightful. I was made Curator, December 8, 1882, so that I have held the office more than nine years."

The literary results of his Curatorship were three very interesting little pamphlets, "Twelve Months in a Curatorship, by One who has tried it"; "Three years in a Curatorship, by One whom it has tried"; and "Curiosissima Curatoria, by 'Rude Donatus,'" all printed for private circulation, and couched in the same serio-comic vein. As a logician he naturally liked to see his thoughts in print, for, just as the mathematical mind craves for a black-board and a piece of chalk, so the logical mind must have its paper and printing-press wherewith to set forth its deductions effectively.

A few extracts must suffice to show the style of these pamphlets, and the opportunity offered for the display of humour.

In the arrangement of the prices at which wines were to be sold to members of Common Room, he found a fine scope for the exercise of his mathematical talents and his sense of proportion. In one of the pamphlets he takes old Port and Chablis as illustrations.

The original cost of each is about 3s. a bottle; but the present value of the old Port is about 11s. a bottle. Let us suppose, then, that we have to sell to Common Room one bottle of old Port and three of Chablis, the original cost of the whole being 12s., and the present value 20s. These are our data. We have now two questions to answer. First, what sum shall we ask for the whole? Secondly, how shall we apportion that sum between the two kinds of wine?

The sum to be asked for the whole he decides, following precedent, is to be the present market-value of the wine; as to the second question, he goes on to say—

We have, as so often happens in the lives of distinguished premiers, three courses before us: (1) to charge the *present* value for each kind of wine; (2) to put on a certain percentage to the *original* value of each kind; (3) to make a compromise between these two courses.

Course 1 seems to me perfectly reasonable; but a very plausible objection has been made to it—that it puts a prohibitory price on the valuable wines, and that they would remain unconsumed. This would not, however, involve any loss to our finances; we could obviously realise the enhanced values of the old wines by selling them to outsiders, if the members of Common Room would not buy them. But I do not advocate this course.

Course 2 would lead to charging 5s. a bottle for Port and Chablis alike. The Port-drinker would be "in clover," while the Chablis-drinker would probably begin getting his wine direct from the merchant instead of from the Common Room cellar, which would be a *reductio ad absurdum* of the tariff. Yet I have heard this course advocated, repeatedly, as an abstract principle. "You ought to consider the *original* value only," I have been told. "You ought to regard the Port-drinker as a private individual, who has laid the wine in for himself, and who ought to have all the advantages of its enhanced value. You cannot fairly ask him for more than what you need to refill the bins with Port, *plus* the percentage thereon needed to meet the contingent expenses." I have listened to such arguments, but have never been convinced that the course is just. It seems to me that the 8s. additional value which the bottle of Port has acquired, is the property of *Common Room*, and that Common Room has the power to give it to whom it chooses; and it does not seem to me fair to give it all to the Port-drinker. What merit is there in preferring Port to Chablis, that could justify our selling the Port-drinker his wine at less than half what he would have to give outside, and charging the Chablis-drinker five-thirds of what he would have to give outside? At all events, I, as a Port-drinker, do not wish to absorb the whole advantage, and would gladly share it with the Chablis-drinker. The course I recommend is

Course 3, which is a compromise between 1 and 2, its essential principle being to sell the new wines *above* their value, in order to be able to sell the old *below* their value. And it is clearly desirable, as far as possible, to make the reductions *where they will be felt*, and the additions *where they will not be felt*. Moreover it seems to me that reduction is most felt where it *goes down to the next round sum,* and an addition in the reverse case, *i.e.,* when it *starts from a round sum*. Thus, if we were to take 2d. off a 5s. 8d. wine, and add it to a 4s. 4d.—thus selling them at 5s. 6d. and 4s. 6d. the reduction would be welcomed, and the addition unnoticed; and the change would be a popular one.

The next extract shows with what light-hearted frivolity he could approach this tremendous subject of wine:—

The consumption of Madeira (B) has been during the past year, zero. After careful calculation I estimate that, if this rate of consumption be steadily maintained, our present stock will last us an infinite number of years. And although there may be something monotonous and dreary in the prospect of such vast cycles spent in drinking second-class Madeira, we may yet cheer ourselves with the thought of how economically it can be done.

To assist the Curator in the discharge of his duties, there was a Wine Committee, and for its guidance a series of rules was drawn up. The first runs as follows: "There shall be a Wine Committee, consisting of five persons, including the Curator, whose duty it shall be to assist the Curator in the management of the cellar." "Hence," wrote Mr. Dodgson, "logically it is the bounden duty of the Curator 'to assist himself.' I decline to say whether this clause has ever brightened existence for me—or whether, in the shades of evening, I may ever have been observed leaving the Common Room cellars with a small but suspicious-looking bundle, and murmuring, 'Assist thyself, assist thyself!'"

Every Christmas at Christ Church the children of the College servants have a party in the Hall. This year he was asked to entertain them, and gladly consented to do so. He hired a magic lantern and a large number of slides, and with their help told the children the three following stories: (1) "The Epiphany"; (2) "The Children Lost in the Bush"; (3) "Bruno's Picnic."

I have already referred to the services held in Christ Church for the College servants, at which Mr. Dodgson used frequently to preach. The way in which he regarded this work is very characteristic of the man. "Once more," he writes, "I have to thank my Heavenly Father for the great blessing and privilege of being allowed to speak for Him! May He bless my words to help some soul on its heavenward way." After one of these addresses he received a note from a member of the congregation, thanking him for what he had said. "It is very sweet," he said, "to get such words now and then; but there is danger in them if more such come, I must beg for silence."

During the year Mr. Dodgson wrote the following letter to the Rev. C.A. Goodhart, Rector of Lambourne, Essex:—

Dear Sir,—Your kind, sympathising and most encouraging letter about "Sylvie and Bruno" has deserved a better treatment from me than to have been thus kept waiting more than two years for an answer. But life is short; and one has many other things to do; and I have been for years almost hopelessly in arrears in correspondence. I keep a register, so that letters which I intend to answer do somehow come to the front at last.

In "Sylvie and Bruno" I took courage to introduce what I had entirely avoided in the two "Alice" books—some reference to subjects which are, after all, the *only* subjects of real interest in life, subjects which are so intimately bound up with every topic of human interest that it needs more effort to avoid them than to touch on them; and I felt that such a book was more suitable to a clerical writer than one of mere fun.

I hope I have not offended many (evidently I have not offended *you*) by putting scenes of mere fun, and talk about God, into the same book.

Only one of all my correspondents ever guessed there was more to come of the book. She was a child, personally unknown to me, who wrote to "Lewis Carroll" a sweet letter about the book, in which she said, "I'm so glad it hasn't got a regular wind-up, as it shows there is more to come!"

There is indeed "more to come." When I came to piece together the mass of accumulated material I found it was quite *double* what could be put into one volume. So I divided it in the middle; and I hope to bring out "Sylvie and Bruno Concluded" next Christmas—if, that is, my Heavenly Master gives me the time and the strength for the task; but I am nearly 60, and have no right to count on years to come.

In signing my real name, let me beg you not to let the information go further—I have an *intense* dislike to personal publicity; and, the more people there are who know nothing of "Lewis Carroll" save his books, the happier I am.

Believe me, sincerely yours,

Charles L. Dodgson.

I have made no attempt to chronicle all the games and puzzles which Lewis Carroll invented. A list of such as have been published will be found in the Bibliographical chapter. He intended to bring out a book of "Original Games and Puzzles," with illustrations by Miss E. Gertrude Thomson. The MS. was, I believe, almost complete before his death, and one, at least, of the pictures had been drawn. On June 30th he wrote in his Diary, "Invented what I think is a new kind of riddle. A Russian had three sons. The first, named Rab, became a lawyer; the second, Ymra, became a soldier; the third became a sailor. What was his name?"

The following letter written to a child-friend, Miss E. Drury, illustrates Lewis Carroll's hatred of bazaars:—

Ch. Ch., Oxford, *Nov.* 10, 1892.

My dear Emmie,—I object to *all* bazaars on the general principle that they are very undesirable schools for young ladies, in which they learn to be "too fast" and forward, and are more exposed to undesirable acquaintances than in ordinary society. And I have, besides that, special objections to bazaars connected with charitable or religious purposes. It seems to me that they desecrate the religious object by their undesirable features, and that they take the reality out of all charity by getting people to think that they are doing a good action, when their true motive is amusement for themselves. Ruskin has put all this far better than I can possibly do, and, if I can find the passage, and find the time to copy it, I will send it you. But *time* is a very scarce luxury for me!

Always yours affectionately,

C.L. Dodgson.

In his later years he used often to give lectures on various subjects to children. He gave a series on "Logic" at the Oxford Girls' High School, but he sometimes went further afield, as in the following instance:—

Went, as arranged with Miss A. Ottley, to the High School at Worcester, on a visit. At half-past three I had an audience of about a hundred little girls, aged, I should think, from about six to fourteen. I showed them two arithmetic puzzles on the black-board, and told them "Bruno's Picnic." At half-past seven I addressed some serious words to a second audience of about a hundred elder girls, probably from fifteen to twenty—an experience of the deepest interest to me.

The illustration on the next page will be best explained by the following letter which I have received from Mr. Walter Lindsay, of Philadelphia, U.S.:—

Phila., *September* 12, 1898.

Dear Sir,—I shall be very glad to furnish what information I can with respect to the "Mechanical Humpty Dumpty" which I constructed a few years ago, but I must begin by acknowledging that, in one sense at least, I did not "invent" the figure. The idea was first put into my head by an article in the *Cosmopolitan*, somewhere about 1891, I suppose, describing a similar contrivance. As a devoted admirer of the "Alice" books, I determined to build a Humpty Dumpty of my own; but I left the model set by the author of the article mentioned, and constructed the figure on entirely different lines. In the first place, the figure as described in the magazine had very few movements, and not very satisfactory ones at that; and in the second place, no attempt whatever was made to reproduce, even in a general way, the well-known appearance of Tenniel's drawing. Humpty, when completed, was about two feet and a half high. His face, of course, was white; the lower half of the egg was dressed in brilliant blue. His stockings were grey, and the famous cravat orange, with a zigzag pattern in blue. I am sorry to say that the photograph hardly does him justice; but he had travelled to so many different places during his career, that he began to be decidedly out of shape before he sat for his portrait.

When Humpty was about to perform, a short "talk" was usually given before the curtain rose, explaining the way in which the Sheep put the egg on the shelf at the back of the little shop, and how Alice went groping along to it. And then, just as the explanation had reached the opening of the chapter on Humpty Dumpty, the curtain rose, and Humpty was discovered, sitting on the wall, and gazing into vacancy. As soon as the audience had had time to recover, Alice entered, and the conversation was carried on just as it is in the book. Humpty Dumpty gesticulated with his arms, rolled his eyes, raised his eyebrows, frowned, turned up his nose in scorn at Alice's ignorance, and smiled from ear to ear when he shook hands with her. Besides this, his mouth kept time with his words all through the dialogue, which added very greatly to his life-like appearance.

The effect of his huge face, as it changed from one expression to another, was ludicrous in the extreme, and we were often obliged to repeat sentences in the conversation (to "go back to the last remark but one") because the audience laughed so loudly over Humpty Dumpty's expression of face that they drowned what he was trying to say. The funniest effect was the change from the look of self-satisfied complacency with which he accompanied the words: "The king has promised me—" to that of towering rage when Alice innocently betrays her knowledge of the secret. At the close of the scene, when Alice has vainly endeavoured to draw him into further conversation, and at last walks away in disgust, Humpty loses his balance on the wall, recovers himself, totters again, and then falls off backwards; at the same time a box full of broken glass is dropped on the floor behind the scenes, to represent the "heavy crash," which "shook the forest from end to end";—and the curtain falls.

Now, as to how it was all done. Humpty was made of barrel hoops, and covered with stiff paper and muslin. His eyes were round balls of rags, covered with muslin, drawn smoothly, and with the pupil and iris marked on the front. These eyes were pivoted to a board, fastened just behind the eye-openings in the face. To the eyeballs were sewed strong pieces of tape, which passed through screw-eyes on the edges of the board, and so down to a row of levers which were hinged in the lower part of the figure. One lever raised both eyes upward, another moved them both to the left, and so on. The eyebrows were of worsted and indiarubber knitted together. They were fastened at the ends, and raised and lowered by fine white threads passing through small holes in the face, and also operated by levers. The arms projected into the interior of the machine, and the gestures were made by moving the short ends inside. The right hand contained a spring clothe-pin, by which he was enabled to hold the note— book in which Alice set down the celebrated problem—

The movement of the mouth, in talking, was produced by a long tape, running down to a pedal, which was controlled by the foot of the performer. And the smile consisted of long strips of red tape, which were drawn out through slits at the corners of the mouth by means of threads which passed through holes in the sides of the head. The performer—who was always your humble servant—stood on a box behind the wall, his head just reaching the top of the egg, which was open all the way up the back. At the lower end of the figure, convenient to the hands of the performer, was the row of levers, like a little keyboard; and by striking different chords on the keys, any desired expression could be produced on the face.

Of course, a performance of this kind without a good Alice would be unutterably flat; but the little girl who played opposite to Humpty, Miss Nellie K—, was so exactly the counterpart of Alice, both in appearance and disposition, that most children thought she was the original, right out of the book.

Humpty still exists, but he has not seen active life for some years. His own popularity was the cause of his retirement; for having given a number of performances (for Charity, of course), and delighted many thousands of children of all ages, the demands upon his time, from Sunday-schools and other institutions, became so numerous that the performers were obliged to withdraw him in self-defence. He was a great deal of trouble to build, but the success he met with and the pleasure he gave more than repaid me for the bother; and I am sure that any one else who tries it will reach the same conclusion.

Yours sincerely,

Walter Lindsay.

At the beginning of 1893 a fierce logical battle was being waged between Lewis Carroll and Mr. Cook Wilson, Professor of Logic at Oxford. The Professor, in spite of the countless arguments that Mr. Dodgson hurled at his head, would not confess that he had committed a fallacy.

On February 5th the Professor appears to have conceded a point, for Mr. Dodgson writes: "Heard from Cook Wilson, who has long declined to read a paper which I sent January 12th, and which seems to me to prove the fallacy of a view of his about Hypotheticals. He now offers to read it, if *I* will study a proof he sent, that another problem of mine had contradictory *data*. I have accepted his offer, and studied and answered his paper. So I now look forward hopefully to the result of his reading mine."

The hopes which he entertained were doomed to be disappointed; the controversy bore no fruits save a few pamphlets and an enormous amount of correspondence, and finally the two antagonists had to agree to differ.

As a rule Mr. Dodgson was a stern opponent of music-halls and music-hall singers; but he made one or two exceptions with regard to the latter. For Chevalier he had nothing but praise; he heard him at one of his recitals, for he never in his life entered a "Variety Theatre." I give the passage from his Diary:—

Went to hear Mr. Albert Chevalier's Recital. I only knew of him as being now recognised as *facile princeps* among music-hall singers, and did not remember that I had seen him twice or oftener on the stage—first as "Mr. Hobbs" in "Little Lord Fauntleroy," and afterwards as a "horsy" young man in a *matinée* in which Violet Vanbrugh appeared. He was decidedly *good* as an actor; but as a comic singer (with considerable powers of pathos as well) he is quite first-rate. His chief merit seems to be the earnestness with which he throws himself into the work. The songs (mostly his own writing) were quite inoffensive, and very funny. I am very glad to be able to think that his influence on public taste is towards refinement and purity. I liked best "The Future Mrs. 'Awkins," with its taking tune, and "My Old Dutch," which revealed powers that, I should think, would come out grandly in Robsonian parts, such as "The Porter's Knot." "The Little Nipper" was also well worth hearing.

Mr. Dodgson's views on Sunday Observance were old-fashioned, but he lived up to them, and did not try to force them upon people with whose actions he had no concern. They were purely matters of "private opinion" with him. On October 2nd he wrote to Miss E.G. Thomson, who was illustrating his "Three Sunsets":—

Would you kindly do *no* sketches, or photos, for *me*, on a Sunday? It is, in *my* view (of *course* I don't condemn any one who differs from me) inconsistent with keeping the day holy. I do *not* hold it to be the Jewish "Sabbath," but I *do* hold it to be "the Lord's Day," and so to be made very distinct from the other days.

In December, the Logical controversy being over for a time, Mr. Dodgson invented a new problem to puzzle his mathematical friends with, which was called "The Monkey and Weight Problem." A rope is supposed to be hung over a wheel fixed to the roof of a building; at one end of the rope a weight is fixed, which exactly counterbalances a monkey which is hanging on to the other end. Suppose that the monkey begins to climb the rope, what will be the result? The following extract from the Diary illustrates the several possible answers which may be given:—

Got Professor Clifton's answer to the "Monkey and Weight Problem." It is very curious, the different views taken by good mathematicians. Price says the weight goes *up*, with increasing velocity; Clifton (and Harcourt) that it goes *up*, at the same rate as the monkey; while Sampson says that it goes *down*.

On December 24th Mr. Dodgson received the first twelve copies of "Sylvie and Bruno Concluded," just about four years after the appearance of the first part of the story. In this second volume the two fairy children are as delightful as ever; it also contains what I think most people will agree to be the most beautiful poem Lewis Carroll ever wrote, "Say, what is the spell, when her fledglings are cheeping?" (p. 305). In the preface he pays a well-deserved compliment to Mr. Harry Furniss for his wonderfully clever pictures; he also explains how the book was written, showing that many of the amusing remarks of Bruno had been uttered by real children. He makes allusion to two books, which only his death prevented him from finishing—"Original Games and Puzzles," and a paper on "Sport," viewed from the standpoint of the humanitarian. From a literary point of view the second volume of "Sylvie and Bruno" lacks unity; a fairy tale is all very well, and a novel also is all very well, but the combination of the two is surely a mistake. However, the reader who cares more for the spirit than the letter will not notice this blemish; to him "Sylvie and Bruno Concluded" will be interesting and helpful, as the revelation of a very beautiful personality.

You have made everything turn out just as I should have chosen [writes a friend to whom he had sent a copy], and made right all that disappointed me in the first part. I have not only to thank you for writing an interesting book, but for writing a helpful one too. I am sure that "Sylvie and Bruno" has given me many thoughts that will help me all life through. One cannot know "Sylvie" without being the better for it. You may say that "Mister Sir" is not consciously meant to be yourself, but I cannot help feeling that he is. As "Mister Sir" talks, I hear your voice in every word. I think, perhaps, that is why I like the book so much.

I have received an interesting letter from Mr. Furniss, bearing upon the subject of "Sylvie and Bruno," and Lewis Carroll's methods of work. The letter runs as follows:—

I have illustrated stories of most of our leading authors, and I can safely say that Lewis Carroll was the only one who cared to understand the illustrations to his own book. He was the W. S. Gilbert for children, and, like Gilbert producing one of his operas, Lewis Carroll took infinite pains to study every detail in producing his extraordinary and delightful books. Mr. Gilbert, as every one knows, has a model of the stage; he puts up the scenery, draws every figure, moves them about just as he wishes the real actors to move about. Lewis Carroll was precisely the same. This, of course, led to a great deal of work and trouble, and made the illustrating of his books more a matter of artistic interest than of professional profit. I was *seven years* illustrating his last work, and during that time I had the pleasure of many an interesting meeting with the fascinating author, and I was quite repaid for the trouble I took, not only by his generous appreciation of my efforts, but by the liberal remuneration he gave for the work, and also by the charm of having intercourse with the interesting, if somewhat erratic genius.

A book very different in character from "Sylvie and Bruno," but under the same well-known pseudonym, appeared about the same time. I refer to "Pillow Problems," the second part of the series entitled "Curiosa Mathematica."

"Pillow Problems thought out during wakeful hours" is a collection of mathematical problems, which Mr. Dodgson solved while lying awake at night. A few there are to which the title is not strictly applicable, but all alike were worked out mentally before any diagram or word of the solution was committed to paper.

The author says that his usual practice was to write down the *answer* first of all, and afterwards the question and its solution. His motive, he says, for publishing these problems was not from any desire to display his powers of mental calculation. Those who knew him will readily believe this, though they will hardly be inclined to accept his own modest estimate of those powers.

Still the book was intended, not for the select few who can scale the mountain heights of advanced mathematics, but for the much larger class of ordinary mathematicians, and they at least will be able to appreciate the gifted author, and to wonder how he could follow so clearly in his head the mental diagrams and intricate calculations involved in some of these "Pillow Problems."

His chief motive in publishing the book was to show how, by a little determination, the mind "can be made to concentrate itself on some intellectual subject (not necessarily mathematics), and thus banish those petty troubles and vexations which most people experience, and which—unless the mind be otherwise occupied—*will* persist in invading the hours of night." And this remedy, as he shows, serves a higher purpose still. In a paragraph which deserves quoting at length, as it gives us a momentary glimpse of his refined and beautiful character, he says:—

Perhaps I may venture for a moment to use a more serious tone, and to point out that there are mental troubles, much worse than mere worry, for which an absorbing object of thought may serve as a remedy. There are sceptical thoughts, which seem for the moment to uproot the firmest faith: there are blasphemous thoughts, which dart unbidden into the most reverent souls: there are unholy thoughts, which torture with their hateful presence the fancy that would fain be pure. Against all these some real mental work is a most helpful ally. That "unclean spirit" of the parable, who brought back with him seven others more wicked than himself, only did so because he found the chamber "swept and garnished," and its owner sitting with folded hands. Had he found it all alive with the "busy hum" of active *work*, there would have been scant welcome for him and his seven!

It would have robbed the book of its true character if Lewis Carroll had attempted to improve on the work done in his head, and consequently we have the solutions exactly as he worked them out before setting them down on paper. Of the Problems themselves there is not much to be said here; they are original, and some of them (e.g., No. 52) expressed in a style peculiarly the author's own. The subjects included in their range are Arithmetic, Algebra, Pure Geometry (Plane), Trigonometry, Algebraic Geometry, and Differential Calculus; and there is one Problem to which Mr. Dodgson says he "can proudly point," in "Transcendental Probabilities," which is here given: "A bag contains two counters, as to which nothing is known except that each is either black or white. Ascertain their colour without taking them out of the bag." The answer is, "One is black and the other white." For the solution the reader is referred to the book itself, a study of which will well repay him, apart from the chance he may have of discovering some mistake, and the consequent joy thereat!

A few extracts from the Diary follow, written during the early part of 1894:—

Feb. 1st.—Dies notandus. As Ragg was reading Prayers, and Bayne and I were the only M.A.'s in the stalls, I tried the experiment of going to the lectern and reading the lesson. I did not hesitate much, but feel it too great a strain on the nerves to be tried often. Then I went to the Latin Chapel for Holy Communion. Only Paget (Dean) and Dr. Huntley came: so, for the first time in my recollection, it had to be given up. Then I returned to my rooms, and found in *The Standard* the very important communication from Gladstone denying the rumour that he has decided upon resigning the Premiership, but admitting that, owing to failing powers, it may come at any moment. It will make a complete change in the position of politics! Then I got, from Cook Wilson, what I have been so long trying for—an accepted transcript of the fallacious argument over which we have had an (apparently) endless fight. I think the end is near, *now*.

Feb. 4th.—The idea occurred to me that it might be a pleasant variation in Backgammon to throw *three* dice, and choose any two of the three numbers. The average quality of the throws would be much raised. I reckon that the chance of "6, 6" would be about two and a half what it now is. It would also furnish a means, similar to giving points in billiards, for equalising players: the weaker might use three dice, the other using two. I think of calling it "Thirdie Backgammon."

March 31st.—Have just got printed, as a leaflet, "A Disputed Point in Logic"—the point Professor Wilson and I have been arguing so long. This paper is wholly in his own words, and puts the point very clearly. I think of submitting it to all my logical friends.

"A Disputed Point in Logic" appeared also, I believe, in *Mind*, July, 1894.

This seems a fitting place in which to speak of a side of Mr. Dodgson's character of which he himself was naturally very reticent—his wonderful generosity. My own experience of him was of a man who was always ready to do one a kindness, even though it put him to great expense and inconvenience; but of course I did not know, during his lifetime, that my experience of him was the same as that of all his other friends. The income from his books and other sources, which might have been spent in a life of luxury and selfishness, he distributed lavishly where he saw it was needed, and in order to do this he always lived in the most simple way. To make others happy was the Golden Rule of his life. On August 31st he wrote, in a letter to a friend, Miss Mary Brown: "And now what am I to tell you about myself? To say I am quite well 'goes without saying' with me. In fact, my life is so strangely free from all trial and trouble that I cannot doubt my own happiness is one of the talents entrusted to me to 'occupy' with, till the Master shall return, by doing something to make other lives happy."

In several instances, where friends in needy circumstances have written to him for loans of money, he has answered them, "I will not *lend*, but I will *give* you the £100 you ask for." To help child-friends who wanted to go on the stage, or to take up music as a profession, he has introduced them to leading actors and actresses, paid for them having lessons in singing from the best masters, sent round circulars to his numerous acquaintances begging them to patronise the first concert or recital.

In writing his books he never attempted to win popularity by acceding to the prejudices and frailties of the age—his one object was to make his books useful and helpful and ennobling. Like the great Master, in whose steps he so earnestly strove to follow, he "went about doing good." And one is glad to think that even his memory is being made to serve the same purpose. The "Alice" cots are a worthy sequel to his generous life.

Even Mr. Dodgson, with all his boasted health, was not absolutely proof against disease, for on February 12, 1895, he writes:—

Tenth day of a rather bad attack of influenza of the ague type. Last night the fever rose to a great height, partly caused by a succession of *five* visitors. One, however, was of my own seeking—Dean Paget, to whom I was thankful to be able to tell all I have had in my mind for a year or more, as to our Chapel services *not* being as helpful as they could be made. The chief fault is extreme *rapidity*. I long ago gave up the attempt to say the Confession at that pace; and now I say it, and the Lord's Prayer, close together, and never hear a word of the Absolution. Also many of the Lessons are quite unedifying.

On July 11th he wrote to my brother on the subject of a paper about Eternal Punishment, which was to form the first of a series of essays on Religious Difficulties:—

I am sending you the article on "Eternal Punishment" as it is. There is plenty of matter for consideration, as to which I shall be glad to know your views.

Also if there are other points, connected with religion, where you feel that perplexing difficulties exist, I should be glad to know of them in order to see whether I can see my way to saying anything helpful.

But I had better add that I do not want to deal with any such difficulties, *unless* they tend to affect *life*. *Speculative* difficulties which do not affect conduct, and which come into collision with any of the principles which I intend to state as axioms, lie outside the scope of my book. These axioms are:—

(1) Human conduct is capable of being *right*, and of being *wrong*.

(2) I possess Free-Will, and am able to choose between right and wrong.

(3) I have in some cases chosen wrong.

(4) I am responsible for choosing wrong.

(5) I am responsible to a person.

(6) This person is perfectly good.

I call them axioms, because I have no *proofs* to offer for them. There will probably be others, but these are all I can think of just now.

The Rev. H. Hopley, Vicar of Westham, has sent me the following interesting account of a sermon Mr. Dodgson preached at his church:—

In the autumn of 1895 the Vicar of Eastbourne was to have preached my Harvest Sermon at Westham, a village five miles away; but something or other intervened, and in the middle of the week I learned he could not come. A mutual friend suggested my asking Mr. Dodgson, who was then in Eastbourne, to help me, and I went with him to his rooms. I was quite a stranger to Mr. Dodgson; but knowing from hearsay how reluctant he usually was to preach, I apologised and explained my position—with Sunday so near at hand. After a moment's hesitation he consented, and in a most genial manner made me feel quite at ease as to the abruptness of my petition. On the morrow he came over to my vicarage, and made friends with my daughters, teaching them some new manner of playing croquet [probably Castle Croquet], and writing out for them puzzles and anagrams that he had composed.

The following letter was forwarded on the Saturday:—
"7, Lushington Road, Eastbourne,

September 26, 1895.

Dear Mr. Hopley,—I think you will excuse the liberty I am taking in asking you to give me some food after the service on Sunday, so that I may have no need to catch the train, but can walk back at leisure. This will save me from the worry of trying to conclude at an exact minute, and you, perhaps, from the trouble of finding short hymns, to save time. It will not, I hope, cause your cook any trouble, as my regular rule here is *cold* dinner on Sundays. This not from any "Sabbatarian" theory, but from the wish to let our *employés* have the day *wholly* at their own disposal.

I beg Miss Hopley's acceptance of the enclosed papers— (puzzles and diagrams.)

Believe me, very truly yours,

C.L. Dodgson."

On Sunday our grand old church was crowded, and, although our villagers are mostly agricultural labourers, yet they breathlessly listened to a sermon forty minutes long, and apparently took in every word of it. It was quite extempore, in very simple words, and illustrated by some delightful and most touching stories of children. I only wish there had been a shorthand-writer there.

In the vestry after service, while he was signing his name in the Preachers' Book, a church officer handed him a bit of paper. "Mr. Dodgson, would you very kindly write your name on that?" "Sir!" drawing himself up sternly—"Sir, I never do that for any one"—and then, more kindly, "You see, if I did it for one, I must do it for all."

An amusing incident in Mr. Dodgson's life is connected with the well-known drama, "Two Little Vagabonds." I give the story as he wrote it in his Diary:—

Nov. 28th.—*Matinée* at the Princess's of "Two Little Vagabonds," a very sensational melodrama, capitally acted. "Dick" and "Wally" were played by Kate Tyndall and Sydney Fairbrother, whom I guess to be about fifteen and twelve. Both were excellent, and the latter remarkable for the perfect realism of her acting. There was some beautiful religious dialogue between "Wally" and a hospital nurse— most reverently spoken, and reverently received by the audience.

Dec. 17th.—I have given books to Kate Tyndall and Sydney Fairbrother, and have heard from them, and find I was entirely mistaken in taking them for children. Both are married women!

The following is an extract from a letter written in 1896 to one of his sisters, in allusion to a death which had recently occurred in the family:—

It is getting increasingly difficult now to remember *which* of one's friends remain alive, and *which* have gone "into the land of the great departed, into the silent land." Also, such news comes less and less as a shock, and more and more one realises that it is an experience each of *us* has to face before long. That fact is getting *less* dreamlike to me now, and I sometimes think what a grand thing it will be to be able to say to oneself, "Death is *over* now; there is not *that* experience to be faced again."

I am beginning to think that, if the *books I* am still hoping to write are to be done *at all,* they must be done *now,* and that I am *meant* thus to utilise the splendid health I have had, unbroken, for the last year and a half, and the working powers that are fully as great as, if not greater, than I have ever had. I brought with me here (this letter was written from Eastbourne) the MS., such as it is (very fragmentary and unarranged) for the book about religious difficulties, and I meant, when I came here, to devote myself to that, but I have changed my plan. It seems to me that *that* subject is one that hundreds of living men could do, if they would only try, *much* better than I could, whereas there is no living man who could (or at any rate who would take the trouble to) arrange and finish and publish the second part of the "Logic." Also, I *have* the Logic book in my head; it will only need three or four months to write out, and I have *not* got the other book in my head, and it might take years to think out. So I have decided to get Part ii. finished *first*, and I am working at it day and night. I have taken to early rising, and sometimes sit down to my work before seven, and have one and a half hours at it before breakfast. The book will be a great novelty, and will help, I fully believe, to make the study of Logic *far* easier than it now is. And it will, I also believe, be a help to religious thought by giving *clearness* of conception and of expression, which may enable many people to face, and conquer, many religious difficulties for themselves. So I do really regard it as work for *God*.

Another letter, written a few months later to Miss Dora Abdy, deals with the subject of "Reverence," which Mr. Dodgson considered a virtue not held in sufficient esteem nowadays:—

My Dear Dora,—In correcting the proofs of "Through the Looking-Glass" (which is to have "An Easter Greeting" inserted at the end), I am reminded that in that letter (I enclose a copy), I had tried to express my thoughts on the very subject we talked about last night—the relation of *laughter* to religious thought. One of the hardest things in the world is to convey a meaning accurately from one mind to another, but the *sort* of meaning I want to convey to other minds is that while the laughter of *joy* is in full harmony with our deeper life, the laughter of amusement should be kept apart from it. The danger is too great of thus learning to look at solemn things in a spirit of *mockery*, and to seek in them opportunities for exercising *wit*. That is the spirit which has spoiled, for me, the beauty of some of the Bible. Surely there is a deep meaning in our prayer, "Give us an heart to love and *dread* Thee." We do not mean *terror*: but a dread that will harmonise with love; "respect" we should call it as towards a human being, "reverence" as towards God and all religious things.

Yours   affectionately,

C.L. Dodgson.

In his "Game of Logic" Lewis Carroll introduced an original method of working logical problems by means of diagrams; this method he superseded in after years for a much simpler one, the method of "Subscripts."

In "Symbolic Logic, Part i." (London: Macmillan, 1896) he employed both methods. The Introduction is specially addressed "to Learners," whom Lewis Carroll advises to read the book straight through, without *dipping*.

This Rule [he says] is very desirable with other kinds of books—such as novels, for instance, where you may easily spoil much of the enjoyment you would otherwise get from the story by dipping into it further on, so that what the author meant to be a pleasant surprise comes to you as a matter of course. Some people, I know, make a practice of looking into vol. iii. first, just to see how the story ends; and perhaps it *is* as well just to know that all ends *happily*—that the much persecuted lovers *do* marry after all, that he is proved to be quite innocent of the murder, that the wicked cousin is completely foiled in his plot, and gets the punishment he deserves, and that the rich uncle in India (*Qu.* Why in *India ? Ans.* Because, somehow, uncles never *can* get rich anywhere else) dies at exactly the right moment—before taking the trouble to read vol i. This, I say, is *just* permissible with a *novel*, where vol. iii. has a *meaning*, even for those who have not read the earlier part of the story; but with a *scientific* book, it is sheer insanity. You will find the latter part *hopelessly* unintelligible, if you read it before reaching it in regular course.

CHAPTER IX

(1897—1898)

Logic-lectures—Irreverent anecdotes—Tolerance of his religious views—A mathematical discovery—"The Little Minister" Sir George Baden-Powell—Last illness—"Thy will be done"—"Wonderland" at last!—Letters from friends "Three Sunsets"—"Of such is the kingdom of Heaven."

The year 1897, the last complete year which he was destined to spend, began for Mr. Dodgson at Guildford. On January 3rd he preached in the morning at the beautiful old church of S. Mary's, the church which he always attended when he was staying with his sisters at the Chestnuts.

On the 5th he began a course of Logic Lectures at Abbot's Hospital. The Rev. A. Kingston, late curate of Holy Trinity and S. Mary's Parishes, Guildford, had requested him to do this, and he had given his promise if as many as six people could be got together to hear him. Mr. Kingston canvassed the town so well that an audience of about thirty attended the first lecture.

A long Sunday walk was always a feature of Mr. Dodgson's life in the vacations. In earlier years the late Mr. W. Watson was his usual companion at Guildford. The two men were in some respects very much alike; a peculiar gentleness of character, a winning charm of manner which no one could resist, distinguished them both. After Mr. Watson's death his companion was usually one of the following Guildford clergymen: the Rev. J.H. Robson, LL.D., the Rev. H.R. Ware, and the Rev. A. Kingston.

On the 26th Mr. Dodgson paid a visit to the Girls' High School, to show the pupils some mathematical puzzles, and to teach the elder ones his "Memoria Technica." On the 28th he returned to Oxford, so as to be up in time for term.

I have said that he always refused invitations to dinner; accordingly his friends who knew of this peculiarity, and wished to secure him for a special evening, dared not actually invite him, but wrote him little notes stating that on such and such days they would be dining at home. Thus there is an entry in his Journal for February 10th:

"Dined with Mrs. G—(She had not sent an 'invitation'—only 'information')."

His system of symbolic logic enabled him to work out the most complex problems with absolute certainty in a surprisingly short time. Thus he wrote on the 15th: "Made a splendid logic-problem, about "great-grandsons" (modelled on one by De Morgan). My method of solution is quite new, and I greatly doubt if any one will solve the Problem. I have sent it to Cook Wilson."

On March 7th he preached in the University Church, the first occasion on which he had done so:—

There is now [he writes] a system established of a course of six sermons at S. Mary's each year, for University men *only*, and specially meant for undergraduates. They are preached, preceded by a few prayers and a hymn, at half-past eight. This evening ended the course for this term: and it was my great privilege to preach. It has been the most formidable sermon I have ever had to preach, and it is a *great* relief to have it over. I took, as text, Job xxviii. 28, "And unto man he said, The fear of the Lord, that is wisdom"—and the prayer in the Litany "Give us an heart to love and dread thee." It lasted three-quarters of an hour.

One can imagine how he would have treated the subject. The views which he held on the subject of reverence were, so at least it appears to me, somewhat exaggerated; they are well expressed in a letter which he wrote to a friend of his, during the year, and which runs as follows:—

Dear—, After changing my mind several times, I have at last decided to venture to ask a favour of you, and to trust that you will not misinterpret my motives in doing   so.

The favour I would ask is, that you will not tell me any more stories, such as you did on Friday, of remarks which children are said to have made on very sacred subjects—remarks which most people would recognise as irreverent, if made by *grown-up people*, but which are assumed to be innocent when made by children who are unconscious of any irreverence, the strange conclusion being drawn that they are therefore innocent when *repeated* by a grown-up person.

The misinterpretation I would guard against is, your supposing that I regard such repetition as always *wrong* in any grown-up person. Let me assure you that I do *not* so regard it. I am always willing to believe that those who repeat such stories differ wholly from myself in their views of what is, and what is not, fitting treatment of sacred things, and I fully recognise that what would certainly be wrong in *me*, is not necessarily so in *them*.

So I simply ask it as a personal favour to myself. The hearing of that anecdote gave me so much pain, and spoiled so much the pleasure of my tiny dinner-party, that I feel sure you will kindly spare me such in future.

One further remark. There are quantities of such anecdotes going about. I don't in the least believe that 5 per cent. of them were ever said by *children*. I feel sure that most of them are concocted by people who *wish* to bring sacred subjects into ridicule—sometimes by people who *wish* to undermine the belief that others have in religious truths: for there is no surer way of making one's beliefs *unreal* than by learning to associate them with ludicrous ideas.

Forgive the freedom with which I have said all this.

Sincerely yours,

C.L. Dodgson.

The entry in the Diary for April 11th (Sunday) is interesting:—

Went my eighteen-mile round by Besilsleigh. From my rooms back to them again, took me five hours and twenty-seven minutes. Had "high tea" at twenty minutes past seven. This entails only leaving a plate of cold meat, and gives much less trouble than hot dinner at six.

Dinner at six has been my rule since January 31st, when it began—I then abandoned the seven o'clock Sunday dinner, of which I entirely disapprove. It has prevented, for two terms, the College Servants' Service.

On May 12th he wrote:—

As the Prince of Wales comes this afternoon to open the Town Hall, I went round to the Deanery to invite them to come through my rooms upon the roof, to see the procession arrive.... A party of about twenty were on my roof in the afternoon, including Mrs. Moberly, Mrs. Driver, and Mrs. Baynes, and most, if not all, of the children in Christ Church. Dinner in Hall at eight. The Dean had the Prince on his right, and Lord Salisbury on his left. My place was almost *vis—à—vis* with the Prince. He and the Dean were the only speakers. We did not get out of Hall till nearly ten.

In June he bought a "Whiteley Exerciser," and fixed it up in his rooms. One would have thought that he would have found his long walks sufficient exercise (an eighteen-mile round was, as we have seen, no unusual thing for him to undertake), but apparently it was not so. He was so pleased with the "Exerciser," that he bought several more of them, and made presents of them to his friends.

As an instance of his broad-mindedness, the following extract from his Diary for June 20th is interesting. It must be premised that E—was a young friend of his who had recently become a member of the Roman Catholic Church, and that their place of worship in Oxford is dedicated to S. Aloysius.

I went with E— to S. Aloysius. There was much beauty in the service, part of which consisted in a procession, with banner, all round the church, carrying the Host, preceded by a number of girls in white, with veils (who had all had their first communion that morning), strewing flowers. Many of them were quite little things of about seven. The sermon (by Father Richardson) was good and interesting, and in a very loyal tone about the Queen.

A letter he wrote some years before to a friend who had asked him about his religious opinions reveals the same catholicity of mind:—

I am a member of the English Church, and have taken Deacon's Orders, but did not think fit (for reasons I need not go into) to take Priest's Orders. My dear father was what is called a "High Churchman," and I naturally adopted those views, but have always felt repelled by the yet higher development called "Ritualism."

But I doubt if I am fully a "High Churchman" now. I find that as life slips away (I am over fifty now), and the life on the other side of the great river becomes more and more the reality, of which *this* is only a shadow, that the petty distinctions of the many creeds of Christendom tend to slip away as well—leaving only the great truths which all Christians believe alike. More and more, as I read of the Christian religion, as Christ preached it, I stand amazed at the forms men have given to it, and the fictitious barriers they have built up between themselves and their brethren. I believe that when you and I come to lie down for the last time, if only we can keep firm hold of the great truths Christ taught us—our own utter worthlessness and His infinite worth; and that He has brought us back to our one Father, and made us His brethren, and so brethren to one another—we shall have all we need to guide us through the shadows.

Most assuredly I accept to the full the doctrines you refer to—that Christ died to save us, that we have no other way of salvation open to us but through His death, and that it is by faith in Him, and through no merit of ours, that we are reconciled to God; and most assuredly I can cordially say, "I owe all to Him who loved me, and died on the Cross of Calvary."

He spent the Long Vacation at Eastbourne as usual, frequently walking over to Hastings, which is about twenty miles off. A good many of his mornings were spent in giving lectures and telling stories at schools.

A letter to the widow of an old college friend reveals the extraordinary sensitiveness of his nature:—

2, Bedford Well Road, Eastbourne, *August* 2, 1897.

My Dear Mrs. Woodhouse,—Your letter, with its mournful news, followed me down here, and I only got it on Saturday night; so I was not able to be with you in thought when the mortal remains of my dear old friend were being committed to the ground; to await the time when our Heavenly Father shall have accomplished the number of His elect, and when you and I shall once more meet the loved ones from whom we are, for a little while only—what a little while even a long human life lasts!—parted in sorrow, yet *not* sorrowing as those without hope.

You will be sure without words of mine, that you have my true and deep sympathy. Of all the friends I made at Ch. Ch., your husband was the very *first* who spoke to me—across the dinner-table in Hall. That is forty-six years ago, but I remember, as if it were only yesterday, the kindly smile with which he spoke....

September 27th and 28th are marked in his Diary "with a white stone":—

Sept. 27th.—*Dies notandus.* Discovered rule for dividing a number by 9, by mere addition and subtraction. I felt sure there must be an analogous one for 11, and found it, and proved first rule by algebra, after working about nine hours!

Sept. 28th.—*Dies cretâ notandus.* I have actually *superseded* the rules discovered yesterday! My new rules require to ascertain the 9—remainder, and the 11—remainder, which the others did *not* require; but the new ones are much the quickest. I shall send them to *The Educational Times* , with date of discovery.

On November 4th he wrote:—

Completed a rule for dividing a given number by any divisor that is within 10 of a power of 10, either way. The *principle* of it is not my discovery, but was sent me by Bertram Collingwood—a rule for dividing by a divisor which is within 10 of a power of 10, *below* it.

My readers will not be surprised to learn that only eight days after this he had superseded his rule:—

An inventive morning! After waking, and before I had finished dressing, I had devised a new and much neater form in which to work my Rules for Long Division, and also decided to bring out my "Games and Puzzles," and Part iii. of "Curiosa Mathematica," in *Numbers*, in paper covers, paged consecutively, to be ultimately issued in boards.

On November 20th he spent the day in London, with the object of seeing "The Little Minister" at the Haymarket. "A beautiful play, beautifully acted," he calls it, and says that he should like to see it "again and again." He especially admired the acting of Mrs. Cyril Maude (Miss Winifred Emery) as Lady Babbie. This was the last theatrical performance he ever witnessed.

He apparently kept rough notes for his Diary, and only wrote it up every few weeks, as there are no entries at all for 1898, nor even for the last week of 1897. The concluding page runs as follows:—

Dec. (W.) 10 a.m.—I am in my large room, with no fire, and open window—temperature 54°.

Dec. 17 (F.).—Maggie [one of his sisters], and our nieces Nella and Violet, came to dinner.

Dec. 19 (Sun.).—Sat up last night till 4 a.m., over a tempting problem, sent me from New York, "to find 3 equal rational-sided rt.-angled *triangles* ." I found *two*, whose sides are 20, 21, 29; 12, 35, 37; but could not find *three*.

Dec. 23(Th.).—I start for Guildford by the 2.7 today.

As my story of Lewis Carroll's life draws near its end, I have received some "Stray Reminiscences" from Sir George Baden-Powell, M.P., which, as they refer to several different periods of time, are as appropriate here as in any other part of the book. The Rev. E.H. Dodgson, referred to in these reminiscences, is a younger brother of Lewis Carroll's; he spent several years of his life upon the remote island of Tristan d'Acunha, where there were only about seventy or eighty inhabitants besides himself. About once a year a ship used to call, when the island-folk would exchange their cattle for cloth, corn, tea, &c., which they could not produce themselves. The island is volcanic in origin, and is exposed to the most terrific gales; the building used as a church stood at some distance from Mr. Dodgson's dwelling, and on one occasion the wind was so strong that he had to crawl on his hands and knees for the whole distance that separated the two buildings.

My first introduction (writes Sir George Baden-Powell) to the author of "Through the Looking-Glass" was about the year 1870 or 1871, and under appropriate conditions! I was then coaching at Oxford with the well-known Rev. E. Hatch, and was on friendly terms with his bright and pretty children. Entering his house one day, and facing the dining-room, I heard mysterious noises under the table, and saw the cloth move as if some one were hiding. Children's legs revealed it as no burglar, and there was nothing for it but to crawl upon them, roaring as a lion. Bursting in upon them in their strong-hold under the table, I was met by the staid but amused gaze of a reverend gentleman. Frequently afterwards did I see and hear "Lewis Carroll" entertaining the youngsters in his inimitable way.

We became friends, and greatly did I enjoy intercourse with him over various minor Oxford matters. In later years, at one time I saw much of him, in quite another *rôle*—namely that of ardent sympathy with the, as he thought, ill-treated and deserted islanders of Tristan d'Acunha. His brother, it will be remembered, had voluntarily been left at that island with a view to ministering to the spiritual and educational needs of the few settlers, and sent home such graphic accounts and urgent demands for aid, that "Lewis Carroll" spared no pains to organise assistance and relief. At his instance I brought the matter before Government and the House of Commons, and from that day to this frequent communication has been held with the islanders, and material assistance has been rendered them—thanks to the warm heart of "Lewis Carroll."

On December 23, 1897, as the note in his Diary states, he went down, in accordance with his usual custom, to Guildford, to spend Christmas with his sisters at the Chestnuts. He seemed to be in his ordinary health, and in the best of spirits, and there was nothing to show that the end was so near.

At Guildford he was hard at work upon the second part of his "Symbolic Logic," spending most of the day over this task. This book, alas! he was not destined to finish, which is the more to be regretted as it will be exceedingly difficult for any one else to take up the thread of the argument, even if any one could be found willing to give the great amount of time and trouble which would be needed.

On January 5th my father, the Rev. C.S. Collingwood, Rector of Southwick, near Sunderland, died after a very short illness. The telegram which brought Mr. Dodgson the news of this contained the request that he would come at once. He determined to travel north the next day—but it was not to be so. An attack of influenza, which began only with slight hoarseness, yet enough to prevent him from following his usual habit of reading family prayers, was pronounced next morning to be sufficiently serious to forbid his undertaking a journey. At first his illness seemed a trifle, but before a week had passed bronchial symptoms had developed, and Dr. Gabb, the family physician, ordered him to keep his bed. His breathing rapidly became hard and laborious, and he had to be propped up with pillows. A few days before his death he asked one of his sisters to read him that well-known hymn, every verse of which ends with 'Thy Will be done.' To another he said that his illness was a great trial of his patience. How great a trial it must have been it is hard for us to understand. With the work he had set himself still uncompleted, with a sense of youth and joyousness, which sixty years of the battle of life had in no way dulled, Lewis Carroll had to face death. He seemed to know that the struggle was over. "Take away those pillows," he said on the 13th, "I shall need them no more." The end came about half-past two on the afternoon of the 14th. One of his sisters was in the room at the time, and she only noticed that the hard breathing suddenly ceased. The nurse, whom she summoned, at first hoped that this was a sign that he had taken a turn for the better. And so, indeed, he had—he had passed from a world of incompleteness and disappointment, to another where God is putting his beautiful soul to nobler and grander work than was possible for him here, where he is learning to comprehend those difficulties which used to puzzle him so much, and where that infinite Love, which he mirrored so wonderfully in his own life, is being revealed to him "face to face."

In accordance with his expressed wish, the funeral was simple in the extreme—flowers, and flowers only, adorned the plain coffin. There was no hearse to drag it up the steep incline that leads to the beautiful cemetery where he lies. The service was taken by Dean Paget and Canon Grant, Rector of Holy Trinity and S. Mary's, Guildford. The mourners who followed him in the quiet procession were few—but the mourners who were not there, and many of whom had never seen him—who shall tell *their* number?

After the grave had been filled up, the wreaths which had covered the coffin were placed upon it. Many were from "child-friends" and bore such inscriptions as "From two of his child-friends"—"To the sweetest soul that ever looked with human eyes," &c. Then the mourners left him alone there—up on the pleasant downs where he had so often walked.

A marble cross, under the shadow of a pine, marks the spot, and beneath his own name they have engraved the name of "Lewis Carroll," that the children who pass by may remember their friend, who is now—himself a child in all that makes childhood most attractive—in that "Wonderland" which outstrips all our dreams and hopes.

I cannot forbear quoting from Professor Sanday's sermon at Christ Church on the Sunday after his death:—

The world will think of Lewis Carroll as one who opened out a new vein in literature, a new and a delightful vein, which added at once mirth and refinement to life.... May we not say that from our courts at Christ Church there has flowed into the literature of our time a rill, bright and sparkling, health-giving and purifying, wherever its waters extend? On the following Sunday Dean Paget, in the course of a sermon on the "Virtue of Simplicity," said:—

We may differ, according to our difference of taste or temperament, in appraising Charles Dodgson's genius; but that that great gift was his, that his best work ranks with the very best of its kind, this has been owned with a recognition too wide and spontaneous to leave room for doubt. The brilliant, venturesome imagination, defying forecast with ever-fresh surprise; the sense of humour in its finest and most naïve form; the power to touch with lightest hand the undercurrent of pathos in the midst of fun; the audacity of creative fancy, and the delicacy of insight—these are rare gifts; and surely they were his. Yes, but it was his simplicity of mind and heart that raised them all, not only in his work but in his life, in all his ways, in the man as we knew him, to something higher than any mere enumeration of them tells: that almost curious simplicity, at times, that real and touching child-likeness that marked him in all fields of thought, appearing in his love of children and in their love of him, in his dread of giving pain to any living creature, in a certain disproportion, now and then, of the view he took of things—yes, and also in that deepest life, where the pure in heart and those who become as little children see the very truth and walk in the fear and love of God.

Some extracts from the numerous sympathetic letters received by Mr. Dodgson's brothers and sisters will show how greatly his loss was felt. Thus Canon Jelf writes:—

It was quite a shock to me to see in the paper to-day the death of your dear, good brother, to whom we owe so much of the brightening of our lives with pure, innocent fun. Personally I feel his loss very much indeed. We were together in old Ch. Ch. days from 1852 onwards; and he was always such a loyal, faithful friend to me. I rejoice to think of the *serious* talks we had together—of the grand, brave way in which he used the opportunities he had as a man of humour, to reach the consciences of a host of readers—of his love for children—his simplicity of heart—of his care for servants—his spiritual care for them. Who can doubt that he was fully prepared for a change however sudden—for the one clear call which took him away from us? Yet the world seems darker for his going; we can only get back our brightness by realising Who gave him all his talent, all his mirth of heart—the One who never leaves us. In deep sympathy,

Yours very sincerely,

George E. Jelf.

P.S.—When you have time tell me a little about him; he was so dear to me.

Mr. Frederic Harrison writes as follows:—

The occasional visits that I received from your late brother showed me a side of his nature which to my mind was more interesting and more worthy of remembrance even than his wonderful and delightful humour—I mean his intense sympathy with all who suffer and are in need.

He came to see me several times on sundry errands of mercy, and it has been a lesson to me through life to remember his zeal to help others in difficulty, his boundless generosity, and his inexhaustible patience with folly and error.

My young daughter, like all young people in civilised countries, was brought up on his beautiful fancies and humours. But for my part I remember him mainly as a sort of missionary to all in need. We all alike grieve, and offer you our heartfelt sympathy.

I am, faithfully yours,

Frederic Harrison.

His old friend and tutor, Dr. Price, writes:—

... I feel his removal from among us as the loss of an old and dear friend and pupil, to whom I have been most warmly attached ever since he was with me at Whitby, reading mathematics, in, I think, 1853—44 years ago! And 44 years of uninterrupted friendship .... I was pleased to read yesterday in *The Times* newspaper the kindly obituary notice: perfectly just and true; appreciative, as it should be, as to the unusual combination of deep mathematical ability and taste with the genius that led to the writing of "Alice's Adventures."

Only the other day [writes a lady friend] he wrote to me about his admiration for my dear husband, and he ended his letter thus: "I trust that when *my* time comes, I may be found, like him, working to the last, and ready for the Master's call"—and truly so he was.

A friend at Oxford writes:—

Mr. Dodgson was ever the kindest and gentlest of friends, bringing sunshine into the house with him. We shall mourn his loss deeply, and my two girls are quite overcome with grief. All day memories of countless acts of kindness shown to me, and to people I have known, have crowded my mind, and I feel it almost impossible to realise that he has passed beyond the reach of our gratitude and affection.

The following are extracts from letters written by some of his "child-friends," now grown up:—

How beautiful to think of the track of light and love he has left behind him, and the amount of happiness he brought into the lives of all those he came in contact with! I shall never forget all his kindness to us, from the time he first met us as little mites in the railway train, and one feels glad to have had the privilege of knowing him.

One of Mr. Dodgson's oldest "child-friends" writes:—

He was to me a dear and true friend, and it has been my great privilege to see a good deal of him ever since I was a tiny child, and especially during the last two years. I cannot tell you how much we shall miss him here. Ch. Ch. without Mr. Dodgson will be a strange place, and it is difficult to realise it even while we listen to the special solemn anthems and hymns to his memory in our cathedral.

One who had visited him at Guildford, writes:—

It must be quite sixteen years now since he first made friends with my sister and myself as children on the beach at Eastbourne, and since then his friendship has been and must always be one of my most valued possessions. It culminated, I think, in the summer of 1892—the year when he brought me to spend a very happy Sunday at Guildford. I had not seen him before, that year, for some time; and it was then, I think, that the childish delight in his kindness, and pride in his friendship, changed into higher love and reverence, when in our long walks over the downs I saw more and more into the great tenderness and gentleness of his nature.

Shortly after Mr. Dodgson's death, his "Three Sunsets" was published by Messrs. Macmillan. The twelve "Fairy Fancies," which illustrate it, were drawn by Miss E. G. Thomson. Though they are entirely unconnected with the text, they are so thoroughly in accordance with the author's delicate refinement, and so beautiful in themselves, that they do not strike one as inappropriate.

Some of the verses are strangely in keeping with the time at which they are published.

I could not see, for blinding tears,
The glories of the west:
A heavenly music filled my ears,
A heavenly peace my breast.
"Come unto me, come unto me—
All ye that labour, unto me—
Ye heavy-laden, come to me—
And I will give you rest."

One cannot read this little volume without feeling that the shadow of some disappointment lay over Lewis Carroll's life. Such I believe to have been the case, and it was this that gave him his wonderful sympathy with all who suffered. But those who loved him would not wish to lift the veil from these dead sanctities, nor would any purpose be served by so doing. The proper use of sympathy is not to weep over sorrows that are over, and whose very memory is perhaps obliterated for him in the first joy of possessing new and higher faculties.

Before leaving the subject of this book, I should like to draw attention to a few lines on "woman's mission," lines full of the noblest chivalry, reminding one of Tennyson's "Idylls of the King":—

In the darkest path of man's despair,
Where War and Terror shake the troubled earth,
Lies woman's mission; with unblenching brow
To pass through scenes of horror and affright
Where men grow sick and tremble: unto her
All things are sanctified, for all are good.
Nothing so mean, but shall deserve her care:
Nothing so great, but she may bear her part.
No life is vain: each hath his place assigned:
Do thou thy task, and leave the rest to God.

Of the unpublished works which Mr. Dodgson left behind him, I may mention "Original Games and Puzzles"; "Symbolic Logic, Part ii.," and a portion of a mathematical book, the proofs of which are now in the hands of the Controller of the Oxford University Press.

I will conclude this chapter with a poem which appeared in *Punch* for January 29th, a fortnight after Lewis Carroll's death. It expresses, with all the grace and insight of the true poet, what I have tried, so feebly and ineffectually, to say:—
LEWIS CARROLL.

Born 1832. *Died January* 14, 1898.

Lover of children! Fellow-heir with those
Of whom the imperishable kingdom is!
Beyond all dreaming now your spirit knows
The unimagined mysteries.

Darkly as in a glass our faces look
To read ourselves, if so we may, aright;
You, like the maiden in your faërie book—
You step behind and see the light!

The heart you wore beneath your pedant's cloak
Only to children's hearts you gave away;
Yet unaware in half the world you woke
The slumbering charm of childhood's day.

We older children, too, our loss lament,
We of the "Table Round," remembering well
How he, our comrade, with his pencil lent
Your fancy's speech a firmer spell.

Master of rare woodcraft, by sympathy's
Sure touch he caught your visionary gleams,
And made your fame, the dreamer's, one with his.
The wise interpreter of dreams.

Farewell! But near our hearts we have you yet,
Holding our heritage with loving hand,
Who may not follow where your feet are set
Upon the ways of Wonderland.[025]

CHAPTER X

CHILD FRIENDS

Mr. Dodgson's fondness for children—Miss Isabel Standen—Puzzles—"Me and Myself"—A double acrostic—"Father William"—Of drinking healths—Kisses by post—Tired in the face—The unripe plum—Eccentricities—"Sylvie and Bruno"—"Mr. Dodgson is going on *well*."

This chapter, and the next will deal with Mr. Dodgson's friendships with children. It would have been impossible to arrange them in chronological sequence in the earlier part of this book, and the fact that they exhibit a very important and distinct side of his nature seems to justify me in assigning them a special and individual position.

For the contents of these two chapters, both my readers and myself owe a debt of gratitude to those child-friends of his, without whose ever-ready help this book could never have been written.

From very early college days began to emerge that beautiful side of Lewis Carroll's character which afterwards was to be, next to his fame as an author, the one for which he was best known—his attitude towards children, and the strong attraction they had for him. I shall attempt to point out the various influences which led him in this direction; but if I were asked for one comprehensive word wide enough to explain this tendency of his nature, I would answer unhesitatingly—Love. My readers will remember a beautiful verse in "Sylvie and Bruno"; trite though it is, I cannot forbear to quote it—

Say, whose is the skill that paints valley and hill,
Like a picture so fair to the sight?
That flecks the green meadow with sunshine and shadow,
Till the little lambs leap with delight?
'Tis a secret untold to hearts cruel and cold,
Though 'tis sung by the angels above,
In notes that ring clear for the ears that can hear,
And the name of the secret is Love!

That "secret"—an open secret for him—explains this side of his character. As *he* read everything in its light, so it is only in its light that *we* can properly understand *him*. I think that the following quotation from a letter to the Rev. F. H. Atkinson, accompanying a copy of "Alice" for his little daughter Gertrude, sufficiently proves the truth of what I have just stated:—

Many thanks to Mrs. Atkinson and to you for the sight of the tinted photograph of your Gertrude. As you say, the picture speaks for itself, and I can see exactly what sort of a child she is, in proof of which I send her my love and a kiss herewith. It is possible I may be the first (unseen) gentleman from whom she has had so ridiculous a message; but I can't say she is the first unseen child to whom I have sent one! I think the most precious message of the kind I ever got from a child I never saw (and never shall see in this world) was to the effect that she liked me when she read about Alice, "but please tell him, whenever I read that Easter letter he sent me I *do* love him!" She was in a hospital, and a lady friend who visited there had asked me to send the letter to her and some other sick children.

And now as to the secondary causes which attracted him to children. First, I think children appealed to him because he was pre-eminently a teacher, and he saw in their unspoiled minds the best material for him to work upon. In later years one of his favourite recreations was to lecture at schools on logic; he used to give personal attention to each of his pupils, and one can well imagine with what eager anticipation the children would have looked forward to the visits of a schoolmaster who knew how to make even the dullest subjects interesting and amusing.

Again, children appealed to his æsthetic faculties, for he was a keen admirer of the beautiful in every form. Poetry, music, the drama, all delighted him, but pictures more than all put together. I remember his once showing me "The Lady with the Lilacs," which Arthur Hughes had painted for him, and how he dwelt with intense pleasure on the exquisite contrasts of colour which it contained—the gold hair of a girl standing out against the purple of lilac-blossom. But with those who find in such things as these a complete satisfaction of their desire for the beautiful he had no sympathy; for no imperfect representations of life could, for him, take the place of life itself, life as God has made it—the babbling of the brook, the singing of the birds, the laughter and sweet faces of the children. And yet, recognising, as he did, what Mr. Pater aptly terms "the curious perfection of the human form," in man, as in nature, it was the soul that attracted him more than the body. His intense admiration, one might almost call it adoration, for the white innocence and uncontaminated spirituality of childhood emerges most clearly in "Sylvie and Bruno." He says very little of the personal beauty of his heroine; he might have asked, with Mr. Francis Thompson—

How can I tell what beauty is her dole,
Who cannot see her countenance for her soul?

So entirely occupied is he with her gentleness, her pity, her sincerity, and her love.

Again, the reality of children appealed strongly to the simplicity and genuineness of his own nature. I believe that he understood children even better than he understood men and women; civilisation has made adult humanity very incomprehensible, for convention is as a veil which hides the divine spark that is in each of us, and so this strange thing has come to be, that the imperfect mirrors perfection more completely than the perfected, that we see more of God in the child than in the man.

And in those moments of depression of which he had his full share, when old age seemed to mock him with all its futility and feebleness, it was the thought that the children still loved him which nerved him again to continue his life-work, which renewed his youth, so that to his friends he never seemed an old man. Even the hand of death itself only made his face look more boyish—the word is not too strong. "How wonderfully young your brother looks!" were the first words the doctor said, as he returned from the room where Lewis Carroll's body lay, to speak to the mourners below. And so he loved children because their friendship was the true source of his perennial youth and unflagging vigour. This idea is expressed in the following poem—an acrostic, which he wrote for a friend some twenty years ago:—

Around my lonely hearth, to-night,
Ghostlike the shadows wander:
Now here, now there, a childish sprite,
Earthborn and yet as angel bright,
Seems near me as I ponder.

Gaily she shouts: the laughing air
Echoes her note of gladness—
Or bends herself with earnest care
Round fairy-fortress to prepare
Grim battlement or turret-stair—
In childhood's merry madness!

New raptures still hath youth in store:
Age may but fondly cherish
Half-faded memories of yore—
Up, craven heart! repine no more!
Love stretches hands from shore to shore:
Love is, and shall not perish!

His first child-friend, so far as I know, was Miss Alice Liddell, the little companion whose innocent talk was one of the chief pleasures of his early life at Oxford, and to whom he told the tale that was to make him famous. In December, 1885, Miss M.E. Manners presented him with a little volume, of which she was the authoress, "Aunt Agatha Ann and Other Verses," and which contained a poem (which I quoted in Chapter VI.), about "Alice." Writing to acknowledge this gift, Lewis Carroll said:—

Permit me to offer you my sincere thanks for the very sweet verses you have written about my dream-child (named after a real Alice, but none the less a dream-child) and her Wonderland. That children love the book is a very precious thought to me, and, next to their love, I value the sympathy of those who come with a child's heart to what I have tried to write about a child's thoughts. Next to what conversing with an angel *might* be—for it is hard to imagine it—comes, I think, the privilege of having a real child's thoughts uttered to one. I have known some few *real* children (you have too, I am sure), and their friendship is a blessing and a help in life.

It is interesting to note how in "Sylvie and Bruno" his idea of the thoughts of a child has become deeper and more spiritual. Yet in the earlier tale, told "all in a golden afternoon," to the plash of oars and the swish of a boat through the waters of Cherwell or Thames, the ideal child is strangely beautiful; she has all Sylvie's genuineness and honesty, all her keen appreciation of the interest of life; only there lacks that mysterious charm of deep insight into the hidden forces of nature, the gentle power that makes the sky "such a darling blue," which almost links Sylvie with the angels.

Another of Lewis Carroll's early favourites was Miss Alexandra (Xie) Kitchin, daughter of the Dean of Durham. Her father was for fifteen years the Censor of the unattached members of the University of Oxford, so that Mr. Dodgson had plenty of opportunities of photographing his little friend, and it is only fair to him to say that he did not neglect them.

It would be futile to attempt even a bare list of the children whom he loved, and who loved him; during forty years of his life he was constantly adding to their number. Some remained friends for life, but in a large proportion of cases the friendship ended with the end of childhood. To one of those few, whose affection for him had not waned with increasing years, he wrote:—

I always feel specially grateful to friends who, like you, have given me a child-friendship and a woman—friendship. About nine out of ten, I think, of my child-friendships get ship-wrecked at the critical point, "where the stream and river meet," and the child-friends, once so affectionate, become uninteresting acquaintances, whom I have no wish to set eyes on again.

These friendships usually began all very much in the same way. A chance meeting on the sea-shore, in the street, at some friend's house, led to conversation; then followed a call on the parents, and after that all sorts of kindnesses on Lewis Carroll's part, presents of books, invitations to stay with him at Oxford, or at Eastbourne, visits with him to the theatre. For the amusement of his little guests he kept a large assortment of musical-boxes, and an organette which had to be fed with paper tunes. On one occasion he ordered about twelve dozen of these tunes "on approval," and asked one of the other dons, who was considered a judge of music, to come in and hear them played over. In addition to these attractions there were clock-work bears, mice, and frogs, and games and puzzles in infinite variety.

One of his little friends, Miss Isabel Standen, has sent me the following account of her first meeting with him:—

We met for the first time in the Forbury Gardens, Reading. He was, I believe, waiting for a train. I was playing with my brothers and sisters in the Gardens. I remember his taking me on his knee and showing me puzzles, one of which he refers to in the letter (given below. This puzzle was, by the way, a great favourite of his; the problem is to draw three interlaced squares without going over the same lines twice, or taking the pen off the paper), which is so thoroughly characteristic of him in its quaint humour:—

"The Chestnuts, Guildford,
August 22, 1869.

My Dear Isabel,—Though I have only been acquainted with you for fifteen minutes, yet, as there is no one else in Reading I have known so long, I hope you will not mind my troubling you. Before I met you in the Gardens yesterday I bought some old books at a shop in Reading, which I left to be called for, and had not time to go back for them. I didn't even remark the name of the shop, but I can tell *where* it was, and if you know the name of the woman who keeps the shop, and would put it into the blank I have left in this note, and direct it to her I should be much obliged ... A friend of mine, called Mr. Lewis Carroll, tells me he means to send you a book. He is a *very* dear friend of mine. I have known him all my life (we are the same age) and have *never* left him. Of course he was with me in the Gardens, not a yard off—even while I was drawing those puzzles for you. I wonder if you saw him?

Your fifteen-minute friend,

C.L. Dodgson.

Have you succeeded in drawing the three squares?"

Another favourite puzzle was the following—I give it in his own words:—

A is to draw a fictitious map divided into counties.

B is to colour it (or rather mark the counties with *names* of colours) using as few colours as possible.

Two adjacent counties must have *different* colours.

A's object is to force B to use as *many* colours as possible.

How many can he force B to use?

One of his most amusing letters was to a little girl called Magdalen, to whom he had given a copy of his "Hunting of the Snark":—

Christ Church,
December 15, 1875.

My dear Magdalen,—I want to explain to you why I did not call yesterday. I was sorry to miss you, but you see I had so many conversations on the way. I tried to explain to the people in the street that I was going to see you, but they wouldn't listen; they said they were in a hurry, which was rude. At last I met a wheelbarrow that I thought would attend to me, but I couldn't make out what was in it. I saw some features at first, then I looked through a telescope, and found it was a countenance; then I looked through a microscope, and found it was a face! I thought it was father like me, so I fetched a large looking-glass to make sure, and then to my great joy I found it was me. We shook hands, and were just beginning to talk, when myself came up and joined us, and we had quite a pleasant conversation. I said, "Do you remember when we all met at Sandown?" and myself said, "It was very jolly there; there was a child called Magdalen," and me said, "I used to like her a little; not much, you know—only a little." Then it was time for us to go to the train, and who do you think came to the station to see us off? You would never guess, so I must tell you. They were two very dear friends of mine, who happen to be here just now, and beg to be allowed to sign this letter as your affectionate friends,

Lewis Carroll and C.L. Dodgson.

Another child-friend, Miss F. Bremer, writes as follows:—

Our acquaintance began in a somewhat singular manner. We were playing on the Fort at Margate, and a gentleman on a seat near asked us if we could make a paper boat, with a seat at each end, and a basket in the middle for fish! We were, of course, enchanted with the idea, and our new friend—after achieving the feat—gave us his card, which we at once carried to our mother. He asked if he might call where we were staying, and then presented my elder sister with a copy of "Alice in Wonderland," inscribed "From the Author." He kindly organised many little excursions for us—chiefly in the pursuit of knowledge. One memorable visit to a light house is still fresh in our memories.

It was while calling one day upon Mrs. Bremer that he scribbled off the following double acrostic on the names of her two daughters—

```
          DOUBLE ACROSTIC—FIVE LETTERS.

          Two little girls near London dwell,
          More naughty than I like to tell.
                         1.
          Upon the lawn the hoops are seen:
          The balls are rolling on the green.        T   ur   F
                         2.
          The Thames is running deep and wide:
          And boats are rowing on the tide.          R   ive  R
                         3.
          In winter-time, all in a row,
          The happy skaters come and go.             I   c    E
                         4.
          "Papa!" they cry, "Do let us stay!"
          He does not speak, but says they may.      N   o    D
                         5.
          "There is a land," he says, "my dear,
          Which is too hot to skate, I fear."        A   fric A
```

At Margate also he met Miss Adelaide Paine, who afterwards became one of his greatest favourites. He could not bear to see the healthy pleasures of childhood spoiled by conventional restraint. "One piece of advice given to my parents," writes Miss Paine, "gave me very great glee, and that was not to make little girls wear gloves at the seaside; they took the advice, and I enjoyed the result." *Apropos* of this I may mention that, when staying at Eastbourne, he never went down to the beach without providing himself with a supply of safety-pins. Then if he saw any little girl who wanted to wade in the sea, but was afraid of spoiling her frock, he would gravely go up to her and present her with a safety-pin, so that she might fasten up her skirts out of harm's way.

Tight boots were a great aversion of his, especially for children. One little girl who was staying with him at Eastbourne had occasion to buy a new pair of boots. Lewis Carroll gave instructions to the bootmaker as to how they were to be made, so as to be thoroughly comfortable, with the result that when they came home they were more useful than ornamental, being very nearly as broad as they were long! Which shows that even hygienic principles may be pushed too far.

The first meeting with Miss Paine took place in 1876. When Lewis Carroll returned to Christ Church he sent her a copy of "The Hunting of the Snark," with the following acrostic written in the fly-leaf:—

```
'A re you deaf, Father William?' the young man said,
'D id you hear what I told you just now?
 E xcuse me for shouting! Don't waggle your head
 L ike a blundering, sleepy old cow!
 A little maid dwelling in Wallington Town,
 I s my friend, so I beg to remark:
 D o you think she'd be pleased if a book were sent down
 E ntitled "The Hunt of the Snark?"'

'P ack it up in brown paper!' the old man cried,
'A nd seal it with olive-and-dove.
 I command you to do it!' he added with pride,
'N or forget, my good fellow, to send her beside
 E aster Greetings, and give her my love.'
```

This was followed by a letter, dated June 7, 1876:—

My dear Adelaide,—Did you try if the letters at the beginnings of the lines about Father William would spell anything? Sometimes it happens that you can spell out words that way, which is very curious.

I wish you could have heard him when he shouted out "Pack it up in brown paper!" It quite shook the house. And he threw one of his shoes at his son's head (just to make him attend, you know), but it missed him.

He was glad to hear you had got the book safe, but his eyes filled with tears as he said, "I sent *her* my love, but she never—" he couldn't say any more, his mouth was so full of bones (he was just finishing a roast goose).

Another letter to Miss Paine is very characteristic of his quaint humour:—

Christ Church, Oxford,
March 8, 1880.

My dear Ada,—(Isn't that your short name? "Adelaide" is all very well, but you see when one's *dreadfully* busy one hasn't time to write such long words—particularly when it takes one half an hour to remember how to spell it—and even then one has to go and get a dictionary to see if one has spelt it right, and of course the dictionary is in another room, at the top of a high bookcase—where it has been for months and months, and has got all covered with dust—so one has to get a duster first of all, and nearly choke oneself in dusting it—and when one *has* made out at last which is dictionary and which is dust, even *then* there's the job of remembering which end of the alphabet "A" comes—for one feels pretty certain it isn't in the *middle*—then one has to go and wash one's hands before turning over the leaves—for they've got so thick with dust one hardly knows them by sight—and, as likely as not, the soap is lost, and the jug is empty, and there's no towel, and one has to spend hours and hours in finding things—and perhaps after all one has to go off to the shop to buy a new cake of soap—so, with all this bother, I hope you won't mind my writing it short and saying, "My dear Ada"). You said in your last letter you would like a likeness of me: so here it is, and I hope you will like it—I won't forget to call the next time but one I'm in Wallington.

Your very affectionate friend,

Lewis Carroll.

It was quite against Mr. Dodgson's usual rule to give away photographs of himself; he hated publicity, and the above letter was accompanied by another to Mrs. Paine, which ran as follows:—

I am very unwilling, usually, to give my photograph, for I don't want people, who have heard of Lewis Carroll, to be able to recognise him in the street—but I can't refuse Ada. Will you kindly take care, if any of your ordinary acquaintances (I don't speak of intimate friends) see it, that they are *not* told anything about the name of "Lewis Carroll"?

He even objected to having his books discussed in his presence; thus he writes to a friend:—

Your friend, Miss—was very kind and complimentary about my books, but may I confess that I would rather have them ignored? Perhaps I am too fanciful, but I have somehow taken a dislike to being talked to about them; and consequently have some trials to bear in society, which otherwise would be no trials at all.... I don't think any of my many little stage-friends have any shyness at all about being talked to of their performances. *They* thoroughly enjoy the publicity that I shrink from.

The child to whom the three following letters were addressed, Miss Gaynor Simpson, was one of Lewis Carroll's Guildford friends. The correct answer to the riddle propounded in the second letter is "Copal":—

December 27, 1873.

My dear Gaynor,—My name is spelt with a "G," that is to say "*Dodgson* ." Any one who spells it the same as that wretch (I mean of course the Chairman of Committees in the House of Commons) offends me *deeply* , and *for ever!* It is a thing I *can* forget, but *never can forgive!* If you do it again, I shall call you "'aynor." Could you live happy with such a name?

As to dancing, my dear, I *never* dance, unless I am allowed to do it *in my own peculiar way.* There is no use trying to describe it: it has to be seen to be believed. The last house I tried it in, the floor broke through. But then it was a poor sort of floor—the beams were only six inches thick, hardly worth calling beams at all: stone arches are much more sensible, when any dancing, *of my peculiar kind*, is to be done. Did you ever see the Rhinoceros, and the Hippopotamus, at the Zoölogical Gardens, trying to dance a minuet together? It is a touching sight.

Give any message from me to Amy that you think will be most likely to surprise her, and, believe me,

Your affectionate friend,

Lewis Carroll.

My dear Gaynor,—So you would like to know the answer to that riddle? Don't be in a hurry to tell it to Amy and Frances: triumph over them for a while!

My first lends its aid when you plunge into trade.
Gain. Who would go into trade if there were no gain in it?

My second in jollifications—
Or [The French for "gold"—] Your jollifications would
be *very* limited if you had no money.

My whole, laid on thinnish, imparts a neat finish
To pictorial representations.

Gaynor. Because she will be an ornament to the Shakespeare Charades—only she must be "laid on thinnish," that is, *there musn't be too much of her.*

Yours affectionately,

C. L. Dodgson.

My dear Gaynor,—Forgive me for having sent you a sham answer to begin with.

My first—*Sea*. It carries the ships of the merchants.

My second—*Weed*. That is, a cigar, an article much used in jollifications.

My whole—*Seaweed*. Take a newly painted oil—picture; lay it on its back on the floor, and spread over it, "thinnish," some wet seaweed. You will find you have "finished" that picture.

Yours affectionately,

C.L. Dodgson.

 Lewis Carroll during the last fifteen years of his life always spent the Long Vacation at Eastbourne; in earlier times, Sandown, a pleasant little seaside resort in the Isle of Wight, was his summer abode. He loved the sea both for its own sake and because of the number of children whom he met at seaside places. Here is another "first meeting"; this time it is at Sandown, and Miss Gertrude Chataway is the narrator:—

I first met Mr. Lewis Carroll on the sea-shore at Sandown in the Isle of Wight, in the summer of 1875, when I was quite a little child.

We had all been taken there for change of air, and next door there was an old gentlemen—to me at any rate he seemed old—who interested me immensely. He would come on to his balcony, which joined ours, sniffing the sea-air with his head thrown back, and would walk right down the steps on to the beach with his chin in air, drinking in the fresh breezes as if he could never have enough. I do not know why this excited such keen curiosity on my part, but I remember well that whenever I heard his footstep I flew out to see him coming, and when one day he spoke to me my joy was complete.

Thus we made friends, and in a very little while I was as familiar with the interior of his lodgings as with our own.

I had the usual child's love for fairy-tales and marvels, and his power of telling stories naturally fascinated me. We used to sit for hours on the wooden steps which led from our garden on to the beach, whilst he told the most lovely tales that could possibly be imagined, often illustrating the exciting situations with a pencil as he went along.

One thing that made his stories particularly charming to a child was that he often took his cue from her remarks—a question would set him off on quite a new trail of ideas, so that one felt that one had somehow helped to make the story, and it seemed a personal possession It was the most lovely nonsense conceivable, and I naturally revelled in it. His vivid imagination would fly from one subject to another, and was never tied down in any way by the probabilities of life.

To *me* it was of course all perfect, but it is astonishing that *he* never seemed either tired or to want other society. I spoke to him once of this since I have been grown up, and he told me it was the greatest pleasure he could have to converse freely with a child, and feel the depths of her mind.

He used to write to me and I to him after that summer, and the friendship, thus begun, lasted. His letters were one of the greatest joys of my childhood.

I don't think that he ever really understood that we, whom he had known as children, could not always remain such. I stayed with him only a few years ago, at Eastbourne, and felt for the time that I was once more a child. He never appeared to realise that I had grown up, except when I reminded him of the fact, and then he only said, "Never mind: you will always be a child to me, even when your hair is grey."

Some of the letters, to which Miss Chataway refers in these reminiscences, I am enabled, through her kindness, to give below:—

Christ Church, Oxford,
October 13, 1875.

My dear Gertrude,—I never give birthday *presents*, but you see I *do* sometimes write a birthday *letter* : so, as I've just arrived here, I am writing this to wish you many and many a happy return of your birthday to-morrow. I will drink your health, if only I can remember, and if you don't mind—but perhaps you object? You see, if I were to sit by you at breakfast, and to drink your tea, you wouldn't like *that*, would you? You would say "Boo! hoo! Here's Mr. Dodgson's drunk all my tea, and I haven't got any left!" So I am very much afraid, next time Sybil looks for you, she'll find you sitting by the sad sea-wave, and crying "Boo! hoo! Here's Mr. Dodgson has drunk my health, and I haven't got any left!" And how it will puzzle Dr. Maund, when he is sent for to see you! "My dear Madam, I'm very sorry to say your little girl has got *no health at all*! I never saw such a thing in my life!" "Oh, I can easily explain it!" your mother will say. "You see she would go and make friends with a strange gentleman, and yesterday he drank her health!" "Well, Mrs. Chataway," he will say, "the only way to cure her is to wait till his next birthday, and then for *her* to drink *his* health."

And then we shall have changed healths. I wonder how you'll like mine! Oh, Gertrude, I wish you wouldn't talk such nonsense!...

Your loving friend,

Lewis Carroll.

Christ Church, Oxford,
Dec. 9, 1875.

My dear Gertrude,—This really will *not* do, you know, sending one more kiss every time by post: the parcel gets so heavy it is quite expensive. When the postman brought in the last letter, he looked quite grave. "Two pounds to pay, sir!" he said. "*Extra weight*, sir!" (I think he cheats a little, by the way. He often makes me pay two *pounds* , when I think it should be *pence*). "Oh, if you please, Mr. Postman!" I said, going down gracefully on one knee (I wish you could see me go down on one knee to a postman—it's a very pretty sight), "do excuse me just this once! It's only from a little girl!"

"Only from a little girl!" he growled. "What are little girls made of?" "Sugar and spice," I began to say, "and all that's ni—" but he interrupted me. "No! I don't mean *that*. I mean, what's the good of little girls, when they send such heavy letters?" "Well, they're not *much* good, certainly," I said, rather sadly.

"Mind you don't get any more such letters," he said, "at least, not from that particular little girl. *I know her well, and she's a regular bad one*!" That's not true, is it? I don't believe he ever saw you, and you're not a bad one, are you? However, I promised him we would send each other *very* few more letters— "Only two thousand four hundred and seventy, or so," I said. "Oh!" he said, "a little number like *that* doesn't signify. What I meant is, you mustn't send *many* ."

So you see we must keep count now, and when we get to two thousand four hundred and seventy, we mustn't write any more, unless the postman gives us leave.

I sometimes wish I was back on the shore at Sandown; don't you?

Your loving friend,

Lewis Carroll.

Why is a pig that has lost its tail like a little girl on the sea-shore?

Because it says, "I should like another tale, please!"

Christ Church, Oxford,
July 21, 1876.

My dear Gertrude,—Explain to me how I am to enjoy Sandown without *you* . How can I walk on the beach alone? How can I sit all alone on those wooden steps? So you see, as I shan't be able to do without you, you will have to come. If Violet comes, I shall tell her to invite you to stay with her, and then I shall come over in the Heather-Bell and fetch you.

If I ever *do* come over, I see I couldn't go back the same day, so you will have to engage me a bed somewhere in Swanage; and if you can't find one, I shall expect *you* to spend the night on the beach, and give up your room to *me*. Guests of course must be thought of before children; and I'm sure in these warm nights the beach will be quite good enough for *you*. If you *did* feel a little chilly, of course you could go into a bathing-machine, which everybody knows is *very* comfortable to sleep in—you know they make the floor of soft wood on purpose. I send you seven kisses (to last a week) and remain

Your loving friend,

Lewis Carroll.

Christ Church, Oxford,
October 28, 1876.

My dearest Gertrude,—You will be sorry, and surprised, and puzzled, to hear what a queer illness I have had ever since you went. I sent for the doctor, and said, "Give me some medicine, for I'm tired." He said, "Nonsense and stuff! You don't want medicine: go to bed!" I said, "No; it isn't the sort of tiredness that wants bed. I'm tired in the *face*." He looked a little grave, and said, "Oh, it's your *nose* that's tired: a person often talks too much when he thinks he nose a great deal." I said, "No; it isn't the nose. Perhaps it's the *hair*." Then he looked rather grave, and said, "*Now* I understand: you've been playing too many hairs on the piano-forte." "No, indeed I haven't!" I said, "and it isn't exactly the *hair*: it's more about the nose and chin." Then he looked a good deal graver, and said, "Have you been walking much on your chin lately?" I said, "No." "Well!" he said, "it puzzles me very much. Do you think that it's in the lips?" "Of course!" I said. "That's exactly what it is!" Then he looked very grave indeed, and said, "I think you must have been giving too many kisses." "Well," I said, "I did give *one* kiss to a baby child, a little friend of mine." "Think again," he said; "are you sure it was only *one*?" I thought again, and said, "Perhaps it was eleven times." Then the doctor said, "You must not give her *any* more till your lips are quite rested again." "But what am I to do?" I said, "because you see, I owe her a hundred and eighty-two more." Then he looked so grave that the tears ran down his cheeks, and he said, "You may send them to her in a box." Then I remembered a little box that I once bought at Dover, and thought I would some day give it to *some* little girl or other. So I have packed them all in it very carefully. Tell me if they come safe, or if any are lost on the way.

Reading Station,
April 13, 1878.

My dear Gertrude,—As I have to wait here for half an hour, I have been studying Bradshaw (most things, you know, ought to be studied: even a trunk is studded with nails), and the result is that it seems I could come, any day next week, to Winckfield, so as to arrive there about one; and that, by leaving Winckfield again about half-past six, I could reach Guildford again for dinner. The next question is, *How far is it from Winckfield to Rotherwick*? Now do not deceive me, you wretched child! If it is more than a hundred miles, I can't come to see you, and there is no use to talk about it. If it is less, the next question is, *How much less?* These are serious questions, and you must be as serious as a judge in answering them. There mustn't be a smile in your pen, or a wink in your ink (perhaps you'll say, "There can't be a *wink* in *ink*: but there *may* be *ink* in a *wink*"—but this is trifling; you mustn't make jokes like that when I tell you to be serious) while you write to Guildford and answer these two questions. You might as well tell me at the same time whether you are still living at Rotherwick—and whether you are at home—and whether you get my letter—and whether you're still a child, or a grown-up person—and whether you're going to the seaside next summer—and anything else (except the alphabet and the multiplication table) that you happen to know. I send you 10,000,000 kisses, and remain.

Your loving friend,

C. L. Dodgson.

The Chestnuts, Guildford,
April 19, 1878.

My dear Gertrude,—I'm afraid it's "no go"—I've had such a bad cold all the week that I've hardly been out for some days, and I don't think it would be wise to try the expedition this time, and I leave here on Tuesday. But after all, what does it signify? Perhaps there are ten or twenty gentlemen, all living within a few miles of Rotherwick, and any one of them would do just as well! When a little girl is hoping to take a plum off a dish, and finds that she can't have that one, because it's bad or unripe, what does she do? Is she sorry, or disappointed? Not a bit! She just takes another instead, and grins from one little ear to the other as she puts it to her lips! This is a little fable to do you good; the little girl means *you*—the bad plum means *me*—the other plum means some other friend—and all that about the little girl putting plums to her lips means—well, it means—but you know you can't expect *every bit* of a fable to mean something! And the little girl grinning means that dear little smile of yours, that just reaches from the tip of one ear to the tip of the other!

Your loving friend,

C.L. Dodgson.

I send you 4—3/4 kisses.

   The next letter is a good example of the dainty little notes Lewis Carroll used to scribble off on any scrap of paper that lay to his hand:—

Chestnuts,   Guildford,
January 15,   1886.

Yes, my child, if all be well, I shall hope, and you may fear, that the train reaching Hook at two eleven, will contain

Your loving friend,

C.L. Dodgson.

   Only a few years ago, illness prevented him from fulfilling his usual custom of spending Christmas with his sisters at Guildford. This is the allusion in the following letter:—

My dear old Friend,—(The friendship is old, though the child is young.) I wish a very happy New Year, and many of them, to you and yours; but specially to you, because I know you best and love you most. And I pray God to bless you, dear child, in this bright New Year, and many a year to come. ... I write all this from my sofa, where I have been confined a prisoner for six weeks, and as I dreaded the railway journey, my doctor and I agreed that I had better not go to spend Christmas with my sisters at Guildford. So I had my Christmas dinner all alone, in my room here, and (pity me, Gertrude!) it wasn't a Christmas dinner at all—I suppose the cook thought I should not care for roast beef or plum pudding, so he sent me (he has general orders to send either fish and meat, or meat and pudding) some fried sole and some roast mutton! Never, never have I dined before, on Christmas Day, without *plum pudding*. Wasn't it sad? Now I think you must be content; this is a longer letter than most will get. Love to Olive. My clearest memory of her is of a little girl calling out "Good-night" from her room, and of your mother taking me in to see her in her bed, and wish her good-night. I have a yet clearer memory (like a dream of fifty years ago) of a little bare-legged girl in a sailor's jersey, who used to run up into my lodgings by the sea. But why should

I trouble you with foolish reminiscences of *mine* that *cannot* interest you?

Yours always lovingly,

C. L. Dodgson.

It was a writer in *The National Review* who, after eulogising the talents of Lewis Carroll, and stating that *he* would never be forgotten, added the harsh prophecy that "future generations will not waste a single thought upon the Rev. C.L. Dodgson."

If this prediction is destined to be fulfilled, I think my readers will agree with me that it will be solely on account of his extraordinary diffidence about asserting himself. But such an unnatural division of Lewis Carroll, the author, from the Rev. C.L. Dodgson, the man, is forced in the extreme. His books are simply the expression of his normal habit of mind, as these letters show. In literature, as in everything else, he was absolutely natural.

To refer to such criticisms as this (I am thankful to say they have been very few) is not agreeable; but I feel that it is owing to Mr. Dodgson to do what I can to vindicate the real unity which underlay both his life and all his writings.

Of many anecdotes which might be adduced to show the lovable character of the man, the following little story has reached me through one of his child-friends:—

My sister and I [she writes] were spending a day of delightful sightseeing in town with him, on our way to his home at Guildford, where we were going to pass a day or two with him. We were both children, and were much interested when he took us into an American shop where the cakes for sale were cooked by a very rapid process before your eyes, and handed to you straight from the cook's hands. As the preparation of them could easily be seen from outside the window, a small crowd of little ragamuffins naturally assembled there, and I well remember his piling up seven of the cakes on one arm, and himself taking them out and doling them round to the seven hungry little youngsters. The simple kindness of his act impressed its charm on his child-friends inside the shop as much as on his little stranger friends outside.

It was only to those who had but few personal dealings with him that he seemed stiff and "donnish"; to his more intimate acquaintances, who really understood him, each little eccentricity of manner or of habits was a delightful addition to his charming and interesting personality. That he was, in some respects, eccentric cannot be denied; for instance he hardly ever wore an overcoat, and always wore a tall hat, whatever might be the climatic conditions. At dinner in his rooms small pieces of cardboard took the place of table-mats; they answered the purpose perfectly well, he said, and to buy anything else would be a mere waste of money. On the other hand, when purchasing books for himself, or giving treats to the children he loved, he never seemed to consider expense at all.

He very seldom sat down to write, preferring to stand while thus engaged. When making tea for his friends, he used, in order, I suppose, to expedite the process, to walk up and down the room waving the teapot about, and telling meanwhile those delightful anecdotes of which he had an inexhaustible supply.

Great were his preparations before going a journey; each separate article used to be carefully wrapped up in a piece of paper all to itself, so that his trunks contained nearly as much paper as of the more useful things. The bulk of the luggage was sent on a day or two before by goods train, while he himself followed on the appointed day, laden only with his well-known little black bag, which he always insisted on carrying himself.

He had a strong objection to staring colours in dress, his favourite combination being pink and grey. One little girl who came to stay with him was absolutely forbidden to wear a red frock, of a somewhat pronounced hue, while out in his company.

At meals he was very abstemious always, while he took nothing in the middle of the day except a glass of wine and a biscuit. Under these circumstances it is not very surprising that the healthy appetites of his little friends filled him with wonder, and even with alarm. When he took a certain one of them out with him to a friend's house to dinner, he used to give the host or hostess a gentle warning, to the mixed amazement and indignation of the child, "Please be careful, because she eats a good deal too much."

Another peculiarity, which I have already referred to, was his objection to being invited to dinners or any other social gatherings; he made a rule of never accepting invitations. "Because you have invited me, therefore I cannot come," was the usual form of his refusal. I suppose the reason of this was his hatred of the interference with work which engagements of this sort occasion.

He had an extreme horror of infection, as will appear from the following illustration. Miss Isa Bowman and her sister, Nellie, were at one time staying with him at Eastbourne, when news came from home that their youngest sister had caught the scarlet fever. From that day every letter which came from Mrs. Bowman to the children was held up by Mr. Dodgson, while the two little girls, standing at the opposite end of the room, had to read it as best they could. Mr. Dodgson, who was the soul of honour, used always to turn his head to one side during these readings, lest he might inadvertently see some words that were not meant for his eyes.

Some extracts from letters of his to a child-friend, who prefers to remain anonymous, follow:

November 30, 1879.

I have been awfully busy, and I've had to write *heaps* of letters—wheelbarrows full, almost. And it tires me so that generally I go to bed again the next minute after I get up: and sometimes I go to bed again a minute *before* I get up! Did you ever hear of any one being so tired as *that?* ...

November 7, 1882.

My dear E—, How often you must find yourself in want of a pin! For instance, you go into a shop, and you say to the man, "I want the largest penny bun you can let me have for a halfpenny." And perhaps the man looks stupid, and doesn't quite understand what you mean. Then how convenient it is to have a pin ready to stick into the back of his hand, while you say, "Now then! Look sharp, stupid!"... and even when you don't happen to want a pin, how often you think to yourself, "They say Interlacken is a very pretty place. I wonder what it looks like!" (That is the place that is painted on this pincushion.)

When you don't happen to want either a pin or pictures, it may just remind you of a friend who sometimes thinks of his dear little friend E—, and who is just now thinking of the day he met her on the parade, the first time she had been allowed to come out alone to look for him....

December 26, 1886.

My dear E—, Though rushing, rapid rivers roar between us (if you refer to the map of England, I think you'll find that to be correct), we still remember each other, and feel a sort of shivery affection for each other....

March 31, 1890.

I *do* sympathise so heartily with you in what you say about feeling shy with children when you have to entertain them! Sometimes they are a real *terror* to me—especially boys: little girls I can now and then get on with, when they're few enough. They easily become "de trop." But with little *boys* I'm out of my element altogether. I sent "Sylvie and Bruno" to an Oxford friend, and, in writing his thanks, he added, "I think I must bring my little boy to see you." So I wrote to say "*don't*," or words to that effect: and he wrote again that he could hardly believe his eyes when he got my note. He thought I doted on *all* children. But I'm *not* omnivorous!—like a pig. I pick and choose....

You are a lucky girl, and I am rather inclined to envy you, in having the leisure to read Dante—*I* have never read a page of him; yet I am sure the "Divina Commedia" is one of the grandest books in the world—though I am *not* sure whether the reading of it would *raise* one's life and give it a nobler purpose, or simply be a grand poetical treat. That is a question you are beginning to be able to answer: I doubt if *I* shall ever (at least in this life) have the opportunity of reading it; my life seems to be all torn into little bits among the host of things I want to do! It seems hard to settle what to do *first. One* piece of work, at any rate, I am clear ought to be done this year, and it will take months of hard work: I mean the second volume of "Sylvie and Bruno." I fully *mean* , if I have life and health till Xmas next, to bring it out then. When one is close on sixty years old, it seems presumptuous to count on years and years of work yet to be done....

She is rather the exception among the hundred or so of child-friends who have brightened my life. Usually the child becomes so entirely a different being as she grows into a woman, that our friendship has to change too: and *that* it usually does by gliding down from a loving intimacy into an acquaintance that merely consists of a smile and a bow when we meet!...

January   1,   1895.

... You are quite correct in saying it is a long time since you have heard from me: in fact, I find that I have not written to you since the 13th of last November. But what of that? You have access to the daily papers. Surely you can find out negatively, that I am all right! Go carefully through the list of bankruptcies; then run your eye down the police cases; and, if you fail to find my name anywhere, you can say to your mother in a tone of calm satisfaction, "Mr. Dodgson is going on *well*."

CHAPTER XI

(THE SAME—*continued*.)

Books for children—"The Lost Plum-Cake"—"An Unexpected Guest"—Miss Isa Bowman—Interviews—"Matilda Jane"—Miss Edith Rix—Miss Kathleen Eschwege.

Lewis Carroll's own position as an author did not prevent him from taking a great interest in children's books and their writers. He had very strong ideas on what was or was not suitable in such books, but, when once his somewhat exacting taste was satisfied, he was never tired of recommending a story to his friends. His cousin, Mrs. Egerton Allen, who has herself written several charming tales for young readers, has sent me the following letter which she received from him some years ago:—

Dear Georgie,—*Many* thanks. The book was at Ch. Ch. I've done an unusual thing, in thanking for a book, namely, *waited to read it*. I've read it *right through*! In fact, I found it very refreshing, when jaded with my own work at "Sylvie and Bruno" (coming out at Xmas, I hope) to lie down on the sofa and read a chapter of "Evie." I like it very much: and am so glad to have helped to bring it out. It would have been a real loss to the children of England, if you had burned the MS., as you once thought of doing....

The very last words of his that appeared in print took the form of a preface to one of Mrs. Allen's tales, "The Lost Plum-Cake," (Macmillan & Co., 1898). So far as I know, this was the only occasion on which he wrote a preface for another author's book, and his remarks are doubly interesting as being his last service to the children whom he loved. No apology, then, is needed for quoting from them here:—

Let me seize this opportunity of saying one earnest word to the mothers in whose hands this little book may chance to come, who are in the habit of taking their children to church with them. However well and reverently those dear little ones have been taught to behave, there is no doubt that so long a period of enforced quietude is a severe tax on their patience. The hymns, perhaps, tax it least: and what a pathetic beauty there is in the sweet fresh voices of the children, and how earnestly they sing! I took a little girl of six to church with me one day: they had told me she could hardly read at all—but she made me find all the places for her! And afterwards I said to her elder sister "What made you say Barbara couldn't read? Why, I heard her joining in, all through the hymn!" And the little sister gravely replied, "She knows the *tunes*, but not the *words*." Well, to return to my subject—children in church. The lessons, and the prayers, are not wholly beyond them: often they can catch little bits that come within the range of their small minds. But the sermons! It goes to one's heart to see, as I so often do, little darlings of five or six years old, forced to sit still through a weary half-hour, with nothing to do, and not one word of the sermon that they can understand. Most heartily can I sympathise with the little charity-girl who is said to have written to some friend, "I think, when I grows up, I'll never go to church no more. I think I'se getting sermons enough to last me all my life!" But need it be so? Would it be so *very* irreverent to let your child have a story—book to read during the sermon, to while away that tedious half-hour, and to make church—going a bright and happy memory, instead of rousing the thought, "I'll never go to church no more"? I think not. For my part, I should love to see the experiment tried. I am quite sure it would be a success. My advice would be to *keep* some books for that special purpose. I would call such books "Sunday-treats"—and your little boy or girl would soon learn to look forward with eager hope to that half-hour, once so tedious. If I were the preacher, dealing with some subject too hard for the little ones, I should love to see them all enjoying their picture-books. And if *this* little book should ever come to be used as a "Sunday-treat" for some sweet baby reader, I don't think it could serve a better purpose.

Lewis Carroll.

Miss M.E. Manners was another writer for children whose books pleased him. She gives an amusing account of two visits which he paid to her house in 1889:—

An Unexpected Guest.

"Mr. Dobson wants to see you, miss."

I was in the kitchen looking after the dinner, and did not feel that I particularly wished to see anybody.

"He wants a vote, or he is an agent for a special kind of tea," thought I. "I don't know him; ask him to send a message."

Presently the maid returned—

"He says he is Mr. Dodgson, of Oxford."

"Lewis Carroll!" I exclaimed; and somebody else had to superintend the cooking that day.

My apologies were soon made and cheerfully accepted. I believe I was unconventional enough to tell the exact truth concerning my occupation, and matters were soon on a friendly footing. Indeed I may say at once that the stately college don we have heard so much about never made his appearance during our intercourse with him.

He did not talk "Alice," of course; authors don't generally *talk* their books, I imagine; but it was undoubtedly Lewis Carroll who was present with us.

A portrait of Ellen Terry on the wall had attracted his attention, and one of the first questions he asked was, "Do you ever go to the theatre?" I explained that such things were done, occasionally, even among Quakers, but they were not considered quite orthodox.

"Oh, well, then you will not be shocked, and I may venture to produce my photographs." And out into the hall he went, and soon returned with a little black bag containing character portraits of his child-friends, Isa and Nellie Bowman.

"Isa used to be Alice until she grew too big," he said. "Nellie was one of the oyster—fairies, and Emsie, the tiny one of all, was the Dormouse."

"When 'Alice' was first dramatised," he said, "the poem of the 'Walrus and the Carpenter' fell rather flat, for people did not know when it was finished, and did not clap in the right place; so I had to write a song for the ghosts of the oysters to sing, which made it all right."

He was then on his way to London, to fetch Isa to stay with him at Eastbourne. She was evidently a great favourite, and had visited him before. Of that earlier time he said:—

"When people ask me why I have never married, I tell them I have never met the young lady whom I could endure for a fortnight—but Isa and I got on so well together that I said I should keep her a month, the length of the honeymoon, and we didn't get tired of each other."

Nellie afterwards joined her sister "for a few days," but the days spread to some weeks, for the poor little dormouse developed scarlet fever, and the elder children had to be kept out of harm's way until fear of infection was over.

Of Emsie he had a funny little story to tell. He had taken her to the Aquarium, and they had been watching the seals coming up dripping out of the water. With a very pitiful look she turned to him and said, "Don't they give them any towels?" [The same little girl commiserated the bear, because it had got no tail.]

Asked to stay to dinner, he assured us that he never took anything in the middle of the day but a glass of wine and a biscuit; but he would be happy to sit down with us, which he accordingly did and kindly volunteered to carve for us. His offer was gladly accepted, but the appearance of a rather diminutive piece of neck of mutton was somewhat of a puzzle to him. He had evidently never seen such a joint in his life before, and had frankly to confess that he did not know how to set about carving it. Directions only made things worse, and he bravely cut it to pieces in entirely the wrong fashion, relating meanwhile the story of a shy young man who had been asked to carve a fowl, the joints of which had been carefully wired together beforehand by his too attentive friends.

The task and the story being both finished, our visitor gazed on the mangled remains, and remarked quaintly: "I think it is just as well I don't want anything, for I don't know where I should find it."

At least one member of the party felt she could have managed matters better; but that was a point of very little consequence.

A day or two after the first call came a note saying that he would be taking Isa home before long, and if we would like to see her he would stop on the way again.

Of course we were only too delighted to have the opportunity, and, though the visit was postponed more than once, it did take place early in August, when he brought both Isa and Nellie up to town to see a performance of "Sweet Lavender." It is needless to remark that we took care, this time, to be provided with something at once substantial and carvable.

The children were bright, healthy, happy and childlike little maidens, quite devoted to their good friend, whom they called "Uncle"; and very interesting it was to see them together.

But he did not allow any undue liberties either, as a little incident showed.

He had been describing a particular kind of collapsible tumbler, which you put in your pocket and carried with you for use on a railway journey.

"There now," he continued, turning to the children, "I forgot to bring it with me after all."
"Oh Goosie," broke in Isa; "you've been talking about that tumbler for days, and now you have forgotten it."
He pulled himself up, and looked at her steadily with an air of grave reproof.

Much abashed, she hastily substituted a very subdued "Uncle" for the objectionable "Goosie," and the matter dropped.
The principal anecdote on this occasion was about a dog which had been sent into the sea after sticks. He brought them back very properly for some time, and then there appeared to be a little difficulty, and he returned swimming in a very curious manner. On closer inspection it appeared that he had caught hold of his own tail by mistake, and was bringing it to land in triumph.

This was told with the utmost gravity, and though we had been requested beforehand not to mention "Lewis Carroll's" books, the temptation was too strong. I could not help saying to the child next me—

"That was like the Whiting, wasn't it?"

Our visitor, however, took up the remark, and seemed quite willing to talk about it.

"When I wrote that," he said, "I believed that whiting really did have their tails in their mouths, but I have since been told that fishmongers put the tail through the eye, not in the mouth at all."

He was not a very good carver, for Miss Bremer also describes a little difficulty he had—this time with the pastry: "An amusing incident occurred when he was at lunch with us. He was requested to serve some pastry, and, using a knife, as it was evidently rather hard, the knife penetrated the d'oyley beneath—and his consternation was extreme when he saw the slice of linen and lace he served as an addition to the tart!"

It was, I think, through her connection with the "Alice" play that Mr. Dodgson first came to know Miss Isa Bowman. Her childish friendship for him was one of the joys of his later years, and one of the last letters he wrote was addressed to her. The poem at the beginning of "Sylvie and Bruno" is an acrostic on her name—

Is all our Life, then, but a dream,
Seen faintly in the golden gleam
Athwart Times's dark, resistless stream?

Bowed to the earth with bitter woe,
Or laughing at some raree-show,
We flutter idly to and fro.

Man's little Day in haste we spend,
And, from the merry noontide, send
No glance to meet the silent end.

Every one has heard of Lewis Carroll's hatred of interviewers; the following letter to Miss Manners makes one feel that in some cases, at least, his feeling was justifiable:—

If your Manchester relatives ever go to the play, tell them they ought to see Isa as "Cinderella"—she is evidently a success. And she has actually been "interviewed" by one of those dreadful newspapers reporters, and the "interview" is published with her picture! And such rubbish he makes her talk! She tells him that something or other was "tacitly conceded": and that "I love to see a great actress give expression to the wonderful ideas of the immortal master!"

(N.B.—I never let her talk like that when she is with *me*!)

Emsie recovered in time to go to America, with her mother and Isa and Nellie: and they all enjoyed the trip much; and Emsie has a London engagement.

Only once was an interviewer bold enough to enter Lewis Carroll's *sanctum*. The story has been told in *The Guardian* (January 19, 1898), but will bear repetition:—

Not long ago Mr. Dodgson happened to get into correspondence with a man whom he had never seen, on some question of religious difficulty, and he invited him to come to his rooms and have a talk on the subject. When, therefore, a Mr.

X— was announced to him one morning, he advanced to meet him with outstretched hand and smiles of welcome. "Come in Mr. X—, I have been expecting you." The delighted visitor thought this a promising beginning, and immediately pulled out a note-book and pencil, and proceeded to ask "the usual questions." Great was Mr. Dodgson's disgust! Instead of his expected friend, here was another man of the same name, and one of the much-dreaded interviewers, actually sitting in his chair! The mistake was soon explained, and the representative of the Press was bowed out as quickly as he had come in.

It was while Isa and one of her sisters were staying at Eastbourne that the visit to America was mooted. Mr. Dodgson suggested that it would be well for them to grow gradually accustomed to seafaring, and therefore proposed to take them by steamer to Hastings. This plan was carried out, and the weather was unspeakably bad—far worse than anything they experienced in their subsequent trip across the Atlantic. The two children, who were neither of them very good sailors, experienced sensations that were the reverse of pleasant. Mr. Dodgson did his best to console them, while he continually repeated, "Crossing the Atlantic will be much worse than this."

However, even this terrible lesson on the horrors of the sea did not act as a deterrent; it was as unsuccessful as the effort of the old lady in one of his stories: "An old lady I once knew tried to check the military ardour of a little boy by showing him a picture of a battlefield, and describing some of its horrors. But the only answer she got was, 'I'll be a soldier. Tell it again!'"

The Bowman children sometimes came over to visit him at Oxford, and he used to delight in showing them over the colleges, and pointing out the famous people whom they encountered. On one of these occasions he was walking with Maggie, then a mere child, when they met the Bishop of Oxford, to whom Mr. Dodgson introduced his little guest. His lordship asked her what she thought of Oxford. "I think," said the little actress, with quite a professional *aplomb*, "it's the best place in the Provinces!" At which the Bishop was much amused. After the child had returned to town, the Bishop sent her a copy of a little book called "Golden Dust," inscribed "From W. Oxon," which considerably mystified her, as she knew nobody of that name!

Another little stage-friend of Lewis Carroll's was Miss Vera Beringer, the "Little Lord Fauntleroy," whose acting delighted all theatre-goers eight or nine years ago. Once, when she was spending a holiday in the Isle of Man, he sent her the following lines:—

There was a young lady of station,
"I love man" was her sole exclamation;

But when men cried, "You flatter,"
She replied, "Oh! no matter,
Isle of Man is the true explanation."

Many of his friendships with children began in a railway carriage, for he always took about with him a stock of puzzles when he travelled, to amuse any little companions whom chance might send him. Once he was in a carriage with a lady and her little daughter, both complete strangers to him. The child was reading "Alice in Wonderland," and when she put her book down, he began talking to her about it. The mother soon joined in the conversation, of course without the least idea who the stranger was with whom she was talking. "Isn't it sad," she said, "about poor Mr. Lewis Carroll? He's gone mad, you know." "Indeed," replied Mr. Dodgson, "I had never heard that." "Oh, I assure you it is quite true," the lady answered. "I have it on the best authority." Before Mr. Dodgson parted with her, he obtained her leave to send a present to the little girl, and a few days afterwards she received a copy of "Through the Looking-Glass," inscribed with her name, and "From the Author, in memory of a pleasant journey."

When he gave books to children, he very often wrote acrostics on their names on the fly-leaf. One of the prettiest was inscribed in a copy of Miss Yonge's "Little Lucy's Wonderful Globe," which he gave to Miss Ruth Dymes:—

R ound the wondrous globe I wander wild,
U p and down-hill—Age succeeds to youth—
T oiling all in vain to find a child
H alf so loving, half so dear as Ruth.

In another book, given to her sister Margaret, he wrote:—

M aidens, if a maid you meet
A lways free from pout and pet,
R eady smile and temper sweet,
G reet my little Margaret.
A nd if loved by all she be
R ightly, not a pampered pet,
E asily you then may see
'Tis my little Margaret.

Here are two letters to children, the one interesting as a specimen of pure nonsense of the sort which children always like, the other as showing his dislike of being praised. The first was written to Miss Gertrude Atkinson, daughter of an old College friend, but otherwise unknown to Lewis Carroll except by her photograph:—

My dear Gertrude,—So many things have happened since we met last, really I don't know *which* to begin talking about! For instance, England has been conquered by William the Conqueror. We haven't met since *that* happened, you know. How did you like it? Were you frightened?

And one more thing has happened: I have got your photograph. Thank you very much for it. I like it "awfully." Do they let you say "awfully"? or do they say, "No, my dear; little girls mustn't say 'awfully'; they should say 'very much indeed'"?

I wonder if you will ever get as far as Jersey? If not, how *are* we to meet?

Your affectionate friend,

C.L. Dodgson.

From the second letter, to Miss Florence Jackson, I take the following extract:—

I have two reasons for sending you this fable; one is, that in a letter you wrote me you said something about my being "clever"; and the other is that, when you wrote again you said it again! And *each* time I thought, "Really, I *must* write and ask her *not* to say such things; it is not wholesome reading for me."

The fable is this. The cold, frosty, bracing air is the treatment one gets from the world generally—such as contempt, or blame, or neglect; all those are very wholesome. And the hot dry air, that you breathe when you rush to the fire, is the praise that one gets from one's young, happy, rosy, I may even say *florid* friends! And that's very bad for me, and gives pride-fever, and conceit-cough, and such-like diseases. Now I'm sure you don't want me to be laid up with all these diseases; so please don't praise me *any* more!

The verses to "Matilda Jane" certainly deserve a place in this chapter. To make their meaning clear, I must state that Lewis Carroll wrote them for a little cousin of his, and that Matilda Jane was the somewhat prosaic name of her doll. The poem expresses finely the blind, unreasoning devotion which the infant mind professes for inanimate objects:—

Matilda Jane, you never look
At any toy or picture-book;
I show you pretty things in vain,
You must be blind, Matilda Jane!

I ask you riddles, tell you tales,
But all our conversation fails;
You never answer me again,
I fear you're dumb, Matilda Jane!

Matilda, darling, when I call
You never seem to hear at all;
I shout with all my might and main,
But you're *so* deaf, Matilda Jane!

Matilda Jane, you needn't mind,
For though you're deaf, and dumb, and blind,
There's some one loves you, it is plain,
And that is *me*, Matilda Jane!

    In an earlier chapter I gave some of Mr. Dodgson's letters to Miss Edith Rix; the two which follow, being largely about children, seem more appropriate here:—

My dear Edith,—Would you tell your mother I was aghast at seeing the address of her letter to me: and I would much prefer "Rev. C.L. Dodgson, Ch. Ch., Oxford." When a letter comes addressed "Lewis Carroll, Ch. Ch.," it either goes to the Dead Letter Office, or it impresses on the minds of all letter-carriers, &c., through whose hands it goes, the very fact I least want them to know.

Please offer to your sister all the necessary apologies for the liberty I have taken with her name. My only excuse is, that I know no other; and how *am* I to guess what the full name is? It *may* be Carlotta, or Zealot, or Ballot, or Lotus-blossom (a very pretty name), or even Charlotte. Never have I sent anything to a young lady of whom I have a more shadowy idea. Name, an enigma; age, somewhere between 1 and 19 (you've no idea how bewildering it is, alternately picturing her as a little toddling thing of 5, and a tall girl of 15!); disposition—well, I *have* a fragment of information on *that* question—your mother says, as to my coming, "It must be when Lottie is at home, or she would never forgive us." Still, I *cannot* consider the mere fact that she is of an unforgiving disposition as a complete view of her character. I feel sure she has some other qualities besides.

Believe me,

Yrs affectionately,

C.L. Dodgson.

My dear child,—It seems quite within the bounds of possibility, if we go on long in this style, that our correspondence may at last assume a really friendly tone. I don't of course say it will actually do so—that would be too bold a prophecy, but only that it may tend to shape itself in that direction.

Your remark, that slippers for elephants *could* be made, only they would not be slippers, but boots, convinces me that there is a branch of your family in *Ireland*. Who are (oh dear, oh dear, I am going distracted! There's a lady in the opposite house who simply sings *all* day. All her songs are wails, and their tunes, such as they have, are much the same. She has one strong note in her voice, and she knows it! I *think* it's "A natural," but I haven't much ear. And when she gets to that note, she howls!) they? The O'Rixes, I suppose?

About your uninteresting neighbours, I sympathise with you much; but oh, I wish I had you here, that I might teach you *not* to say "It is difficult to visit one's district regularly, like every one else does!"

And now I come to the most interesting part of your letter—May you treat me as a perfect friend, and write anything you like to me, and ask my advice? Why, *of course* you may, my child! What else am I good for? But oh, my dear child-friend, you cannot guess how such words sound to *me*! That any one should look up to *me*, or think of asking *my* advice—well, it makes one feel humble, I think, rather than proud—humble to remember, while others think so well of me, what I really *am*, in myself. "Thou, that teachest another, teachest thou not thyself?" Well, I won't talk about myself, it is not a healthy topic. Perhaps it may be true of *any* two people, that, if one could see the other through and through, love would perish. I don't know. Anyhow, I like to *have* the love of my child-friends, tho' I know I don't deserve it. Please write as freely as *ever* you like.

I went up to town and fetched Phoebe down here on Friday in last week; and we spent *most* of Saturday upon the beach—Phoebe wading and digging, and "as happy as a bird upon the wing" (to quote the song she sang when first I saw her). Tuesday evening brought a telegram to say she was wanted at the theatre next morning. So, instead of going to bed, Phoebe packed her things, and we left by the last train, reaching her home by a quarter to 1 a.m. However, even four days of sea-air, and a new kind of happiness, did her good, I think. I am rather lonely now she is gone. She is a very sweet child, and a thoughtful child, too. It was very touching to see (we had a little Bible-reading every day: I tried to remember that my little friend had a soul to be cared for, as well as a body) the far-away look in her eyes, when we talked of God and of heaven—as if her angel, who beholds His face continually, were whispering to her.

Of course, there isn't *much* companionship possible, after all, between an old man's mind and a little child's, but what there is is sweet—and wholesome, I think.

Three letters of his to a child-friend, Miss Kathleen Eschwege, now Mrs. Round, illustrate one of those friendships which endure: the sort of friendship that he always longed for, and so often failed to secure:—

Ch. Ch., Oxford,
October 24, 1879.

My dear Kathleen,—I was really pleased to get your letter, as I had quite supposed I should never see or hear of you again. You see I knew only your Christian name—not the ghost of a surname, or the shadow of an address—and I was not prepared to spend my little all in advertisements—"If the young lady, who was travelling on the G.W. Railway, &c." —or to devote the remainder of my life to going about repeating "Kathleen," like that young woman who came from some foreign land to look for her lover, but only knew that he was called "Edward" (or "Richard" was it? I dare say you know History better than I do) and that he lived in England; so that naturally it took her some time to find him. All I knew was that *you* could, if you chose, write to me through Macmillan: but it is three months since we met, so I was *not* expecting it, and it was a pleasant surprise.

Well, so I hope I may now count you as one of my child-friends. I am fond of children (except boys), and have more child-friends than I could possibly count on my fingers, even if I were a centipede (by the way, *have* they fingers? I'm afraid they're only feet, but, of course, they use them for the same purpose, and that is why no other insects, *except centipedes*, ever succeed in doing *Long Multiplication*), and I have several not so very far from you—one at Beckenham, two at Balham, two at Herne Hill, one at Peckham—so there is every chance of my being somewhere near you *before the year* 1979. If so, may I call? I am *very* sorry your neck is no better, and I wish they would take you to Margate: Margate air will make *any* body well of *any* thing.

It seems you have already got my two books about "Alice." Have you also got "The Hunting of the Snark"? If not, I should be very glad to send you one. The pictures (by Mr. Holiday) are pretty: and you needn't read the verses unless you like.

How do you pronounce your surname? "esk-weej"? or how? Is it a German name?

If you can do "Doublets," with how many links do you turn KATH into LEEN?

With kind remembrances to your mother, I am

Your affectionate friend,

Charles L. Dodgson

(*alias* "Lewis Carroll").

Ch. Ch., Oxford,
January 20, 1892.

My dear Kathleen,—Some months ago I heard, from my cousin, May Wilcox, that you were engaged to be married. And, ever since, I have cherished the intention of writing to offer my congratulations. Some might say, "Why not write *at once?*" To such unreasoning creatures, the obvious reply is, "When you have bottled some peculiarly fine Port, do you usually begin to drink it *at once?*" Is not that a beautiful simile? Of course, I need not remark that my congratulations are like fine old Port—only finer, and *older!*

Accept, my dear old friend, my *heartiest* wishes for happiness, of all sorts and sizes, for yourself, and for him whom you have chosen as your other self. And may you love one another with a love second only to your love for God—a love that will last through bright days and dark days, in sickness and in health, through life and through death.

A few years ago I went, in the course of about three months, to the weddings of three of my old child-friends. But weddings are not very exhilarating scenes for a miserable old bachelor; and I think you'll have to excuse me from attending *yours*.

However, I have so far concerned myself in it that I actually *dreamed* about it a few nights ago! I dreamed that you had had a photograph done of the wedding-party, and had sent me a copy of it. At one side stood a group of ladies, among whom I made out the faces of Dolly and Ninty; and in the foreground, seated in a boat, were two people, a gentleman and a lady I *think* (could they have been the bridegroom and the bride?) engaged in the natural and usual occupation for a riverside picnic—pulling a Christmas cracker! I have no idea what put such an idea into my head. *I* never saw crackers used in such a scene!

I hope your mother goes on well. With kindest regards to her and your father, and love to your sisters—and to yourself too, if HE doesn't object!—I am,

Yours affectionately,

C.L. Dodgson.

P.S.—I never give wedding-presents; so please regard the enclosed as an *unwedding* present.

Ch. Ch., Oxford,
December 8, 1897.

My dear Kathleen,—Many thanks for the photo of yourself and your *fiancé*, which duly reached me January 23, 1892. Also for a wedding-card, which reached me August 28, 1892. Neither of these favours, I fear, was ever acknowledged. Our only communication since, has been, that on December 13,

1892, I sent you a biscuit—box adorned with "Looking-Glass" pictures. This *you* never acknowledged; so I was properly served for my negligence. I hope your little daughter, of whose arrival Mrs. Eschwege told me in December, 1893, has been behaving well? How quickly the years slip by! It seems only yesterday that I met, on the railway, a little girl who was taking a sketch of Oxford!

Your affectionate old friend,

C.L. Dodgson.

The following verses were inscribed in a copy of "Alice's Adventures," presented to the three Miss Drurys in August, 1869:—

To three puzzled little girls, from the Author.
Three little maidens weary of the rail,
Three pairs of little ears listening to a tale,
Three little hands held out in readiness,
For three little puzzles very hard to guess.
Three pairs of little eyes, open wonder-wide,
At three little scissors lying side by side.
Three little mouths that thanked an unknown Friend,
For one little book, he undertook to send.
Though whether they'll remember a friend, or book, or day—
In three little weeks is very hard to say.

He took the same three children to German Reed's entertainment, where the triple bill consisted of "Happy Arcadia," "All Abroad," and "Very Catching." A few days afterwards he sent them "Phantasmagoria," with a little poem on the fly-leaf to remind them of their treat:—

Three little maids, one winter day,
While others went to feed,
To sing, to laugh, to dance, to play,
More wisely went to—Reed.

Others, when lesson-time's begun,
Go, half inclined to cry,
Some in a walk, some in a run;
But *these* went in a—Fly.

I give to other little maids
A smile, a kiss, a look,
Presents whose memory quickly fades,
I give to these—a Book.

Happy Arcadia may blind,
While *all abroad,* their eyes;

At home, this book (I trust) they'll find
A *very catching* prize.

The next three letters were addressed to two of Mr. Arthur Hughes' children. They are good examples of the wild and delightful nonsense with which Lewis Carroll used to amuse his little friends:—

My dear Agnes,—You lazy thing! What? I'm to divide the kisses myself, am I? Indeed I won't take the trouble to do anything of the sort! But I'll tell *you* how to do it. First, you must take *four* of the kisses, and—and that reminds me of a very curious thing that happened to me at half-past four yesterday. Three visitors came knocking at my door, begging me to let them in. And when I opened the door, who do you think they were? You'll never guess. Why, they were three cats! Wasn't it curious? However, they all looked so cross and disagreeable that I took up the first thing I could lay my hand on (which happened to be the rolling-pin) and knocked them all down as flat as pan-cakes! "If *you* come knocking at *my* door," I said, "*I* shall come knocking at *your* heads." "That was fair, wasn't it?"

Yours affectionately,

Lewis Carroll.

My dear Agnes,—About the cats, you know. Of course I didn't leave them lying flat on the ground like dried flowers: no, I picked them up, and I was as kind as I could be to them. I lent them the portfolio for a bed—they wouldn't have been comfortable in a real bed, you know: they were too thin—but they were *quite* happy between the sheets of blotting-paper—and each of them had a pen-wiper for a pillow. Well, then I went to bed: but first I lent them the three dinner-bells, to ring if they wanted anything in the night.

You know I have *three* dinner-bells—the first (which is the largest) is rung when dinner is *nearly* ready; the second (which is rather larger) is rung when it is quite ready; and the third (which is as large as the other two put together) is rung all the time I am at dinner. Well, I told them they might ring if they happened to want anything—and, as they rang *all* the bells *all* night, I suppose they did want something or other, only I was too sleepy to attend to them.

In the morning I gave them some rat-tail jelly and buttered mice for breakfast, and they were as discontented as they could be. They wanted some boiled pelican, but of course I knew it wouldn't be good *for* them. So all I said was "Go to Number Two, Finborough Road, and ask for Agnes Hughes, and if it's *really* good for you, she'll give you some." Then I shook hands with them all, and wished them all goodbye, and drove them up the chimney. They seemed very sorry to go, and they took the bells and the portfolio with them. I didn't find this out till after they had gone, and then I was sorry too, and wished for them back again. What do I mean by "them"? Never mind.

How are Arthur, and Amy, and Emily? Do they still go up and down Finborough Road, and teach the cats to be kind to mice? I'm *very* fond of all the cats in Finborough Road.

Give them my love.
Who do I mean by "them"?
Never mind.

Your affectionate friend,

Lewis Carroll.

My dear Amy,—How are you getting on, I wonder, with guessing those puzzles from "Wonderland"? If you think you've found out any of the answers, you may send them to me; and if they're wrong, I won't tell you they're right!

You asked me after those three cats. Ah! The dear creatures! Do you know, ever since that night they first came, they have *never left me?* Isn't it kind of them? Tell Agnes this. She will be interested to hear it. And they *are* so kind and thoughtful! Do you know, when I had gone out for a walk the other day, they got *all* my books out of the bookcase, and opened them on the floor, to be ready for me to read. They opened them all at page 50, because they thought that would be a nice useful page to begin at. It was rather unfortunate, though: because they took my bottle of gum, and tried to gum pictures upon the ceiling (which they thought would please me), and by accident they spilt a quantity of it all over the books. So when they were shut up and put by, the leaves all stuck together, and I can never read page 50 again in any of them!

However, they meant it very kindly, so I wasn't angry. I gave them each a spoonful of ink as a treat; but they were ungrateful for that, and made dreadful faces. But, of course, as it was given them as a treat, they had to drink it. One of them has turned black since: it was a white cat to begin with.

Give my love to any children you happen to meet. Also I send two kisses and a half, for you to divide with Agnes, Emily, and Godfrey. Mind you divide them fairly.

Yours affectionately,

C.L. Dodgson.

The intelligent reader will make a discovery about the first of the two following letters, which Miss Maggie Cunningham, the "child-friend" to whom both were addressed, perhaps did not hit upon at once. Mr. Dodgson wrote these two letters in 1868:—

Dear Maggie,—I found that *the friend,* that the little girl asked me to write to, lived at Ripon, and not at Land's End—a nice sort of place to invite to! It looked rather suspicious to me—and soon after, by dint of incessant inquiries, I found out that *she* was called Maggie, and lived in a Crescent! Of course I declared, "After that" (the language I used doesn't matter), "I will *not* address her, that's flat! So do not expect me to flatter."

Well, I hope you will soon see your beloved Pa come back—for consider, should you be quite content with only Jack? Just suppose they made a blunder! (Such things happen now and then.) Really, now, I shouldn't wonder if your "John" came home again, and your father stayed at school! A most awkward thing, no doubt. How would you receive him? You'll say, perhaps, "you'd turn him out." That would answer well, so far as concerns the boy, you know—but consider your Papa, learning lessons in a row of great inky schoolboys! This (though unlikely) might occur: "Haly" would be grieved to miss him (don't mention it to *her*).

No *carte* has yet been done of me, that does real justice to my *smile*; and so I hardly like, you see, to send you one. However, I'll consider if I will or not—meanwhile, I send a little thing to give you an idea of what I look like when I'm lecturing. The merest sketch, you will allow—yet still I think there's something grand in the expression of the brow and in the action of the hand.

Have you read my fairy tale in *Aunt Judy's Magazine?* If you have you will not fail to discover what I mean when I say "Bruno yesterday came to remind me that *he* was my god-son!"—on the ground that I "gave him a name"!

Your affectionate friend,

C.L. Dodgson.

P.S.—I would send, if I were not too shy, the same message to "Haly" that she (though I do not deserve it, not I!) has sent through her sister to me. My best love to yourself—to your Mother my kindest regards—to your small, fat, impertinent, ignorant brother my hatred. I think that is all.

My dear Maggie,—I am a very bad correspondent, I fear, but I hope you won't leave off writing to me on that account. I got the little book safe, and will do my best about putting my name in, if I can only manage to remember what day my birthday is—but one forgets these things so easily.

Somebody told me (a little bird, I suppose) that you had been having better photographs done of yourselves. If so, I hope you will let me buy copies. Fanny will pay you for them. But, oh Maggie, how *can* you ask for a better one of me than the one I sent! It is one of the best ever done! Such grace, such dignity, such benevolence, such—as a great secret (please don't repeat it) the *Queen* sent to ask for a copy of it, but as it is against my rule to give in such a case, I was obliged to answer—

"Mr. Dodgson presents his compliments to her Majesty, and regrets to say that his rule is never to give his photograph except to *young* ladies." I am told she was annoyed about it, and said, "I'm not so old as all that comes to!" and one doesn't like to annoy Queens; but really I couldn't help it, you know.

I will conclude this chapter with some reminiscences of Lewis Carroll, which have been kindly sent me by an old child-friend of his, Mrs. Maitland, daughter of the late Rev. E.A. Litton, Rector of Naunton, and formerly Fellow of Oriel College and Vice—Principal of Saint Edmund's Hall:—

To my mind Oxford will be never quite the same again now that so many of the dear old friends of one's childhood have "gone over to the great majority."

Often, in the twilight, when the flickering firelight danced on the old wainscotted wall, have we—father and I—chatted over the old Oxford days and friends, and the merry times we all had together in Long Wall Street. I was a nervous, thin, remarkably ugly child then, and for some years I was left almost entirely to the care of Mary Pearson, my own particular attendant. I first remember Mr. Dodgson when I was about seven years old, and from that time until we went to live in Gloucestershire he was one of my most delightful friends.

I shall never forget how Mr. Dodgson and I sat once under a dear old tree in the Botanical Gardens, and how he told me, for the first time, Hans Andersen's story of the "Ugly Duckling." I cannot explain the charm of Mr. Dodgson's way of telling stories; as he spoke, the characters seemed to be real flesh and blood. This particular story made a great impression upon me, and interested me greatly, as I was very sensitive about my ugly little self. I remember his impressing upon me that it was better to be good and truthful and to try not to think of oneself than to be a pretty, selfish child, spoiled and disagreeable; and, after telling me this story, he gave me the name of "Ducky." "Never mind, little Ducky," he used often to say, "perhaps some day you will turn out a swan."

I always attribute my love for animals to the teaching of Mr. Dodgson: his stories about them, his knowledge of their lives and histories, his enthusiasm about birds and butterflies enlivened many a dull hour. The monkeys in the Botanical Gardens were our special pets, and when we fed them with nuts and biscuits he seemed to enjoy the fun as much as I did.

Every day my nurse and I used to take a walk in Christ Church Meadows, and often we would sit down on the soft grass, with the dear old Broad Walk quite close, and, when we raised our eyes, Merton College, with its walls covered with Virginian creeper. And how delighted we used to be to see the well-known figure in cap and gown coming, so swiftly, with his kind smile ready to welcome the "Ugly Duckling." I knew, as he sat beside me, that a book of fairy tales was hidden in his pocket, or that he would have some new game or puzzle to show me—and he would gravely accept a tiny daisy-bouquet for his coat with as much courtesy as if it had been the finest hot-house *boutonnière*.

Two or three times I went fishing with him from the bank near the Old Mill, opposite Addison's Walk, and he quite entered into my happiness when a small fish came wriggling up at the end of my bent pin, just ready for the dinner of the little white kitten "Lily," which he had given me.

My hair was a great trouble to me, as a child, for it would tangle, and Mary was not too patient with me, as I twisted about while she was trying to dress it. One day I received a long blue envelope addressed to myself, which contained a story-letter, full of drawings, from Mr. Dodgson. The first picture was of a little girl—with her hat off and her tumbled hair very much in evidence—asleep on a rustic bench under a big tree by the riverside, and two birds, holding what was evidently a very important conversation, above in the branches, their heads on one side, eyeing the sleeping child. Then there was a picture of the birds flying up to the child with twigs and straw in their beaks, preparing to build their nest in her hair. Next came the awakening, with the nest completed, and the mother-bird sitting on it; while the father-bird flew round the frightened child. And then, lastly, hundreds of birds—the air thick with them—the child fleeing, small boys with tin trumpets raised to their lips to add to the confusion, and Mary, armed with a basket of brushes and combs, bringing up the rear! After this, whenever I was restive while my hair was being arranged, Mary would show me the picture of the child with the nest on her head, and I at once became "as quiet as a lamb."

I had a daily governess, a dear old soul, who used to come every morning to teach me. I disliked particularly the large—lettered copies which she used to set me; and as I confided this to Mr. Dodgson, he came and gave me some copies himself. The only ones which I can remember were "Patience and water-gruel cure gout" (I always wondered what "gout" might be) and "Little girls should be seen and not heard" (which I thought unkind). These were written many times over, and I had to present the pages to him, without one blot or smudge, at the end of the week.

One of the Fellows of Magdalen College at that time was a Mr. Saul, a friend of my father's and of Mr. Dodgson, and a great lover of music—his rooms were full of musical instruments of every sort. Mr. Dodgson and father and I all went one afternoon to pay him a visit. At that time he was much interested in the big drum, and we found him when we arrived in full practice, with his music-book open before him. He made us all join in the concert. Father undertook the 'cello, and Mr. Dodgson hunted up a comb and some paper, and, amidst much fun and laughter, the walls echoed with the finished roll, or shake, of the big drum—a roll that was Mr. Saul's delight.

My father died on August 27, 1897, and Mr. Dodgson on January 14, 1898. And we, who are left behind in this cold, weary world can only hope we may some day meet them again. Till then, oh! Father, and my dear old childhood's friend, *requiescalis in pace!*

www.ingramcontent.com/pod-product-compliance
Lightning Source LLC
La Vergne TN
LVHW032009070526
838202LV00059B/6366